Johnny

THE MAN,
THE MYTH, THE
AMERICAN STORY

Appleseed

HOWARD MEANS

SIMON & SCHUSTER
NEW YORK   LONDON   TORONTO   SYDNEY

Simon & Schuster
1230 Avenue of the Americas
New York, NY 10020

Copyright © 2011 by Howard Means

First Simon & Schuster hardcover edition April 2011

SIMON & SCHUSTER and colophon are registered trademarks of Simon & Schuster, Inc.

Illustrations by Ihrie Means

For information about special discounts for bulk purchases, please contact Simon & Schuster Special Sales at 1-866-506-1949 or business@simonandschuster.com.

The Simon & Schuster Speakers Bureau can bring authors to your live event. For more information or to book an event contact the Simon & Schuster Speakers Bureau at 1-866-248-3049 or visit our website at www.simonspeakers.com.

Designed by Renata Di Biase

Manufactured in the United States of America

10   9   8   7   6   5   4   3   2   1

Library of Congress Cataloging-in-Publication Data
Means, Howard B.
    Johnny Appleseed : the man, the myth, the American story / Howard Means.
        p. cm.
    Summary: "A biography of Johnny Appleseed, both the historical person and the legendary figure"—Provided by publisher.
    1. Appleseed, Johnny, 1774–1845. 2. Apple growers—United States—Biography. 3. Frontier and pioneer life—Middle West. I. Title.
SB63.C46M43 2011
634'.11092—dc22   2011000665
[B]

ISBN 978-1-4391-7825-6
ISBN 978-1-4391-7827-0 (ebook)

For Caper

CONTENTS

1826-1845

1803-1825

Lake Erie

Fran|

Cleveland

Ashland

Mansfield

Pitts

Gree

INDIANA

Fort Wayne

Van Wert

Mount Vernon

Urbana

Newark

Columbus

OHIO

Marietta

Ohio River

N

W E

S

0   50   100 miles

0   50   100 kilometers

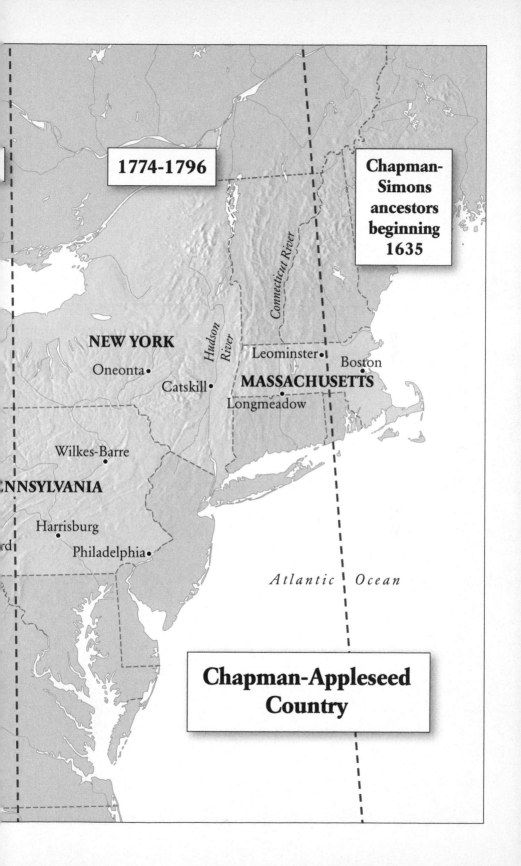

1774-1796

Chapman-
Simons
ancestors
beginning
1635

NEW YORK

Oneonta

Catskill

Hudson River

Connecticut River

Leominster

Boston

MASSACHUSETTS

Longmeadow

Wilkes-Barre

NNSYLVANIA

Harrisburg

Philadelphia

Atlantic Ocean

Chapman-Appleseed Country

Johnny Appleseed

RIGHT FRESH FROM HEAVEN

~

Near sunset, one day in mid-March 1845, a seventy-year-old man named John Chapman appeared at the door of a cabin along the banks of the St. Joseph River, a few miles north of Fort Wayne, Indiana. Barefoot, dressed in coarse pantaloons and a coffee sack with holes cut out for his head and arms, Chapman had walked fifteen miles that day through mixed snow and rain to repair a bramble fence that protected one of his orchards. Now, he sought a roof over his head at the home of William Worth and his family—a request readily granted. Chapman had stayed with the Worths before on those few occasions when he felt a need to be out of the weather, a little more than five weeks in all over the previous five-plus years.

Inside, as was his custom, Chapman refused a place at table, taking a bowl of bread and milk by the hearth—or maybe on the chill of the front stoop, staring at the sunset. Accounts vary. The weather might have cleared. Afterward, also a custom, he regaled his hosts with news "right fresh from heaven" in a voice that, one frontier diarist wrote, "rose denunciatory and thrilling, strong and loud as the roar of wind and waves, then soft and soothing as the balmy airs that quivered the morning-glory leaves about his gray beard."

One version of events has him reciting the Beatitudes, from the

Gospel According to St. Matthew: "Blessed are the poor in spirit, for theirs is the kingdom of heaven. Blessed are they who mourn, for they shall be comforted. Blessed are the meek, for they shall inherit the earth. . . ." That could be, but for last words—and this was to be his final lucid night on earth—the Beatitudes are almost too perfect, like those morning-glory leaves fluttering in the old gray beard. More likely, Chapman expounded for the gathered Worth family on the "spiritual truths" of the Bible, its hidden codex, a subject for him of inexhaustible fascination.

John Chapman slept on the hearth, by the fire, that night. On that everyone agrees. By morning, a fever had "settled on his lungs," according to one person present, and rendered him incapable of speech. Within days, perhaps hours, he was dead, a victim of "winter plague," a catch-all diagnosis that dated back to the Middle Ages and included everything from pneumonia and influenza to the cold-weather rampages of the Black Death. Whatever carried him away, Chapman almost certainly did not suffer. The physician who pronounced him dying later said that he had never seen a man so placid in his final passage. Years afterward, Worth family members would describe the corpse as almost glowing with serenity.

That's overblown, of course, but with John Chapman—or Johnny Appleseed, as he eventually became known throughout the Old Northwest—just about everything is.

❧

He had paddled into the Ohio wilderness in the opening years of the nineteenth century in two lashed-together canoes, a catamaran of his own design, carrying nothing but a few tools and two sacks stuffed with apple seeds. The land then teemed with danger: wolves, wild boars, and especially black rattlesnakes, known to the pioneers as massasaugas. One of the earliest farmers recorded killing two hundred of them in his first year while clearing a small prairie, roughly one every five yards. Bears, too, were bountiful. In an account of his travels along the Ohio River in 1807–1809, Fortescue Cuming tells of meeting a cattle-and-hog dealer named Buffington, who a few years earlier had killed, along with a partner, 135 black bears in only six weeks—skins had been selling for as much as ten dollars each back then. Yet according to virtually every testimony, Chapman took not a whit of precaution against such wilderness dangers, was heedless of his personal safety, would rather have been bitten by a rattler or mauled by a bear than defend himself against one.

It was a land, too, of rough men and harsh ways. British general Thomas Gage, longtime commander in chief of the Crown's North American forces, once described the frontier men and women he encountered as "a Sett of People . . . near as wild as the country they go in, or the People they deal with, and by far more vicious & wicked."

This was John Chapman's world. He was part and parcel of it—adrift on the frontier with men and women at the outer edge of American civilization. Yet he appears to have glided over it all: abided by the vicious and wicked, welcomed even by the Native Americans whose land the settlers were seizing, impervious to isolation, without bodily wants or needs. It's almost as if he drew sustenance from the landscape itself, or maybe he simply absorbed the wilderness and became it, much as he absorbed the myth of Johnny Appleseed and became that, too, in his own lifetime. What the record tells us is that when Chapman was present in whatever setting—a cabin, a town, a clearing—he was a powerful and unavoidable personality. Like many fundamental loners, though, he also was a master of the disappearing act: here one minute, gone the next.

In his 1862 history of Knox County, Ohio, A. Banning Norton

calls Chapman/Appleseed "the oddest character in all our history." That's a toss-up. The competition for "oddest American [anything]" grows stiffer year by year, but of the many odd characters who populate our early history, John Chapman must count among the most singular of them all—nurseryman; religious zealot; real-estate dabbler; medicine man; lord of the open trail, with the stars for a roof and the moon for his night-light; pioneer capitalist; altruist; the list could go on. By tradition, he also seems to have been among the most loved Americans, too. The tributes that followed his death are said to have included this one from Sam Houston, the hero of the War for Texas Independence: "Farewell, dear old eccentric heart. . . . Generations yet to come shall rise up and call you blessed."

As we'll see, there's more than a little reason to doubt whether Sam Houston ever uttered those words, whether he even knew of Chapman or Appleseed. More likely is this traditional eulogy from another much-lauded fighting man, William Tecumseh Sherman: "Johnny Appleseed's name will never be forgotten. . . . We will keep his memory green, and future generations of boys and girls will love him as we, who knew him, have learned to love him." Sherman had been born and raised in Lancaster, Ohio, land that Chapman was still passing through regularly when the Scourge of the South was yet in his teens. Whether we accept the legitimacy of either eulogy, though, the hope they jointly express has been realized, at best, only in part.

John Chapman did not slip unnoticed into the afterlife. His life and death were summarized in a four-paragraph obituary in the March 22, 1845, edition of the *Fort Wayne Sentinel*, a lively account that runs to almost three hundred words. But Chapman lies today effectively forgotten on the cutting-room floor of the national narrative—his name almost as likely to evoke John Lennon's murderer (Mark David Chapman) as it is to bring to mind the true source of that memory Sherman vowed would be ever green.

Johnny Appleseed, of course, does live on, but less as a whole person than as a barometer of the ever-shifting American ideal: by turns a pacifist (extolled by at least one and perhaps two of the most renowned fighting men of the nineteenth century), the White Noble Savage (so remembered long after the Red Savages themselves had been driven from the land), a children's book simpleton, a frontier bootlegger in the fanciful interpretation of Michael Pollan, patron saint of everything from cannabis to evangelical environmentalism and creation care—everything, that is, but the flesh-and-blood man he really was.

This book is their story—John Chapman *and* Johnny Appleseed—and the story of America at the birth of the nation. It's a tale of the wilderness, of the inner frontier and its taming. It explores how our national past gets mythologized and hired out. Mostly, though, it's a tale of two men, one real and one invented; of the times they lived through, the ties that link them, and the gulf that separates them; of the uses to which both have been put; and of what that tells us about ourselves, then and now.

❦

No American folk hero has been more widely and diversely celebrated than Johnny Appleseed. Two of the best-selling poets of the first half of the last century, Vachel Lindsay and Stephen Vincent Benét (working with his wife, Rosemary), wrote wildly popular narrative poems in his honor. He has been the subject of a ballet and an opera, a Broadway show, concertos and a cantata, as well as Mark O'Connor's sweetly lovely "Johnny Appleseed Suite." Over the last sixty years, Johnny also has been featured in a constant parade of children's books and videos, themselves the spawn of one of the most famous cartoons ever turned out by the Walt Disney Studios, the 1948 classic *Melody Time*.

But the ballyhoo, the sheer volume of attention paid over the years to Johnny Appleseed, is very much the point. No American hero—not Davy Crockett, not even Daniel Boone—has become more lost in his own mythologies, more trapped in his many legends than this one. The fact is, John Chapman might well be the best-known figure from our national past about whom most people know almost nothing at all.

I tested that theory with a survey conducted exclusively for this book by Zogby International. Nearly 2,500 adult Americans nationwide were asked about four figures from our distant past— Johnny Appleseed, Daniel Boone, Paul Bunyan, and Davy Crockett: Did they ever exist or were they mythic creations? Of Boone and Crockett, there was little doubt: Roughly 92 percent of those surveyed were sure both men were real figures. Paul Bunyan of the blue ox and mighty ax caused more confusion: 80 percent thought he never existed, 10 percent said he did, and another 10 percent were unsure. Johnny Appleseed, though, walked a middle line: 58 percent said he was an actual historical figure, while 42 percent said either he never existed (29 percent) or they weren't sure if he had (13 percent).

Fewer than one in four of those polled could identify Ohio and Indiana as the primary sites where Johnny Appleseed planted and tended his trees. Only a little more than one in four could place him in the proper half century. Asked what words first came to mind to describe him, respondents opted for the standard children's book version of the man: kindhearted, generous, an environmentalist. Lost was his religious intensity, in many ways the driving force of his life; any sense of an intellectual life, of which he had a very active one; and to some extent the sheer loneliness and self-reliance that defined his five decades on the American frontier. Of Johnny Appleseed, in short, most of us know largely a caricature; of John Chapman, barely a glimmer.

❦

Not that everything can be known. Chapman's early years, particularly, disappear into the mists. Whole sections of his childhood fill blank pages, including where he might have learned to read more than the Bible, which he clearly did, and write with a strong hand, which he had.

Still, hard and fast moments do exist. John Chapman was born September 26, 1774, in Leominster, Massachusetts, to a family with pedigree, if not great means. His father marched with the Minutemen and fought at Bunker Hill. Elizabeth, his mother, died shortly after delivering her third child, in the summer of 1776. (The new baby, a son, died soon after its mother.) Where and with whom John and his older sister, Elizabeth, might have lived until their father returned from service is lost to history, but they are thought to have joined him and his new family in Longmeadow, just south of Springfield, Massachusetts, in about 1781.

A decade and a half later—another of the unfilled gaps in his biography—John Chapman and his half brother Nathaniel fetched up on the edge of western Pennsylvania, almost at the close of the century, just as the new American nation north and west of the Ohio River was being born. The match of man, moment, and opportunity could not have been better.

For at least a half century, the territory's Native American tribes had regarded the Ohio River as the dividing line between their lands and the white man's lands to the east, but transportation routes were steadily opening up across the Pennsylvania Alleghenies—one-time Indian trails widened by Anglo-American soldiers in the 1760s to help defeat the French and Indians and now improved again to carry the settlers that would drive Native Americans out of the territory for good. Population pressures followed the roads west. Manifest Destiny beckoned, and with "Mad

Anthony" Wayne's 1795 victory at the Battle of Fallen Timbers, effective Indian resistance mostly disappeared.

By century's turn, when John Chapman first began poking his nose across the river, Ohio was a massive real-estate event in the offing. Millions of acres in what was known as the Western Reserve and elsewhere had been set aside for Revolutionary War veterans, but much of that had been scooped up by private companies awaiting the day when the "Indian problem" would be resolved and the pent-up demand for holdings in Ohio unleashed. It was a good time for speculators, and John Chapman, it turned out, had plenty of that in him.

It was a good time for nurserymen, too. One strain of the many folk traditions that fill in Chapman's early years has him working as a boy in Longmeadow for a local apple grower. In truth, no one knows for certain where Chapman learned the orchard skills that would eventually ripen into the name and myth of Johnny Appleseed, but however he came about his learning, the Ohio frontier at the start of the new century was an ideal place to exercise it. Apples were a vital diet supplement—whether dried for winter or pressed and fermented into applejack and hard cider, the essential beverages of early American life, just as cider vinegar was the essential medicine. Almost as important, fruit trees were also a frequent legal stipulation of land ownership.

Beginning in 1792, the Ohio Company of Associates (formed, despite its name, in Massachusetts) offered one hundred acres free to anyone willing to settle in the "Donation Tract," a hundred thousand acres of wilderness beyond Ohio's first permanent white settlement, at Marietta, that Congress had given the company to create a buffer zone with still-warring Indian tribes. The only requirement: Settlers had three years to plant fifty apple trees and twenty peach trees. Other land companies struck similar bargains: Orchards ran against the grain of squatters and rank speculators alike; they were improvements on nature, proof a settler meant to stay. Like their trees, orchard men were a valuable commodity.

Chapman was one of many among them, but almost alone among his peers, he had an uncanny sense of where the frontier would migrate next. He would load up with seeds each winter at the cider presses of southwestern Pennsylvania. Then, as the spring thaw came on, he would follow waterways and Indian trails into unclaimed land, make a clearing of a few acres, plant his seeds, and surround the new nursery with a brush fence to keep the deer out. When the settlers arrived a few years later, his seedlings would be waiting for them. On more than one occasion, he bought or leased land in expectation of the settlement to come.

It might have been a nice business model if he had been inclined to run it that way. But Chapman gave too much of his nursery stock away to those who couldn't pay and treated his own property, and interest and tax payments, far too cavalierly. What profits there were from his speculation and apple tree sales often went to secure pasturing for horses he saw being abused as he traveled the frontier's byways. Chapman might have run the first equine rescue operation in the new nation. He couldn't stand to watch an animal suffer, or a plant. That's why he propagated his apple trees by seed rather than by the more tried-and-true method of grafting.

Chapman had the eye of a speculator, the heart of a philanthropist, the courage of a frontiersman, and the wandering instincts of a Bedouin nomad. His nature was almost self-canceling.

❦

But it was the final leg of the great cluster of forces massed on the Ohio River at the start of the nineteenth century that would truly animate John Chapman: the Second Great Awakening. Then as now, this was a land filled with proselytizers, hell-bent on conversions and largely convinced that the Final Days were near.

Chapman could have had his choice of any of them: the Methodists, whose camp-meeting movement had swept into Ohio from Kentucky; Campbellites; Halcyonists; Stonites; later the Millerites and even the Mormons. Instead, he settled on the most intellectually rigorous and in some ways strangest of them all—the Church of the New Jerusalem, or simply New Church, based on the writings of the Swedish mystic Emanuel Swedenborg.

Like Chapman, Swedenborg has largely disappeared from history, but for a century after his death in 1772, he was taken as one of the seminal thinkers of modern history, a man who had done more than any other European of his age to rend the veil between this world and the next. Balzac wrote of Swedenborg: "He alone enables man to touch God." William Blake waged a virtual war against those who sought to codify the Swedish philosopher's teachings into a church, but Swedenborg's cosmology, his insistence on the accessibility of the spiritual world, leaks all through Blake's poetry and art. On this side of the ocean, Ralph Waldo Emerson, in his famous 1837 oration "The American Scholar," praised Swedenborg as "a man of genius who has done much for the philosophy of life. . . . He saw and showed the connection between nature and the affections of the soul. He pierced the emblematic or spiritual character of the visible, audible, tangible world."

Through the angels that populated Swedenborg's dreams, God delivered the secret truths of the Bible and revealed the very architecture of heaven and hell. Through chapters torn from Swedenborg's books and through his own after-dinner orations, John Chapman—the New Church's most famous North American disciple—carried those truths to the cabins and shacks of the frontier. God alone knows what the settlers who lived there must have made of the message, or the messenger, but the *Annals of the New Church* for 1847 gives a hint when it describes Chapman's reading "aloud the strange Gospel to the astonished family around the hearthstone . . . with a glow of enthusiasm such as to affect even those who looked upon him as half-witted or a heretic." This news *was* right fresh from heaven—not Scripture from thousands of years back but truths handed down from on high within the lifetime of many of Chapman's listeners. How thrilling it must have been to be brought so up to date in such a remote setting.

❦

In truth, John Chapman might have been exactly what A. Banning Norton called him: as odd as odd can be. He communed with birds and animals, even with insects, in a way that suggests both Francis of Assisi and a Hindu ascetic. Gentle as a lamb, he became a legendary figure in a land ruled by gun, knife, and fist. Learned enough to read Swedenborg, he was also queer enough to evoke the Holy Fool of the Eastern Orthodox tradition. Chapman was a vegetarian in a raw country where it was far easier to kill game for food than to grow a crop. He lived indoors occasionally, but as little as he had to. In dress and diet, he calls most directly to mind another Voice in the Wilderness: John the Baptist, with his camel hair cloak and meals of locusts and wild honey. Yet unlike that John, there was nothing fierce about this one.

In a time and a place where mass communication was nonexistent and local newspapers still rare, just about everyone seems to have known John Chapman, or known of him, either by his own name or by the nickname that became more common as he migrated from mortal man to immortal myth. Stories of him floated from cabin to cabin, from village to village, just as he did. Some of the best stories he spread himself. In a sense, Chapman was his own wandering minstrel.

To amuse the boys, Chapman stuck pins in his feet and walked on red-hot coals. He seems to have been impervious to most pain. And he was welcomed almost everywhere.

John Chapman never married, had no children, left no heirs, but he was as social as a loner could be. He loved the company of children. To the girls, he doled out bits of ribbon; to amuse the boys, he stuck pins in his feet and walked on red-hot coals. He seems to have been impervious to most pain. And he was welcomed almost everywhere—although, here again, the mythic Appleseed has to be teased out of the flesh-and-blood Chapman.

One rumor had it that he had been promised a settler's young daughter in marriage when she reached an appropriate age. Another held that, in the manner of a Muslim martyr, he had two virgins waiting for him in the afterlife if he took no bride in this one. Whatever the truth, the only thing he really seems to have been wedded to was motion. Even in his seventh decade, Chapman was still living out the restlessness of a young and idealistic nation. It's both fitting and predictable that he should have died by a rented hearth, on someone else's floor.

❧

Some people thought Chapman had been kicked in the head by a horse, perhaps back in Pennsylvania, in his mid- or late twenties. In his somewhat shaky "contemporaneous" recollections of Johnny Appleseed, W. M. Glines, who was born in Marietta, Ohio, in 1806, states outright that "At about the age of 21 years, [Johnny] received a kick from a horse that fractured his skull, which was trepanned at the time. From that time forth he manifested that singular character attributed to him." A horse kick might indeed explain his many extreme oddities. Some people never get over a blow like that, and the fact that he was (or might have been) trepanned—had a piece of the skull cut out to relieve pressure on the brain—suggests the possible severity of the situation. But the injury to Chapman's brain, if there was one, doesn't appear to have affected his higher mental faculties. In its obituary for Chapman, the *Fort Wayne Sentinel* noted that "he always carried with him some works of the doctrine of Swedenborg, with which he was perfectly familiar, and would readily converse and argue on his tenets, evincing much shrewdness and penetration."

In fact, Chapman seems to have conversed freely and incessantly (when he wasn't holed up alone, deep in the woods) about many things, but the one subject he clearly did not address with any frequency and/or accuracy was himself. Robert Price made note of it in his meticulously researched 1954 biography *Johnny Appleseed: Man & Myth:* Chapman's *Fort Wayne Sentinel* obituary is long on color. It has the sidelights of the story down. It notes that Chapman had been a regular visitor to the Fort Wayne area for "upwards of 20 years" and was "well known through this region by his eccentricity and the strange garb he usually wore." But when it comes to details, the man behind the story remains mostly a mystery, a cipher in his time just as he continues to be into our own.

Chapman, the obituary speculates, "lived to an extreme old age, being probably not less than 80 years old at the time of his death—though no person would have judged from his appearance that he was 60." In fact, he was six months shy of turning seventy-one.

"His home—if home he had—was in the neighborhood of Cleveland, Ohio," or so the obituary writer contends, but while John Chapman's name can reasonably be associated with at least sixteen cities and towns in Ohio, Cleveland is not among them.

"He was a native of Pennsylvania." Wrong again, although for nearly a century after his death Pennsylvania seemed as good a guess as any.

2.

ROOTS

Elizabeth Simons Chapman left behind a daughter, also Elizabeth; a very memorable son, as events turned out; and one heartbreaking letter for the world to recall her by. The letter was sent June 3, 1776, from her home in Leominster, Massachusetts, forty miles west of Boston, to her husband, Nathaniel, then serving in the Continental Army, with "Capt. Pollard's Company of Carpenters," somewhere in New York State. Elizabeth was eight months pregnant.

Loving Husband,

These lines come with my affectionate regards to you hoping they will find you in health, tho I still continue in a very weak and low condition. I am no better than I was when you left me but rather worse, and I should be very glad if you could come and see me for I want to see you.

Our children [Elizabeth was then nearly six years old and John still shy of two] *are both well thro the Divine Goodness.*

I have received but two letters from you since you went away—neither knew where you was till last Friday I had one and Sabathday evening after, another, and I rejoice to hear that you are well and I pray you may thus continue and in God's due

*time be returned in safety. I send this letter by Mr. Mullins and I
hope it will reach you and I should be glad if you would send me a
letter back by him.*

*I have wrote that I should be glad you could come to see me
if you could, but if you cannot, I desire you should make yourself
as easy as possible for I am under the care of a kind Providence
who is able to do more for me than I can ask or think and I desire
humbly to submit to His Holy Will with patience and resigna-
tion, patiently to hear what he shall see fit to lay upon me. My
cough is somewhat abated, but I think I grow weaker. I desire
your prayers for me that I may be prepared for the will of God
that I may so improve my remainder of life that I may answer
the great end for which I was made, that I might glorify God here
and finally come to the enjoyment of Him in a world of glory,
thro the merits of Jesus Christ.*

*Remember, I beseech you, that you are a mortall and that you
must submit to death sooner or later and consider that we are
always in danger of our spiritual enemy. Be, therefore, on your
guard continually, and live in a daily preparation for death—
and so I must bid you farewell and if it should be so ordered that
I should not see you again, I hope we shall both be as happy as to
spend an eternity of happiness in the coming world which is my
desire and prayer.*

So I conclude by subscribing myself, your

Ever loving and affectionate wife
Elizabeth Chapman

The letter has two postscripts. In the first, Elizabeth provides
a quick summary of family and friends: Brother Zebedee, her father's family, the Johnsons, the Widow Smith's and Joshua Pierce's
folks are all well. The second postscript gets briefly down to business and hints at the economic condition of the family:

I have not bought a cow for they are very scarce and dear and I think I can do without, and I would not have you uneasy about it or about any money for I have as much as I need for the present.

On June 26, 1776, Leominster town records show, Elizabeth gave birth to a son, her third child, named Nathaniel after his father. Three weeks later, on July 16, a dozen days after America had declared its independence from Great Britain, Elizabeth died, as her last letter so clearly hinted she expected to. Infant Nathaniel followed her to the grave two weeks after that. No record exists to show where the two might have been buried. Nor is there any sure evidence of where the now-fractured Chapman family was living at the time, although it was certainly a rented farm property. Wherever the exact location—and it was somewhere within the Leominster boundaries—it must have been a house of sorrows that summer of 1776.

❦

That we have even this brief window into Elizabeth Chapman's life is largely serendipitous. The last letter she sent her husband survived the war and his deployments, passed into their daughter Elizabeth's hands, was preserved through the generations, and eventually surfaced in Detroit, almost 160 years after it was penned, in the possession of Kitty Dix Humphrey, the great-great-granddaughter of the woman who wrote it—a testimony to her long dead ancestor's Yankee stoicism and piety. That we know of Elizabeth Chapman's role as a handmaiden to America's mythic past is in some ways still more remarkable, a credit to the dogged work of a handful of dedicated women.

Daniel Boone has always been from somewhere, sprung from a specific moment in time: to be exact, the Oley Valley of Berks County, Pennsylvania, where he was born October 22, 1734 (or

November 2 by the Gregorian calendar, which was adopted during his lifetime), the sixth of Squire and Sarah Morgan Boone's eleven children. Davy Crockett—born August 17, 1786, along the Nolichucky River in Greene County, Tennessee—left behind an autobiography that recounts not only the occasional difficulties with his father but also the adventures and wanderings of his youth. Both men entered American folklore anchored in their own realities. Intentionally or not, John Chapman left it to others to establish the coordinates of his birth, his early years, and his ancestry.

The first extensive mention of Johnny Appleseed in print—a lengthy article in 1871 for *Harper's New Monthly Magazine*—gathers together most of what was then known or surmised about Chapman and ventures that "there is good reason for believing" he was born in Boston in 1775. W. M. Glines, who claimed to have known Chapman personally, sets his birthplace more exactly, "near Bunker Hill," but seven years earlier, in 1768. By November 1900, when the first monument to Chapman/Appleseed was erected in Mansfield, Ohio, the birthplace had migrated west-southwest nearly a hundred miles, to Springfield, Massachusetts, near the Connecticut border, according to the lengthy historical sketch delivered by A. J. Baughman.

And so the coordinates went, slip-sliding along, for another third of a century, even as the myth of Johnny Appleseed was planting itself firmly in the American conscience. In his 1923 poem "In Praise of Johnny Appleseed," which relied heavily on the *Harper's* piece, Vachel Lindsay accepts Chapman's birth date as 1775, "in the days of President Washington," but gives up on where. He was simply "A boy / Blew west" from New England who "with prayers and incantations, / And with 'Yankee Doodle Dandy,' / Crossed the Appalachians, / And was 'young John

Chapman.'" That's poetic license, of course—or maybe mythic license, given what Chapman became—but as late as the mid-1930s, the *Dictionary of American Biography*, published by the American Council of Learned Societies, was still using the 1775 date (which the dictionary notes "is generally inferred") and placing Chapman's birth in either Boston or Springfield. "His parentage," the author writes, "[has] not been discovered."

His *Fort Wayne Sentinel* obituary, logically enough, had Chapman born in Pennsylvania, since that is where he first came to any sort of notice. Other accounts name Ohio (even less surprising), Maryland (a stretch), and elsewhere. In the 1904 historical novel *The Quest of John Chapman: The Story of a Forgotten Hero*—published by the Macmillan Company, at a cost new of $1.30—the Reverend Dr. Newell Dwight Hillis makes Chapman the son of a New England minister in the severe Jonathan Edwards mode. In a competing version, Chapman is a half-breed love child. In part, Appleseed seems to have sprung from Chapman's own wildly romantic conception of himself. But, in fact, John Chapman did have coordinates, and in 1937 they at long last struggled to the surface.

The *New York Times* took note, belatedly, in an editorial short for its edition of April 19, 1938:

> It may not be news to anybody else, but it escaped us that Johnny's birthplace has been found. . . . A Durham [NH] dispatch to the Manchester Union says:
>
> The discovery of Johnny Appleseed's birthplace came to its final stage last Summer, following research into vital statistics by Mrs. M.H. Grassley and Mrs. Ernestine Perry of the Garden Club of Springfield, Mass. The actual records prove the birth at Leominster and the date Sept. 24, 1774.

Grassley and Perry, of course, did more than pinpoint the birthplace and, almost, the birth date. (They missed the latter by two days.) They also established Elizabeth Simons Chapman and Nathaniel Chapman as John Chapman's parents, and that was enough of a lead to begin giving Johnny Appleseed a long tail in history and a few notable relatives.

The Simons genealogy was for the most part well recorded in town and church annals. Elizabeth's New World lineage traces back on the male side to William Simonds, who arrived in Massachusetts Bay Colony in 1635, and settled in Woburn, in what are now the northwest suburbs of Boston, about 1644, just about the time he married a widow, Judith Hayward. Their tenth child, James Simonds—born in Woburn on November 1, 1658—married Susanna Blodgett on December 29, 1685. A son, also James, was born ten months later, on November 1, 1686, exactly thirty years after his father's birth, and eventually married Mary Fowle, a dozen years his junior. Their son, yet another James Simons but now (maybe) with the "d" omitted, was born in Woburn in 1717, married Anna Lawrence, and the two of them migrated to Leominster, where Elizabeth Simons was born on the second of February, 1748. Elizabeth, in turn, was six days past her twenty-second birthday when she married Nathaniel Chapman on February 8, 1770, in Leominster.

Histories of Woburn in the colonial era make frequent mention of Simons (and Simonds and Symonds) without dwelling particularly long on any of them—an indication that the family might have been more plentiful than distinguished. But longevity seems to have run in the family. At a time when the average male didn't survive into his forties, James Simons made it almost to age ninety, long enough to see his great-grandchildren Elizabeth and John born and perhaps to witness children and parents fully accepted into the First Congregational Church of Leominster on June 25, 1775, five weeks before the old man's death.

If you trace the female side back far enough and cast a wide-enough net, you can even find a connection to two U.S. presidents. Mary Fowle, John Chapman's maternal great-grandmother, was nine generations removed from Thomas Richardson and Katherine Duxford (died in 1631 and 1633 respectively), who also are great-great-etc. grandparents to George H. W. Bush, the forty-first president of the United States, and George W. Bush, the forty-third. That might mean nothing more than that virtually every living white person of English descent whose parents came to New England before the start of the eighteenth century is probably related in one way or another. Still, the thought of Johnny Appleseed sitting down for a tête-à-tête in the Oval Office with his long-lost and distant cousins is delicious. Would they have made Johnny wear shoes? Or bathe first?

The Simons family tree also provided one family member far more immediate to the moment—a first cousin to Elizabeth—whose story nearly rivals Johnny Appleseed's for color.

Benjamin Thompson, Jr., later Count Rumford of the Holy Roman Empire, was born in Woburn on March 26, 1753, in his grandfather's house, "a humble dwelling," according to Reverend Samuel Sewall, author of an 1868 history of the town. Benjamin's father died before the boy was two. About the time of his third birthday, his mother remarried and moved into a home opposite the town's grandest estate, the Baldwin mansion. Benjamin and his new neighbor and contemporary Loammi Baldwin became fast friends, connected by precocious intellects, particularly in the sciences. The two were first instructed by John Fowle (almost certainly a cousin through the Thompson/Simon family), who ran the local grammar school. Subsequent tutors took up instruction in mathematics and astronomy.

Benjamin was apprenticed at age thirteen to a Salem merchant and, later, to a Boston dry-goods dealer. In both cases, business ground to a near halt as tensions with Great Britain mounted, and the apprenticeships were terminated. Back home in Woburn in 1770, without work, Benjamin, accompanied by Loammi Baldwin, gained permission to attend a series of Harvard University lectures on natural philosophy, delivered by John Winthrop, great-great-grandson of the founder of the Massachusetts Bay Colony and one of the most distinguished scientists of his day. (Winthrop had also influenced another Boston Benjamin—Benjamin Franklin.)

In 1772, not yet twenty years old, Thompson moved to Concord, New Hampshire, then still known as Rumford, to take charge of the local school, and with that, his fortunes changed dramatically. He built an almost instant reputation for brilliance and innovation, introducing physical exercise into the curriculum and holding his students spellbound with his scientific lectures and experiments. But he seems to have been equally or more notable for his physical beauty. One local historian describes Thompson as "nearly six feet tall, erect and finely proportioned, with clear cut features of the Roman type, bright blue eyes and dark auburn hair....A handsomer man never walked our main street." And indeed a portrait later painted by Thomas Gainsborough shows Thompson to be every bit the Adonis described.

Among those who took immediate notice of the new teacher was Sarah Walker Rolfe, widow of the town's richest citizen and, at age thirty-three, fourteen years older than Thompson. The two were married in the fall of 1772, only months after Thompson had arrived in town. Soon, the new schoolmaster was socializing with New Hampshire's royal governor, John Wentworth, who was so impressed (as everyone seems to have been) that he appointed Thompson a major in one of the colony's regiments. The moment was to prove the apex of his life in America.

Jealousies ensued, in Rumford and beyond. As the Revolution

began, Thompson found himself charged with being a Tory spy. Hauled before a local Committee of Correspondence and fearing violence on himself and his family, Thompson fled back to Woburn, leaving his wife, stepson, and new daughter behind, only to meet a similar reception in his hometown. A few years earlier, Thompson had dazzled Woburn with his expensive wardrobe and costly conveyance when he brought his new wife to meet his mother. Now, except for Loammi Baldwin's protection, judgment might well have been rendered on him by an angry mob.

Out of options, Thompson took the only safe course available, fleeing to Boston and then to England, where it seems he charmed the pants off just about everyone.

Within four years of arriving in London, Thompson was serving as undersecretary for the Northern Department of the British Government, with responsibilities for America, and had been elevated to the rank of lieutenant colonel of the King's American Dragoons. In 1784, he accepted an invitation from Karl Theodor, Elector of Bavaria, to join him at his capital in Munich. There, Thompson set about establishing schools, reforming the military establishment, and ridding the capital of beggary—according to Sewall "an enormous evil in Munich"—through a combination of public contributions and training in "honest industry," efforts that appear to have rendered him one of the best-loved men in all of Bavaria. Sewall writes that when Thompson once fell sick with a dangerous illness, the inmates of the workhouse he had established voluntarily proceeded to the cathedral to pray for his recovery.

Sarah Thompson had joined her husband briefly in Woburn but was never to see him again. She died in Concord (Rumford's new name) in early 1792. By the time their daughter, also Sarah, joined her stranger of a father in Munich, honors were flowing his way. Thompson was admitted to the Academy of Science in Berlin, was made a lieutenant general of the Army of Bavaria, and finally with the intercession of his patron, the Elector, was named a Count of the Holy Roman Empire. For his title he chose the place where he had first gained entry into society and from which he had later been forced to flee: Count of Rumford.

More triumphs followed, both in Munich and back in London, where he gained great fame for solving the problem of smoky chimneys and almost single-handedly launched the Royal Institution of Great Britain. Like Benjamin Franklin, Thompson occupied his mind with practical inventions: a drip coffeemaker, double-pane glass, and a more efficient stove, named the Rumford stove, just as Franklin's improvement became known as the Franklin stove.

Had Thompson ever been able to settle down in one place, he might have attained a fame similar to Franklin's: public man, social benefactor, inventor, scientific theorist. But he seems to have been addicted to movement and to seizing the main chance, in life and love. His mistresses were many and bore him at least two children. In 1805, in Paris and with his daughter permanently settled back in America, Thompson married the most famous of his lovers—Marie-Anne Pierette Paulze Lavoisier, the widow of the famed chemist and aristocrat Antoine-Laurent Lavoisier, who had been guillotined in the French Revolution. Marie-Anne had been thirteen when she married Lavoisier, then twenty-eight. In Thompson, she found a husband closer to her own age, but their relationship quickly soured, and Thompson finally retreated to a house in Auteuil, on the outskirts of Paris, where he died in 1814, at age sixty-one.

In a 1998 article for the *Proceedings* of the American Philosophical Society, John Meurig Thomas, master of Peterhouse at Cambridge University and the former director of the Royal Institution of Great Britain, describes its founder thus:

By all accounts he was ruthless and arrogant, callously cunning and devious, an unprincipled spy, a calculating womanizer; moreover, he had been a soldier of fortune and a statesman. But he was also a philanthropist, a brilliantly effective social reformer, an ingenious inventor, and an exceptionally innovative scientist.

In all, it's hard to imagine a wayward branch on a family tree better balanced by Johnny Appleseed—Count Rumford's polar opposite in virtually every regard except in their mutual inability to stay still, to root in any one place. Perhaps it was only the times, but perpetual motion seems to have been built into the family gene pool.

As for Loammi Baldwin, Thompson's youthful best friend and mob protector, he went on to honors of his own, but he is best remembered today for helping to popularize a fruit that first came to Baldwin's attention when he noticed woodpeckers swarming about the tree that bore it: the bright red winter apple that came to be known in Loammi's honor as the Baldwin apple, almost the sole surviving link between the once internationally famous Count Rumford and the young cousin who would eventually gain a reputation that dwarfs his own.

❦

If the Simonses' lineage was mostly an open book, the Chapman genealogy was closer to a gigantic puzzle, filled with blind alleys and conflicting claims. English-born Chapmans arrived in the New World in droves in the seventeenth century, in differing family groups that were related to one another often only in the loosest ways. Once on American soil, they propagated like mad and favored no given name more than Nathaniel or John. Whether one tracks the family through Massachusetts or Virginia, where Chapmans were among the earliest settlers, Johns and Nathaniels spill out of the record books, not infrequently in father-son and son-father combinations. Just to keep things interesting, the earliest Chapman that Johnny Appleseed can be directly tied to took as his first wife Mary Symonds, later Simonds, later Simons, etc.

As Winston Churchill famously said of Russia, John Chapman's family tree was "a riddle wrapped in a mystery inside an enigma." Solving the riddle would take a bulldog-like tenacity, a detective's intuition for the unrecognized clue, and an easy comfort with dry stacks of public records. All those qualities happily came together in the person of Florence E. Wheeler.

Born in 1879, Wheeler served for almost fifty years as Leominster's principal librarian and the first person specifically trained to the work. She was in place when the city's two-story Roman-style temple to books, a library building funded in part by Andrew Carnegie, was completed in 1910. By proxy—Wheeler died in 1962—she's still supporting the cause: The Florence E. Wheeler Cornerstone Society is reserved for the Leominster library's top givers, those who pony up fifty thousand dollars or more. But her most enduring contribution to Leominster, the library, and the nation is this: Florence Wheeler cracked the Chapman code.

In a 1939 article for *Ohio Archeological and Historical Quarterly*, the scholarly publication of the Ohio Historical Society, Wheeler spelled out Johnny Appleseed's paternal heritage in detail for the first time. Edward Chapman, the American fountainhead of the family, was apparently born in Yorkshire, England, in the early part of the seventeenth century and reached Boston about 1639. By 1642, he had become a grantee of the town of Ipswich—colonized only nine years earlier by a group headed by John Winthrop, Jr.— and he went on to become a prosperous farmer and miller there. Edward had two wives: Mary Symonds, who died in 1658, and Dorothy (Swan) Abbott, a widow who would remarry again when Edward died in April 1678.

Edward and Mary had five children: Simon, Mary, Nathaniel, Samuel, and John, the last born three years before his mother's death. John was married near his twentieth birthday, in September 1675, and died a little over two years later, but he did leave behind a son, another John, born July 7, 1676. That John (known as Senior), in turn, had five children by Elizabeth Davis: Martha, Elizabeth, Rebecca, John (Jr. on some records; baptized in Ipswich on December 2, 1714), and Davis. John Jr. would go on to have two wives: Martha Perley Boardman, ten years his senior and already a widow when they married on March 1, 1738; and Martha Hunt, whom he married in July 1756, three or four years after the first Martha's death and four years before his own death of smallpox, on December 7, 1760, five days after his forty-sixth birthday. By the first Martha, John had four children of his own: Perley, Elizabeth, Martha, and Nathaniel, the last born September 13, 1746.

So far, so good. By carefully combing through town and church records, Florence Wheeler had tracked the Edward/John/John/John Chapman family from Ipswich, thirty miles north-northeast of Boston, to Topsfield, about eight miles southwest of Ipswich, to Tewksbury, another eighteen miles west-northwest. Wheeler had the begets and begats down, and they told their own tale of urgency: An astounding number of firstborns in the family had come into the world within the first year of marriage. She had learned that John Chapman, Jr., and his brother had in 1741 purchased a large farming tract "on the road from Billerica to Borland's Farm" in Tewksbury. Wheeler even had uncovered the intimate details of John Jr.'s estate: among the items books, "wareing apparrill," "salted meat & Fat," cows, oxen, young cattle, sheep, lambs, horses, swine, and a one-quarter share of a "nett and other utensils for fishing."

Most important for Wheeler's purposes, she seemed to have

drawn a clear bead on the man she was trying to link to all this history: Nathaniel, son of John, son of John, etc. Now all she had to do was show that the Tewksbury Nathaniel Chapman was one and the same as the Nathaniel Chapman in Leominster, thirty miles west, who was already known to be the father of the future Johnny Appleseed. But here was a problem: The two ends wouldn't connect. Like one of those maddening miswirings of Christmas tree lights, Wheeler had been left with two female plugs facing each other.

The trail working forward from John Jr. stopped cold with his death. The trail working backward from Nathaniel couldn't definitively be linked to his likely father. What happened? The answer, Wheeler discovered, lay in that stock figure of folklore and fairy tales: the stepmother. Of the four children born to John Chapman, Jr., and Martha Perley Boardman Chapman, only two had survived their father—Nathaniel and his older sister, Elizabeth—and neither seems to have been enamored of their father's second wife. While she was trying to levy her late husband's estate for the care and maintenance already expended on her stepchildren, the surviving ones were making their own arrangements. On June 13, 1761, Nathaniel appealed to the local court as follows:

I NATHANIEL CHAPMAN of Tewksbury in the County of Middle & Province of Massachusetts Bay in New England Being Fourteen years of age Do Choose & Desire that my sd Uncle Davis Chapman may be made Guardian For me according to Law as Witness my Hand . . .

Elizabeth, Nathaniel's sister, followed a week later with a similar petition, and the petitions proved to be the critical piece of intelligence. Nathaniels and Johns littered the male side of the family tree. Davis, by contrast, was singular and easy to isolate—the missing link that showed Florence Wheeler the way out of the puzzle palace.

❧

Who might have taken in John and Elizabeth Chapman after their mother died, in whose home they might have lived for the next four years, until their father was released from military duty, is anyone's guess. Chapmans were rare in Leominster, but Simondses and Simonses were all over the place. At least ten births by those names are recorded in the Leominster vital records between 1740 and 1763, and this in a town that by 1765 had a population of only 743 people. Maybe the children, temporarily orphaned, moved in with their dead mother's relatives. Or maybe their great-uncle Davis, then age sixty, took them in. Their paternal grandfather and great-grandfather were both dead, but Davis had been their father's guardian, and his own house would have needed cheering up. His son, also Davis, born within a month of Nathaniel in 1746, had died only two years earlier of "cold in the night."

For nearly half a century after Nathaniel Chapman bobbed to the surface of history as Johnny Appleseed's father, the quality of his military service was at question as well.

The progression of the elder Chapman's army career is fairly forthright, at least as far as the facts are known. In April 1775, he was among three companies of "Minutemen" that set out from Leominster to Lexington, thirty miles to the east. None of the companies arrived in time to take part in the skirmishes there or at Concord, but upon returning to Leominster, Nathaniel immediately enlisted in the Twenty-Third Regiment of Foot; was sent back east, this time to camp in Cambridge; and by all indications took part in the Battle at Bunker Hill, overlooking Boston harbor, in mid-June 1775.

The Bunker Hill service and subsequent duty at Prospect

Hill—the "Citadel" overlooking the strategically important Charlestown Road—and with Washington's army in New York State must have involved artillery, because on March 19, 1777, Nathaniel was assigned as a Captain of Wheelwrights to the newly established armory at Springfield, Massachusetts, where he remained until the end of September 1780.

Those are the bare bones. Nathaniel's release from service—the whys and wherefores behind it—is what's at issue. In his 1954 biography, Robert Price writes of Johnny Appleseed's father: "Whatever his earlier record, the journals of the Continental Congress give only the unpleasant truth that Captain Chapman along with other Springfield officers was released late in 1780 because of unsatisfactory management of the military stores." As further evidence, Price notes that Nathaniel "was given neither a pension nor a land bounty for his services."

That was sufficient insult to the family name to incite a modern-day Chapman descendant, George B. Huff of Indianapolis, Indiana, to launch his own investigation and to hire a fellow of the American College of Genealogists, Mabel Swanson, to sort through the record. The resulting document, more than sixty pages presented to the Storrs Library of Longmeadow, Massachusetts, in November 1994, stops short of being a compelling rebuttal, but it does suggest considerable mitigation.

For starters, Huff and Swanson note that by 1780, the flow of the war had reduced the Springfield Armory to a minor, distant, and expensive role. In early 1777, when the armory was established, the war was being fought largely in New England and across the Middle Atlantic states. The monthlong Battle of Saratoga in New York; the Battle of Bennington, Vermont; Washington's challenging winter at Valley Forge; the back-and-forth fighting around Philadelphia; Monmouth Court House in New

Jersey—they all lay ahead at that point, and the Springfield Armory was a central part of the supply chain.

At the end of 1778, though, the war began to shift dramatically to the south, and by 1780, American soldiers were fighting almost exclusively on southern soil. Not only was the armory at Springfield too far away from the action to be of practical use; it seems also to have fallen under sloppy command, the way outposts often do when they have outlived their usefulness.

The *Journals of the Continental Congress* report that on July 17, 1780, the matter of the Springfield Armory and its staffing was taken up by a Board of War:

> The Board having made inquiry into and considered the state of the department of military stores at Springfield in the State of Massachusetts Bay, are convinced that it is and has long been so very ill conducted that the benefits derived from it have been very inadequate to the expense of supporting it. . . . We are now satisfied that it would be better to break up the post entirely than continue it on its present footing. For, such has been the negligence and mismanagement for some time past, we cannot think it our duty to furnish any more money for the post, while the present principals there are in office.

That has really been the gist of the case against Nathaniel Chapman's military service—that he was part of a team of incompetents and layabouts—and it is clearly what Robert Price had in mind when he wrote of the "unpleasant truth" to be found in the Continental Congress *Journals*. But the *Journals* don't stop there.

The same day, July 17, as part of its plan to "derange" the Armory, the Board of War "excused from farther service at the post" two of its top commanders, Ezekiel Cheever, Esq., and Lieutenant

Colonel David Mason. A little over six weeks later, on August 26, 1780, the Board added Captain Nathaniel Chapman and Major Joseph Eayres to the same list, noting that their service was "altogether unnecessary in our present circumstances." But the Board also resolved at the same time to provide all four men with one year's pay and subsistence—not a pension and land grant, to be sure, but less a dishonorable discharge perhaps than a simple recognition that the war had moved beyond needing them.

❦

One thing Nathaniel Chapman did have to show for his time at the Springfield Armory: a new wife. On July 24, 1780—two months before he was released from service and almost exactly four years after his first wife's death—Nathaniel married Lucy Cooley, of nearby Longmeadow.

Like Nathaniel, Lucy traced her descent from the early decades of European settlement in New England. Benjamin Cooley, known as "Ensign," received a land allotment in Longmeadow in 1642 and by some reckonings was the very first proprietor of the meadow grants that gave the town its name. Of his eight children, two sons, with the wonderful biblical names of Obadiah and Eliakim, settled in Longmeadow, and their progeny were still peopling the town when Lucy and Nathaniel settled there and Nathaniel sent for the daughter who barely knew him and the son he had rarely seen since John was well shy of a year old.

What did Elizabeth and John make of their new circumstances? If local lore is right, they moved into a small, plain, rectangular frame home that dates back to at least 1695. For the four of them—two children, then ten and not quite six, freshly reacquired father, and new stepmother—the house certainly would have been satisfactory, and clearly there were opportunities for schooling in

Longmeadow, quite possibly for Elizabeth to continue hers and for John to start his. But one guesses that what Elizabeth and John were most likely to have recalled in later life about their growing years in Longmeadow were the agonies of childbirth, the constant bawling of children, and the ever-diminishing personal space in their living quarters.

Nathaniel Chapman appears to have been a mostly unsuccessful provider caught in a shrinking postwar economy, but he was a prodigious sire, and in Lucy Cooley, he found a fertile and durable mate. Beginning in December 1781 and through the summer of 1787, Lucy Chapman gave birth to a child every two years on average: Nathaniel came first, named both for his father and for the infant son who had died earlier; then Abner (July 1783); Pierly, which seems to be an alternative spelling of the Perley family name (March 1785); and Lucy, in July 1787. Over the next decade, the pace slowed to a child every three years: Patty (February 1790), Persis (November 1793), Mary (January 1796). Then the reproductive schedule picked up again with Jonathan in February 1798 and Davis, named for the guardian uncle, in April 1800. Three years later, on April 23, 1803, Lucy gave birth for the final time: a girl, Sally.

In all, Lucy had ten children and must, despite her many labors, have been healthy as a horse. (She lived another twenty-seven years after the last of her children was born.) Nathaniel could count thirteen offspring, including the three by his first wife, two of them still living. Because all of Nathaniel and Lucy's brood seem to have survived to adulthood—and since Elizabeth didn't marry until 1799, when she was nearing her late twenties, and almost certainly lived at home until then, helping her stepmother with the constant parade of babies—the possibility exists that by the very late 1790s as many as fourteen people ranging in age from infancy to their late forties were coexisting at the Longmeadow house in, at best, four hundred square feet of indoor living space, plus a low-ceilinged attic floor for sleeping.

Fully occupied, the house would have afforded each of its inmates about twenty-eight square feet during non-sleeping hours, room enough to turn around but not to escape the clatter, the runny noses, the wail of the latest newborn (and the almost constant sight of Lucy pregnant yet again), the aggravations of living not just on top of one another but literally cheek to jowl. By 1796, though, and perhaps as early as 1792, the house was no longer fully occupied. John Chapman had flown the coop. And he'd taken his oldest half brother with him.

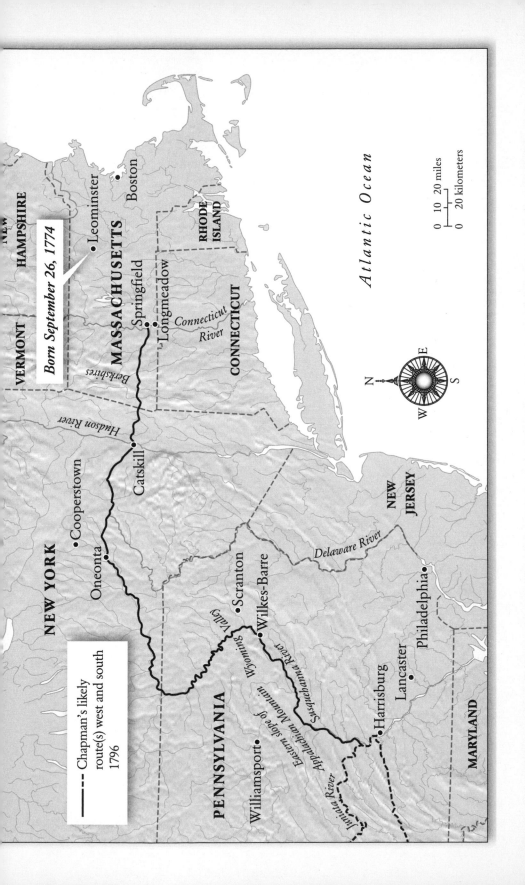

Born September 26, 1774

Chapman's likely
route(s) west and south
1796

NEW HAMPSHIRE

VERMONT

MASSACHUSETTS

Leominster

Boston

RHODE ISLAND

Springfield

Longmeadow

Connecticut River

CONNECTICUT

Berkshires

Hudson River

Catskill

Cooperstown

NEW YORK

Oneonta

Atlantic Ocean

0   10   20 miles
0   20 kilometers

N
W   E
S

NEW JERSEY

Delaware River

Scranton

Wilkes-Barre

Wyoming Valley

Eastern slope of

Appalachian Mountains

Susquehanna River

Philadelphia

Lancaster

Harrisburg

Juniata River

PENNSYLVANIA

Williamsport

MARYLAND

3.

BREAKING AWAY

~

In an October 17, 1883, address celebrating the centennial of Longmeadow, Reverend Charles R. Bliss, a Congregational minister and native son, evoked the majestic landscape that greeted the town's founders "as they wound down the Bay Path to the banks of the Connecticut, the vanguard of the mighty army that for two hundred and fifty years has been marching westward."

"Never can we extol too highly the deeds of our fathers," the reverend went on. "By whatever names our families are known, they all strike their roots into the same rich soil. We are not so much Coltons, or Cooleys, or Keeps, or Blisses, as descendants of the Puritans; of the lineage and household of men who, with cruel persecutions behind them, and hardships and disasters before them, erected here altars whose fires, after two and a half centuries, are to-day burning brightly as ever."

Nine decades earlier, two descendants of that same Puritan lineage—one a half Cooley, the other a step-Cooley/Chapman—joined that mighty army marching westward. Why did John Chapman and his half brother Nathaniel up and leave the Connecticut River Valley? When did they take off and where did they go? Like almost every question involving the early years of Johnny Appleseed, *when* and *where* have multiple answers.

One version has them striking out as early as 1792, picking

up the Old Connecticut Path, which ran from Boston through Springfield, and from there west through Westfield and Great Barrington, Massachusetts, roughly along the line of State Route 23, and on to the Hudson River at present-day Catskill, New York. Albany would have lain a few days' trek to the north once they made the river; New York City, 120 miles due south. Instead, John and Nathaniel are thought to have crossed the Hudson at Catskill (the site today of the Rip Van Winkle Bridge) by one of the many ferries then at work all along the Hudson, and made their way farther due west to the Susquehanna River Valley—perhaps three weeks in all of arduous travel and just the beginning of their journey.

Chances are they would have intersected the Susquehanna River just about at Oneonta, twenty miles below its headwaters at the south end of Otsego Lake, now almost within sight of the National Baseball Hall of Fame. From there, so this version goes, John and Nathaniel followed the Susquehanna Valley as the river meandered, first southwest into Pennsylvania; then back southeast into the Wyoming Valley of current-day Scranton and Wilkes-Barre, where they would have found a host of Connecticut settlers, six thousand or more living in almost twenty settlements, a legacy of Connecticut's long-forgotten claim on northern Pennsylvania. (Hostilities between the two states, which share a northern border interrupted by New York State, resulted in two brief clashes in the immediate post-Revolution years, the so-called Pennamite Wars.)

Hard evidence of the Chapmans' presence in the Wyoming Valley has never been uncovered, but the oral tradition placing them there is strong and the travel logic compelling. Where they went from there is more of a crapshoot.

A biographical sketch put together by J. Appleseed & Co., a publisher of "spiritual growth literature" affiliated with the Swedenborgian Church of North America, posits that the two wanderers might have kept following the Susquehanna, now flowing southwest, to Harrisburg, then only recently incorporated and still better known as the site of John Harris's ferry, and from there back southeast until the river joined the Chesapeake Bay at Havre de Grace, Maryland. Once they reached the bay, the two brothers are supposed to have skirted along its western shore into Virginia, where they tarried for a number of years while John strengthened in faith and learned the rudiments of his future vocation: "There are some early accounts of John speaking of his own activities as 'a Bible missionary' on the Potomac when he was a young man," the J. Appleseed sketch notes, "and Johnny was seen for two or three consecutive years along the banks of the Potomac in eastern Virginia, picking the seeds from the pomace of the cider mills in the late 1790s."

Other versions of the same essential tale set the departure from Longmeadow at 1796, not 1792. John Chapman would have been twenty-two then, not eighteen, and Nathaniel fifteen instead of eleven—a more likely age for undertaking such an adventurous journey, especially in the context of the times. In 1790, the average age of first menstruation for European girls was just about eighteen, almost fifty percent older than today. Comparable historical data on the onset of male puberty doesn't exist, but it's reasonable to suppose that males, too, mature today at about two-thirds the age they did at the end of the eighteenth century. In 1792, Nathaniel would have been only a boy; by 1796, he might have had the sinew and stamina for what lay ahead.

The later departure date, too, doesn't require John and Nathaniel to wander about Virginia for several years before appearing, all but magically, in western Pennsylvania in 1797—and indeed there's not a shred of evidence other than tradition to support the notion that brother and half brother ever reached the banks of the Potomac or even crossed the southern border of

Pennsylvania. Otherwise, the competing versions tend to dovetail: Longmeadow/Springfield across the Hudson to the Susquehanna River Valley; the Valley downstream for hundreds of miles almost to Harrisburg, where they might have turned west toward Pittsburgh along the Juniata River, or perhaps on to Lancaster, an early hotbed of Swedenborgian and New Church enthusiasm, before setting out for the frontier.

Yet another possibility is that the Chapmans left the main route of the Susquehanna at Sunbury, fifty miles north of Harrisburg, and followed the river's western branch through Williamsport, the wonderfully named Jersey Shore, Loch Haven, and on to the Sinnemahoning Creek. According to an 1843 history of Pennsylvania, several "adventurous Irishmen" had taken that route perhaps in 1795, "penetrated the wilderness of McKean co., built canoes, and launched them upon the waters of the Allegheny," eventually floating by the future site of Olean in New York State and reentering Pennsylvania at the northern end of what is now Allegheny National Forest.

The more northerly route would have been a feat of amazing derring-do for two relatively green travelers, one still half a boy—an unmarked and mostly untried trek through what had been hostile Indian territory only a few years earlier. How would they even have heard about the route? And yet in the years to come, Johnny Appleseed would rarely take a road if there was a trail instead to follow, rarely take to a river if a creek beckoned. And what an adventure it would have been, however unlikely it seems.

An even more ingenious—if still less probable—route is the one plotted by Vermont high-school principal Hank Ruppertsberger. Inspired by a biography for juvenile readers—*The Real Johnny Appleseed*, by Laurie Lawlor—and wanting to mark the supposed two hundredth anniversary of the first nursery planted by John Chapman, Ruppertsberger decided to walk the route himself, from

Longmeadow to the Chapman brothers' first known stopping place, Warren, in northwestern Pennsylvania, and from there on into Ohio and Indiana.

"I got out an atlas and ripped out pages for the Northeast," Ruppertsberger told me. "I plotted all the places where Chapman had lived and worked. Then I found a map that had all the roads and Indian trails on it for that part of the country back then. I overlaid that on the atlas pages, and sure enough, a lot of the old trails lined up with the places I had marked. So I figured I would take the most expeditious way out."

Ruppertsberger's hike took him, as other Chapman plottings have, through Great Barrington and across the Hudson River at Catskill. But rather than continue on to Oneonta and follow the Susquehanna River Valley south alongside Interstate 88, he picked up the west branch of the Delaware River at Stamford, took the lightly traveled Route 10 almost to Pennsylvania, and then skirted west on the New York side of the border through Binghamton and Elmira. Below Southport, he finally dropped into Pennsylvania and worked his way west along Routes 328 and 49 to U.S. 6 and State Route 59, which he followed through the northern part of the Allegheny National Forest until he came to Warren.

In effect (and with good cause!), Ruppertsberger made a beeline out of the trip: Mapquest plots the shortest possible distance between the two termini—Longmeadow and Warren—at 420 miles, about nine hours thirty minutes by car. Ruppertsberger walked the same rough distance in a month, from June 20 to July 18, 1998. The Susquehanna, the main "highway" out of New England into Pennsylvania, disappears in his reckoning, except as something to cross. The Wyoming Valley is out as well, of necessity. Put the Wyoming Valley back in, and you've added another hundred miles to the trip. Substitute trails and primitive rutted roads for the rural highways that the Vermont principal mostly followed, and you have certainly doubled the time, even without having to stop and work for food, or hunt and forage for it.

Whichever way the brothers went, whenever they left Longmeadow, however long they meandered before setting their eyes westward and seeing the hard hump of Pennsylvania in front of them, the hardest part of the journey still lay ahead.

❦

The earliest Europeans navigated the Allegheny Mountains on Indian paths, which themselves followed ancient animal trails as deer, bear, and other game migrated back and forth between seasonal feeding grounds and winter shelter. What inspired colonial Americans to improve on the Native Americans' work—and on the work of nature before that—was the same thing that inspired President Dwight Eisenhower to launch the Interstate Highway System in the 1950s: warfare and its possibilities.

In the uncertain early years of the Cold War, before Mutually Assured Destruction pushed ground war into the background, Ike wanted to be able to rush tanks and other matériel from coast to coast. To that end, his planners pulled together and upgraded existing national highways, many of which began themselves as Indian and animal trails; added connectors; and limited access largely to cloverleaf ramps. Almost two centuries earlier, during the French and Indian War, British-American forces under General Edward Braddock commandeered the old Nemacolin Trail, named for a Delaware chief, and widened it to accommodate wagons and artillery for his assault on the French stronghold at Fort Duquesne, later Fort Pitt, later Pittsburgh. (U.S. 40, the "National Highway," follows Braddock's Road from Cumberland, Maryland, westward, as does a long section of Interstate 68.)

Braddock's expedition was a flop, as was a 1758 expedition led by General John Forbes. But like Braddock's before him, Forbes's army widened and exploited an old Indian trading route, this one along the very rough path of today's Pennsylvania Turnpike, also known as Interstate 76. Almost four decades further on, when John and Nathaniel Chapman most likely set out for the same rough destination, those two war roads were still the main paths over the Alleghenies—Braddock's southwesterly approach and Forbes's more due-west one, known as the Pennsylvania Road— and neither route was comfort-filled.

The roads had been partially reclaimed by the surrounding forests in the first several decades since they were first improved. Wagons had disappeared from them. Attention had turned elsewhere with the Revolution. Transport was by horseback, and the ride could be harrowing. In his wonderful multivolume, turn-of-the-century *Historic Highways of America* series, Arthur Butler Hulbert quotes one traveler who braved Braddock's Road during the Revolutionary period:

> The caravan route from the Ohio river to Frederick [Maryland] crossed the stupendous ranges of the . . . mountains. . . . The path, scarcely two feet wide, and traveled by horses in single file, roamed over hill and dale, through mountain defile, over craggy steeps, beneath impending rocks, and around points of dizzy heights, where one false step might hurl horse and rider into the abyss below.

By the fall of 1796, when the Englishman Francis Baily set out on the Pennsylvania Road, bound for Pittsburgh and eventually Cincinnati, wagons could again be found making their way, sometimes painfully, along the highway. Roadhouses, inns, and taverns had begun to dot the trail. Baily would eventually gain distinction as an astronomer and an economist—he reformed the standard

Nautical Almanac, updated a number of star catalogs, and wrote treatises on leases and on interest and annuities—but in 1796, he was a twenty-two-year-old adventurer, riding west on horseback, and even for him, the trip was a haul.

On October 11, he and his traveling party put up for the night at an inn known as McDowell's Mill, thirteen miles west of Chambersburg. Dinner began with warm "sour milk" placed on the table in a single bowl, into which the seven or eight people around the table dipped spoons. Next came stewed pork and "warm slaw . . . devoured in the same hoggish manner, every one trying to help himself first, and two or three eating off the same plate, all in the midst of filth and dirt." Cold milk and warm bread followed, served with the same "habitual nastiness." Afterward, they were shown up a ladder "into a dirty place" and slept not under blankets but between feather-filled mattresses.

The next day brought better and worse. Eight miles west of the miserable tavern, Baily found himself descending from a high hill into the valley of the Juniata River, "one of the most enchanting and romantic scenes I ever experienced," he would later write in *Journal of a Tour in Unsettled Parts of North America in 1796–97.* "From this hill we beheld ourselves in the midst of a mountainous and wooded country; the Junietta [*sic*] winding and flowing on each side of us at the foot of the hill; the distant mountains appearing in all the *wilderness of majesty* and extending just below the horizon." That was the good news. The bad news was the road they traveled on, "which was carried along the side of a tremendously high hill [and] seemed to threaten us with instant death, if our horses should make a false step." And so it went—miserable accommodations with occasional grace notes, majestic mountains "incommoded by the cold winds and rain which generally infest the summit," grand vistas and perilous roads—all the way to Pittsburgh, which Baily's party finally reached on October 18, seven days and about 160 miles after leaving Chambersburg.

Francis Baily and John Chapman were the same age, born half a year apart. There's good reason to suspect they crossed the Alleghenies at just about the same time. John and Nathaniel Chapman would have been seasoned by their long trek thus far from southern Massachusetts. Unless they had been weakened by illness or malnutrition, they should have been Baily's equal in strength and endurance, and John Chapman would later prove the most notable trekker in our national history. But that's the point: He and Nathaniel were on foot, not on horseback, not traveling by other "conveyance."

By the very early nineteenth century, when road improvements had begun to catch up with the migratory push westward, settlers driving ox-carts and horse-drawn wagons were making the trip from Springfield to the Ohio River in about two months on the average (and barring any number of sometimes disastrous complications). John and Nathaniel's trip by foot along the same rough route—the Connecticut-Massachusetts border, through New York to the Susquehanna River Valley, down the river into Pennsylvania, and from there across the mountains—likely consumed on the order of half a year. Francis Baily's weeklong horseback jaunt over the Alleghenies might have taken the two foot travelers a month of hardscrabble trekking, up and down narrow defiles, climbing from ridge to ridge, always sleeping outdoors—a pattern of behavior that was to stay with Johnny Appleseed for a lifetime.

Baily complains occasionally about the fall climate of 1796— those incommodious cold winds, weather so vile they had to seek lodging well before they intended. John and Nathaniel would have been far more exposed to the weather, and for far longer, into the late fall and winter of 1796–97, either still in the mountains or in the sprawling woodlands to the west once they had crossed the Alleghenies. And the winters of the late eighteenth century were by and large truly awful.

The "Hard Winter" of 1779–80 has never been equaled on the East Coast. Thomas Jefferson recalled that in 1780 "the Chesapeake Bay was frozen from its head to the mouth of the Potomac," an astounding distance, over a hundred miles. New York City was so socked in by ice for much of the winter that navigation ceased for a full five weeks and residents—and British and American raiding parties—could walk between lower Manhattan and Staten Island. Meanwhile, George Washington and his army were hunkered down in Morristown, New Jersey, in some of the most miserable conditions in American fighting history. That January, the famous Philadelphia physician Benjamin Rush noted that the temperature in his city never rose above freezing, except for a single day. Out in the western part of the state, in the Laurel Highlands, the snow lay four feet deep.

Winters during the rest of the century were not notably better. From November 1783 through January 1784, Morristown recorded 83.5 inches of snow. On the Delaware River, navigation ceased from just after Christmas to mid-March. Three years later, in December 1786, Philadelphia and Morristown were hit with 41 inches of snow in a single week. In 1798, winter began in mid-November with an 18-inch snowfall in New York City and up to three feet across much of New England. By the end of the year Philadelphia was covered with snow, a white blanket that remained in place until mid-March 1799. Up in the Berkshires of New England, snow was still falling lightly in May.

Weather, of course, is variable, and the fall of 1796—when John and Nathaniel Chapman were likely crossing the Alleghenies— seems to have been far from the worst on record. But we do have a very exact accounting of the weather in eastern Pennsylvania for those closing months of 1796—from the meticulous diary of a Quaker farmer named Joseph Price, in Lower Merion Township outside Philadelphia—and it does suggest the harsh conditions the two travelers would have been facing several hundred miles to the west, where the winter weather is almost always more extreme.

On October 7, Price recorded the first frost; on the eighth, a "Sharp frost"; and on the eighteenth, "white frost." By November 7, the weather was "very Cold Ice plenty." Snow arrived on the twenty-fifth and "very Exstreem Cold" the next day. By December 5, Price was cutting ice off his sawmill waterwheel, which had been frozen ever since November 26. "It was amaising," he writes, "to see the thickness of Ice on the wheel." Eleven inches of snow arrived the seventh, more the fourteenth. The twentieth brought "Remarkable Cold." On the twenty-third, Price slept beneath two "coverlids, two blankets, a sheet, and two great coats." And so it went. If anything, the weather was worse on the Ohio side of the mountains. In his field-note-rich *Pioneer History*, S. P. Hildreth writes that "in December 1796, about Christmas, there was an excessive cold spell of weather. The rivers were frozen over to the depth of nine inches, soon after which fell two feet of snow."

Like the other ranges of the Appalachian chain, the Allegheny Mountains are the worn nubs of a range once every bit as majestic and forbidding as today's Rockies. Drive along the high roads of central and western Pennsylvania, and the prospect is of ridge upon ridge, separated often by sharply defined valleys. The highest point in the entire state is Mount Davis, in the southwest corner near the Maryland line, at a little over 3,200 feet. There was no Donner Pass (7,075 feet) for these Pennsylvania pioneers to get through, headed for the Promised Land of the Old Northwest; no Pikes Peak (14,110 feet) to get around.

Still, it's worth keeping in mind what a formidable barrier the Alleghenies remained for nearly a century and a half after the Chapman brothers crossed them. A railroad company coheaded by William Vanderbilt, grandson of Cornelius, managed to partially excavate seven tunnels through the mountains, trying to connect Harrisburg and Pittsburgh by rail along the same rough route General Forbes's army had cleared 120 years earlier, before Vanderbilt went broke in 1885. (His partner, Andrew Carnegie, managed to ride out the storm.) A little over a half century later the Pennsylvania Turnpike finally pushed through the mountains using much of the Vanderbilt-Carnegie roadbed, but at a staggering cost for the time—$70 million in New Deal, Depression-era grants for a 160-mile stretch of "superhighway"—and with a labor force greater than the entire population of western Pennsylvania at the start of the nineteenth century: fifteen thousand workers from 155 construction companies spread across eighteen states, employing probably enough explosives to level half of modern Pittsburgh.

❦

Why did John and Nathaniel do it? Why leave the known world of Longmeadow for the unknown one of western Pennsylvania and "Ohio Country" beyond it? Why did they join that long parade of early American postcolonialists who risked so much to launch a new life?

According to the later recollection of one of his half sisters, Chapman as a boy had been drawn to the woods, enticed by plants, flowers, and birdsong. Maybe, then, the answer is as simple as nature: By the end of the eighteenth century, Ohio Country had more of it than staid and settled New England.

Or maybe the answer is the one famously attributed to Daniel

Boone: "elbow room." By the start of 1796, the Chapman-Cooley family had swelled to eleven in all, with no end in sight. Farms need hands, and John and Nathaniel must have been hearty and able helpers, judging by the fact that they were soon to make it on foot across the Allegheny Mountains. But the household was fast becoming a sardine can, and the larder must have frequently been nearly empty with so many mouths to feed. Better to lighten the load, John might well have felt.

Remember, too, that John was eventually to become not only the best-known walker in American history but also one of its most notable loners. Whether his aversion to crowds predated the teeming Chapman-Cooley household or was caused by it, living in such packed conditions must have become an increasingly heavy burden to him. As for Nathaniel, younger brothers have been following older ones on perilous adventures since the beginning of time.

Larger issues were at work, as well. Father Nathaniel wasn't alone in postwar New England in feeling the wolf at his farmhouse door. The economy of the region—long the money engine of colonial America—was in steep transition from a traditional rural model to a capitalist one. Wealth and vision were shifting south and west as the new nation found its footing and the frontier pushed inland, and Massachusetts farmers often found themselves caught in the middle.

Beginning in May 1775, Congress had authorized paper "continentals" to help finance the Revolution. The value of the continentals was pegged one-to-one to gold, and in theory, they were to be fully convertible to that durable specie once the war had wound down. In practice, the continentals—which eventually financed some 40 percent of the war effort—were nothing of the sort. By January 1780, more than $240 million in continentals was in circulation. When Congress retired the bills a little over a year later, in April 1781, they were worth less than a penny apiece. By the time New England's farmers started trading their muskets for plowshares and returning to the fields, a deep postwar depression had spread across the region.

That was Problem One. Problem Two was taxes. Another 18 percent of the Revolution had been funded by state debt issues. In the war's aftermath, those debt burdens had to be retired everywhere, but Massachusetts seems to have been more aggressive than any of the other former colonies in the urgency with which it sought to lay its burden to rest. Taxes postwar in the state rose to five times what they had been prewar, and "property"—what farmers have in abundance—was the easiest way to place that load and calculate "fair share."

Overwhelmed, farmers began lying wantonly to tax assessors: Land yet to be put under plow was "unimprovable"; near the coast, prized salt marshes were glibly dismissed as worthless wetlands. (Appropriately in that successor state to the original Puritan colony, the bad-mouthing was known as "dooming.") Unfazed, mostly unfooled, and granted extraordinary powers to recharge the state's coffers, county sheriffs seized farms, animals, equipment, anything salable and put it all on the block to cover unmet obligations.

Shays's Rebellion—the farmer-led uprising that flared up in western Massachusetts in August 1786—was the almost inevitable outcome of turning the screws so tight on the state's agricultural sector. But as Winifred Barr Rothenberg points out in an excellent essay on the subject, Shays's uprising was also an index of sorts of how rapidly economic and social change was overwhelming the state and New England as a whole.

Growing things was on the wane, making them on the rise, and the demographics of the state were rearranging themselves accordingly. By 1800, one in every three residents of Massachusetts was living in an "urban" setting, defined by the U.S. Census then as at least 2,500 people. The old farm-family model—multiple children, sons waiting to take a wife until the father was dead, daughters marrying in order of their birth—was breaking down. Fertility, for many of the reasons just cited, was in statistical collapse. In his much-cited study of Hingham, Massachusetts, back on the coast, Daniel Scott Smith found that family size had dropped from an average of 7.6 children in the seventeenth century to 4.6 in 1715, and down to 2.8 children by the middle of the next century.

Obviously, not all of the state's farm families failed, but many were stressed, especially the undercapitalized ones. With an ever-increasing family, trying to scrape a living out of rented land, Nathaniel and Lucy Chapman were living on the backside of the region's history at a time when fertile lands and longer growing seasons were just beginning to open up down the Susquehanna River Valley and beyond the Appalachians in western Pennsylvania and Ohio. Perhaps John and young Nathaniel sensed that, as their parents (and step-parents) finally seemed to have done. In 1805, with little Sally barely two years old, Nathaniel and Lucy pulled up stakes and went west themselves, settling in on Duck Creek, almost twenty miles above Marietta. Nathaniel died there a little more than two years later, by which time his second oldest living son and namesake appears to have rejoined the family.

One more thing about the Susquehanna River Valley that almost certainly would have lured the young Johnny Appleseed onward: This was a land bursting with religious individualism and Romantic dreams. The Amish were already well established in Lancaster County, near the river's end, as was the Ephrata Cloister, an almost monastic community that, like the Shakers in New York State, practiced a self-defeating celibacy. The river's reputation had traveled abroad as well. At some unspecified spot along its shores, the English poets Samuel Taylor Coleridge and Robert Southey planned to establish their egalitarian community, Pantisocracy (for "all rule"). Conceived in 1794, just as John Chapman and his stepbrother seemed to be getting itchy feet, the project died a few years later, but the river continued to inspire dreamers of a new order. A little over three decades later, upriver at Great Bend near the Pennsylvania–New York border, Joseph Smith settled in at his father-in-law's farm and began translating the Book of Mormon into English.

❦

Was John Chapman among Pennsylvania's early dreamers, or religious crackpots (of which the state has also had many)? He certainly seems to have been ripe for revelation, as were the times, but it's all informed speculation at best: the route the two young men followed, the dates, the reasons.

Almost equally at question are the stories from those earliest months in western Pennsylvania that the future Johnny Appleseed told about himself, or allowed to be told, or the ones he spread the seeds of so that they could grow to fruition in his aftermath. In one such tale, he and Nathaniel braved the westward mountain crossing only to follow the Allegheny River upstream into lower New York State, looking for what proved to be the abandoned cabin of a long-lost uncle. Socked in by winter and desperate for food, John took off through the snow in search of provisions. Nathaniel, for his part, survived only through the care of kind Indians who came upon him when he was near death. In another tale from those opening days on the frontier, this one set near Lake Erie, John escaped less benevolent Native Americans by lying silently for hours among the cattails while his pursuers stalked angrily through the reeds.

In another of his oft-told tales, Chapman lay silently among the cat-tails while Indians stalked angrily nearby.

Chapman is said to have walked for miles barefoot on fro-zen rivers. By his own account, he once dragged his canoe onto a passing ice floe, again escaping Indian pursuers, and promptly fell asleep, only to awake a hundred miles downstream. Like Paul Bunyan, Chapman wielded an ax almost as effectively as King Ar-thur wielded his magic sword, Excalibur. In his 1859 memoir, R. I. Curtis writes that "Chapman could chop as much wood or girdle as many trees in one day as most men could in two." As Robert Price notes, the remarkable thing about these early tales is not their myth-making but the absence of so many of the later elements of the Chapman mythology: apples, religion, reverence for animals, deification by the Indians, etc. This was Chapman unadorned by Appleseed. Or maybe it was Chapman self-mythologizing, the early stirrings of the later myths that would completely subsume his real identity. Chapman apparently entertained the young R. I. Curtis with many such stories of the "hardships he had endured, of his adventures, and hair-breadth escapes by flood and field."

Also notable about these early tales is how thoroughly they omit almost any mention, heroic or otherwise, of Nathaniel. Maybe he was always the little brother along for the adventure, the one left behind when John set out on a heroic quest for food, the boy-man who stood admiringly to the side while his half brother girdled trees and chopped wood at twice the speed of mortal men. Certainly, the operative word is "tales." Who knows what's real or imagined, what actually took place and what was embellishment as the oral tradition spread?

One hard fact, though, does survive from those earliest months in and west of the Alleghenies. On February 14, 1797, John Chapman bought a gimlet—a small auger—at the Craig & O'Hara Stores, a trading post located at the confluence of the Allegheny River and Big Brokenstraw Creek, near Warren, in the northwestern part of the state. Five more transactions followed over the next fifteen months, all duly recorded by John Daniels in his account book, still preserved today in the collection of the Warren County Historical Society. Nathaniel got in the act as well, making four purchases on his own between late June and mid-September 1798.

The transactions were modest in every case, but they do fix the two brothers at long last in place and time, and they point to at least one powerful motivation for their journey through all that harsh terrain, a motivation that cuts through all the "maybes" and "might haves": cheap land.

4.

LAND, HO!

In 1792, Peter Stadnitski, a Dutchman who had profited mightily in American bonds in the immediate post-Revolutionary years, sent out to potential investors a preliminary prospectus for a far more ambitious undertaking in the New World: land speculation.

Stadnitski began by reminding his Dutch audience of the generally favorable investment climate to be found across the Atlantic. America was "a tremendously large country, much of it very fertile and with easy communication between the various parts and, in most cases, with the oceans. These advantages are all of the greatest benefit to trade and agriculture."

To be sure, securing its independence from England had saddled the new nation with debt and placed it, initially, under the authority of "an inefficient government . . . hastily formed." But that, Stadnitski wrote, was to be expected. What mattered was that "as soon as things quieted down, the more sensible citizens felt the necessity for giving the government more power, more authority. Without these it would be impossible to build an establishment based on order, faith and truth, so urgently needed for the welfare of so many citizens. The author of *The Federalist* enlightened the people on this subject, and the whole nation adopted the new constitution with a great plurality. . . . And so the expectations of the experts were realized and the serious speculator was well paid for his skill and industry."

Initially, Stadnitski and his associates had invested in bonds issued to retire the war debt. Now, his attention was focused on a much bigger cash cow: the large tracts of uncultivated land secured from Indian tribes for a pittance and sold off by the individual states and the federal government "from time to time for whatever they could get."

The Dutchman acknowledged to potential investors that speculation in these lands had grown so intense, with people buying land on time and paying exaggerated interest for the privilege, that bubbles had formed and "a great many people were ruined." (And indeed such a land-speculation bubble formed and broke in 1792, as Stadnitski was circulating his final prospectus.) But ultimately, he argued, conditions were ideal in America, where "there are still few rich people . . . but major opportunities to invest money." Bottom line: Land speculation across the Atlantic was a can't-miss deal.

For starters, immigration was sure to increase, the population to grow, and land prices to rise accordingly. New York State's population, he noted, had grown from 96,765 residents in 1756 to 238,897 in 1786, "in spite of all destruction by eight years of war," and to 340,120 as of July 26, 1791—a 42 percent increase in the past five years alone. Individual cities and towns told an even more alluring tale. Hudson, New York, near where John and Nathaniel Chapman were to cross the river of the same name a few years later, "was no more than a rock in 1785 and . . . then could have been bought for ten cents an acre." Now it was "a small city with a bank where house lots sell for £150."

Of even greater importance was internal migration westward, particularly from New England, and here Stadnitski went on to provide a catalog of reasons that parallel almost exactly the condition of the Chapman family. The soil of New England was played out; land to the south and west was more fertile. New England farmers also faced "the necessity of providing for their numerous children, which could be done most easily by settling them with some cattle on new lands in the interior." The relatively dense population of Massachusetts and the lower New England states also meant that pasturage was restricted and the herds of deer and other game were becoming played out. "The New Englander [is eager] to be always on the move. They are very fond of hunting and that is why they always prefer the less populated frontiers."

Stadnitski's final reason for internal migration westward may have been the most applicable of all to the Chapmans: "The majority, having little or no money, have to settle on the cheapest and least settled lands." Stadnitski even went on to provide a template of sorts for John Chapman's future real-estate ventures on the other side of the Ohio River: "Some wholesale buyers of unimproved land who have no capital lease their property undeveloped, waiting for the growth of population and the consequent arrival of settlers and the rise in the value of the land."

The general opinion, based on government estimates that the American population would double every two decades, was "that, within 100 years, all the territory between the seacoast and the Great Lakes, in other words, from Canada to the ocean, will be densely populated and well cultivated." In the meantime, fortunes were already being made. In a matter of only a few years, land along the Mohawk River had grown seven times in value. In Kentucky, "though they are still at war with the Indians," tracts that had sold for roughly six cents an acre in the early to mid-1780s were fetching nearly three dollars an acre by decade's end. Out in western Massachusetts, Robert Morris, the so-called Financier of the American Revolution and a signer of the Declaration of Independence and land speculator par excellence, had flipped more than a million acres for three and a half times what he paid for it. "He had no expenses," Stadnitski marvels. "Nothing was done to improve the land."

All that amounted to a compelling argument to investors, but what really clinched the deal for Stadnitski was the land itself. He had sent his own agents to investigate large tracts of western New York State and western Pennsylvania—men with "enough physical fitness to explore these almost trackless territories in all directions and even to live there for some months during the coldest weather and deepest snow"—and their report clearly pleased him.

From these people we secured much information which very satisfactorily confirmed our belief that the majority of these regions were very fertile, that even without cultivation great profits could be made from the natural products if the area was only settled and that, in several parts of the country, rivers and lakes were found which were already navigable or could be made so at little expense. The different products of the frontier could be sent along these waterways to the more populated states along the seacoast. They could even be sent all over the world and the profits of opening these new farm lands would be incalculable. . . .

The land is almost completely covered by forests. Some of the trees, because of their vigorous growth, are very straight, with an average height of from eighty to 100 feet with some of them as much as 200 feet. Among other varieties there are the black, white and red oak, the water oak, the chestnut oak, beech, elm, black and silver birch, the wild cherry (the wood of which is unusually hard), walnuts, firs, pines as well as a lot of useful shrubs.

But I will not stop here [for a more complete description] since this is not written to entice settlers.

However, I should report that in addition to many natural pastures planted to clover, especially in the valleys, even the forests supply a great deal of food for horses and cattle without the need of cultivation. There are also several medicinal roots such as sarsaparilla, ginseng, etc. But there is a special sugar tree and in many localities it is very plentiful. In addition to its other qualities it provides a quantity of sugar which I know from my own experience is just as good as cane sugar. We have already experimented with it and if my plans are successful it may provide a large income.

No one apparently bothered to inform Stadnitski or his land agents that the sap of America's "special sugar tree"—the sugar maple—couldn't be tapped year-round, but cheap sugar was only the icing on the cake. A subsequent prospectus announced that Stadnitski and Son and five Dutch partners had negotiated to purchase one million acres in western New York State for three million guilders (about $1.2 million). To raise money for the purchase, the enterprise—soon to be renamed the Holland Land Company—was offering to sell three thousand shares at a thousand guilders apiece. The shares first went on sale January 1, 1793. "Within a few days," Paul Evans reports in his history of the Holland Land Company, "all the shares had been sold; many who had planned to buy were turned away empty-handed."

Not long afterward, the Holland Company added another million or so acres of western Pennsylvania to the pot—much of it unclaimed inventory from the "Donation and Depreciation Lands" that had originally been set aside for veterans of the Revolution in lieu of pay and later sold by the state to raise revenue and promote settlement. Soon, the company was advertising heavily throughout New England and along the eastern seaboard, and that's where Johnny Appleseed and Nathaniel Chapman come walking into the story.

When the two brothers wandered down the Susquehanna River Valley in 1796, they were reversing the trail followed by Peter Stadnitski's two agents, Gerrit Boon and Jan Lincklaen, as they traveled from their base in Philadelphia to Lancaster, and then north along the river bank into the virgin woods of western New York State. The two brothers would have crossed between states by the same cultivated fields and meadows that Lincklean describes so warmly in his journals: the ground rich, the wheat abundant. Like the two land agents, they are likely to have marveled at the Okwago Settlement in northernmost Pennsylvania, three hundred and more transplanted New Englanders gathered in a valley ringed by old apple orchards.

Later, when John and Nathaniel had traversed the mountains, moved up the valley of the Allegheny River to Warren, and finally left an indelible marker of their presence, it was Holland Company land they had come to. Other land-holding outfits also claimed vast tracts in the area: the Philadelphia-based North American Land Company (another project of the ever-speculative Robert Morris); the Lancaster Land Company, which would eventually sell off all its acreage by lottery; and still more. But the best tracts, those north and west of the Allegheny, were Holland Company–controlled, and, almost beyond a shadow of a doubt, John and Nathaniel had come to Warren because of what the Holland Land Company had in such abundance to sell: unimproved cheap real estate. No other reason justifies all the trouble of getting there.

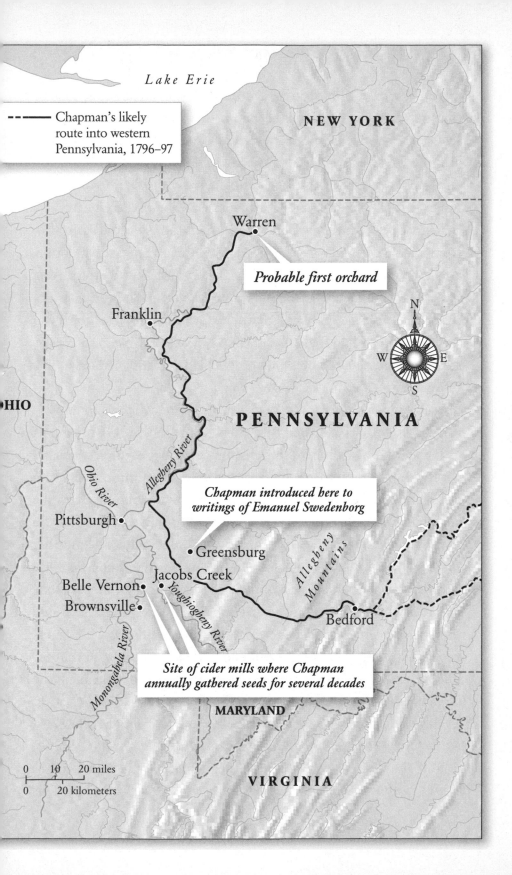

Lake Erie

Chapman's likely
route into western
Pennsylvania, 1796–97

NEW YORK

Warren

Probable first orchard

N

W E

S

Franklin

PENNSYLVANIA

Ohio River

Allegheny River

*Chapman introduced here to
writings of Emanuel Swedenborg*

Pittsburgh

Greensburg

Jacobs Creek

Allegheny Mountains

Belle Vernon

Brownsville

Youghiogheny River

Bedford

Monongahela River

*Site of cider mills where Chapman
annually gathered seeds for several decades*

MARYLAND

OHIO

0   10   20 miles

0   20 kilometers

VIRGINIA

Today, Warren, Pennsylvania, is a pleasant city of about ten thousand residents, located on the banks of the Allegheny, on either side of the mouth of the Conewango Creek. Oil and lumber barons filled Warren with impressive mansions during the nineteenth and early twentieth centuries, and many of them are still nicely preserved in an extensive historic district. A high ridge to its back is said to help protect Warren from the wintry blasts that roll in from Lake Erie, sixty miles to the west-northwest. Sadly, though, almost nothing has been done to preserve the city's waterfront. Instead of walks and parkland for residents to enjoy, a refinery, factories, and ill-conceived urban restoration projects dominate the riverbank. Still, kayakers and canoeists are drawn to the area by the more-protected shores of the Allegheny National Forest, just downstream.

Warren had its beginning on April 18, 1795, when the Pennsylvania legislature established three new towns in the northwest part of the state "to facilitate and promote the progress of settlements within the Commonwealth, and to afford additional security to the frontiers." Soon thereafter, commissioners appointed by the governor began planning a town of three hundred acres, with no city lot larger than one-third of an acre, surrounded by another seven hundred acres of "out lots," none bigger than five acres, and with ten acres reserved for public use. The lots went on the block the following August in Carlisle, Pennsylvania—two hundred miles to the southeast, back across the mountains at the edge of what was then civilization—and over the next decade, all the lots sold, at prices ranging from $2.50 to $6, with one-third of the money required at purchase.

The modern city grew from there, but in late 1796 or early 1797, when John and Nathaniel Chapman first made it to the conjunction of the Conewango and the Allegheny, Warren amounted to almost nothing to behold. Less than two years earlier, a ferocious storm had leveled the forest of white, black, and red oaks that had covered the site since time immemorial. Later, a fire raged through the windfall. To add to the rigor, Indian hostilities had flared up in the summer of 1795. By the time John and Nathaniel arrived, Warren amounted to a single blockhouse surrounded by the early signs of a scrub forest emerging out of the charred remains of the blaze. The first person they are likely to have seen in Warren was the blockhouse's sole permanent resident, a Holland Land Company agent named Dan McQuay—another of those figures from frontier history who seem almost larger than life.

An 1887 history of Warren County describes McQuay as "a genuine son of Erin, full of recklessness and adventure, fond of fun, fight and whiskey." That sounds like a man indulging in the normal recreations of the time and place, but what really seems to have set Dan McQuay apart was his stamina afoot. He might, in fact, have been the one American to equal Johnny Appleseed, and his treks were prodigious.

The Warren County history tells us that McQuay made as many as ten trips from the Warren area to New Orleans in command of virtual floating islands—smaller rafts lashed together to make barges as wide and long as a football field, piled high with lumber. Since the rafts went only with the current, not against it, McQuay traveled the 1,200 miles back home by foot: "a perilous undertaking . . . The few towns along the Ohio and Mississippi rivers were then but insignificant villages, and all else between them tangled thickets, swamps and dense forests infested by Indians, wild animals, and frequently by worse foes—white desperadoes and highwaymen."

Whatever the two young men might have made of Dan McQuay on first meeting, they must have been somewhat enchanted because for the next year, they seem to have tied their fortune and future pretty much to his own.

John and Nathaniel bunked with McQuay in the Holland Land Company blockhouse during the very early part of their time in Warren. Everyone who wandered into Warren did—whether they were drawn by the promise of the city to come or by the large tracts of mostly thick forest that the company was advertising back east. Supplies were brought up by keel boat from Pittsburgh, kept in the blockhouse, and sold there; and McQuay, the proprietor of this all-in-one harbor house, warehouse, convenience store, and ad hoc fortress (not to mention bar), was by all accounts among the most sociable men in western Pennsylvania, so long as there was strong drink to be had.

Holland Land Company policy at the time called for selling its land off in four-hundred-acre tracts, with the stipulation that an actual "resident settlement" had to be constructed on the land within two years of purchase—protection against squatters and second-generation speculators who simply wanted to hold on to the land for resale at some later point. Four hundred acres would have been out of John Chapman's price range, even as cheaply as the land sold, but as the company's sole agent for a vast region of northwestern Pennsylvania, McQuay had considerable latitude. Sometimes settlers were imported and given strategically located hundred-acre tracts free of charge, on the condition that they cleared two acres, built a house, and stayed on the land five years. In essence, these free settlers served as land decoys—by creating the impression that settlement was already well advanced, they were meant to draw paying customers into shooting range.

Maybe that was the link between McQuay and the Chapmans. John seems to have done considerable exploring up and down the Allegheny and its tributaries during his first year in and around

Warren. He could have been looking for the right hundred acres, or he and his brother might have been in McQuay's direct employ. Someone who was learning to move so easily through the wilderness would be a useful policeman for a land agent determined to keep squatters from occupying Holland Company land for free or, worse, lumbermen from stealing the company's timber because trees were the real cash crop of the time. Or maybe John was planning to squat himself, or gave that impression—in later life he showed little regard for traditional property rights—and McQuay simply wanted to hold him close so he could keep an eye on him.

The possibilities are boundless. What's telling is that when McQuay vacated the blockhouse the next year, in 1798, and moved seven miles downriver to the mouth of Brokenstraw Creek, John and Nathaniel moved with him, or at least as close to him as they could remain. McQuay established himself near where the Allegheny and the Brokenstraw joined forces. He seems to have been already plotting the timber business that would take him to New Orleans and back multiple times. With far fewer options in front of them (or maybe because empty spaces were already beckoning), the Chapmans set up camp seven miles up the Brokenstraw, with their backs flat against the wilderness. In between the two appears to have been a large chunk of the semipermanent white population of what was to become Warren County.

John McKinney was two miles downstream. McKinney, another Irishman and a part of the surveying team that first laid out Warren, moved west from Lancaster with his two brothers in the summer of 1795, just about the time Dan McQuay arrived. For three years, McKinney lived alone by the creek, "clearing the woods and subduing the obstinate wilderness," in the words of the Warren County history. Just about the time the Chapmans moved in above him, McKinney—"shrewd, hospitable, genial, and thoroughly democratic"—returned to Lancaster, married the woman he had left behind there, and brought her back to the Brokenstraw, where they raised a large family "prominent . . . for energy and integrity."

Closer to the Allegheny River—and McQuay's nearest neighbor—was Callender Irvine, living on a tract purchased by his father, a Revolutionary War general. Along with "Black Tom," a former slave freed by Irvine's father after the war, Irvine cleared and farmed his land and spent much of his energy constructing a house, to satisfy the Holland Land Company requirement that habitation be raised on the property within two years. (Black Tom, it seems, was the full-time resident settler, while Irvine was able to escape the severe winters common to the area.)

In between the two—McKinney and Irvine—a bachelor Scotsman named Matthew Young pitched a tent in the spring of 1796, apparently without the least idea of what it might take to survive in that obstinate Pennsylvania wilderness, or so an anecdote in the 1887 Warren County history suggests:

> Late in the spring of that year Callender Irvine, anxious to cultivate acquaintance with his neighbors, and to see how they prospered, walked up to see Mr. Young, and found him engaged in opening out what is now the main street of the borough [of Youngsville], and extending it down the creek. He inquired of Young, with real curiosity, what he was about, and why he was not putting in some crops. With the utmost simplicity he replied: "Why, man, I'm more fond of a beautiful prospect." To which Mr. Irvine retorted: "The prospect is, you will either starve or have to leave the country before spring."
>
> Sure enough, when fall came he had no corn and was kept

from starvation only by the surplus of provisions Irvine had and generously furnished him, when he went abroad to winter.

Later historians of the area go lighter on Young, noting that the source of the anecdote, a Judge S. P. Johnson, didn't appear in Warren County until after Young's death. And indeed Young does seem to have had considerably more ambition than the story credits him with. He stayed on the Brokenstraw and in Warren for the rest of his life, built the area's first sawmill, served as the second treasurer of Warren County, and seems to have been widely admired. When he died in August 1825, while visiting a friend many miles downriver, his body was returned by canoe and buried in the local cemetery of Youngsville, the town that by then bore his name.

❦

Thus was John and Nathaniel's first neighborhood, if that word can even be used to encompass six men, one woman, two or three permanent structures, a tent, and whatever lean-to arrangement the Chapmans were relying on, separated by seven miles end to end of sporadically cleared wilderness. Nathaniel would have been sixteen, almost a man; John, twenty-three, the second youngest in that stretched-out clustering.

Little hard and fast is known about their life along the Big Brokenstraw. That's par for Johnny Appleseed, but we can begin to make reasonable speculations based on the accounts ledger that John Daniels meticulously kept at his trading post back where creek and river met.

As noted earlier, John Chapman's first purchase at the trading post, on February 14, 1797, was recorded in the ledger as a "speck gimblet," an older spelling of "spike gimlet." This was a standard tool of the time: T-shaped, with a wooden handle for turning, attached across the top to a forged spike, fluted toward the bottom, with an auger tip. Meriwether Lewis and William Clark took more than a dozen spike gimlets with them on their famous expedition. Annals of War Department stores from the times are littered with requisitions for such tools.

Why a spike gimlet, and why does one appear to have been Chapman's first purchase west of the mountains? Perhaps he and Nathaniel were building a lean-to of some sort to get through the remainder of the winter. That might explain the urgency of the purchase. Spike gimlets were primitive drills, used to ream out holes, especially in soft wood. Imagine a superstructure of pine branches rising in a clearing up the Brokenstraw, soon to be covered by pine boughs, maybe with a hole in the roof to vent a fire.

Just as likely, and perhaps in conjunction with putting together a first, primitive dwelling, a gimlet would have been useful for building a stretching frame for buckskin. John and Nathaniel had come west in Massachusetts farmer clothing: woolen breeches and a full, almost blousy linen shirt, perhaps a linen knee-length smock, or a wool smock for cold weather. Now they were at the edge of the wilderness, where skins were far more plentiful than cloth and animal gut easier to come by than thread. Appleseed reenactors always seem to favor buckskin costumes, something he never wore once he grew into his nickname and strode the countryside half naked, in sacks and cast-off clothing. But here he might well have made his own buckskin clothing, and perhaps moccasins as well, to cover those bare feet that would become so famous in later years.

The Brokenstraw Creek was John and Nathaniel's first neighborhood—six men, one woman, and two or three permanent structures, separated by seven miles end to end of sporadically cleared wilderness. Nathaniel would have been sixteen, almost a man; John, twenty-three, the second youngest in that stretched-out clustering.

Or maybe the answer is simpler than either buckskin or lean-to: A spiked gimlet would have proved a useful seed drill, especially in winter. From his very first arrival in western Pennsylvania, the future Johnny Appleseed might have had a nursery in mind.

John Chapman was back at the trading post a month later, on

March 15, 1797, for a purchase of a completely different sort—one that begins to color in his early schooling, his intellectual life, and his desire to learn. John Daniels recorded the purchase only as "2 Small Historeys." Beyond that, there's no hint of what they might have been about, but now we can begin to imagine him clad in buckskin, sitting by the fire in the backwoods clearing he and Nathaniel shared, maybe deep into some history of the ancient world or struggling through it, word by word; maybe helping his half brother to read, too.

Other trading post visits followed. Two days after he bought the "Small Historeys," he was back to buy some cheese, or to make good on the balance for a cheese already bought—the ledger is unclear. On May 9, he bought what must have been a small wheel of the same: almost six pounds of cheese, at a cost of a little over fourteen shillings.

A year passed before his next visit, on May 14, 1798, when he purchased "sundries," and another year before he picked up more sundries at the trading post, on May 3, 1799. By then, Nathaniel had opened his own account. On July 14, 1798, Nathaniel bought a pair of "mokasins," Daniels's spelling for moccasins, one of four visits to the trading post that year. There's no record of how his older brother settled his accounts, but Nathaniel paid for his purchases by "work," presumably for Daniels himself.

The John Daniels ledger also begins to paint a broader picture of the larger community the Chapman brothers inhabited. Matthew Young and Callender Irvine can both be found in Daniels's pages, but so can Blind Snow and Old Thompson, Jenny Longknife and Freckled Boy. In fact, the log of John Chapman's purchases is virtually surrounded by those others. Blind Snow paid off part of his (or her) account with "mokasins"—maybe Blind Snow was the same primitive artisan who made the moccasins Nathaniel later bought—and part with "peltry," skins with the fur still on it. Old

Thompson and Freckled Boy also paid up in skins; Jenny Long-knife, with peltry.

The 1800 census counted 230 people in all 898 square miles of newly formed Warren County—one person for every four square miles of forest, meadow, scrub, and wilderness—but the U.S. Census Bureau didn't make its first tentative effort to count Native Americans until 1860, and the wildlands of Warren County seem to have been home to as many Indians as Euro-Americans. Within a decade, in the next state west, John Chapman would sprout a reputation among recently subdued tribes as a wise man, a white sachem, an herbalist, filled with the holy spirit of nature. Surely if he didn't begin that education among Old Thompson, Blind Snow, and others, he deepened it there. If the "2 Small Historeys" are a guide, Chapman had an appetite to know. Opportunity was at his doorstep.

John Chapman's prolonged absences from John Daniels's account book begin to fill in yet another blank spot on his resume: the missing years between the springs of 1797–98 and 1798–99. We know from the ledger that Nathaniel was around for the first of those summers, but his older brother was ranging in all directions—as far as fifty miles south to Franklin, where his name can be found in other early trading-post ledgers.

❦

The Allegheny cuts a tight, beautiful valley as it winds down from Warren. The industrial clutter that hogs the banks wherever it flows through a city of any size quickly disappears in the long spaces in between. Small cabins dot the river on either side, canoe and kayak outfitters, lodges for summer vacationers. Just about everything man-made is low cut, unobtrusive. Let your imagination go, and it's easy to see John Chapman moving along the banks, scouting for land, gathering herbs—a long drink of water, as my late father-in-law would have called him, barely making a sound.

Or maybe he's gliding along one of the Indian trails that his tutors would have shown him: the Brokenstraw Path, which followed the creek west and then went overland to Fort Le Boeuf (today's Waterford) and from there, by a connecting path, to Fort Presque Isle, modern Erie; or the Cornplanter-Venango Path, named for the half-breed Seneca chief whom some credit with being Warren County's very first settler. The Cornplanter Path took off south from the Big Brokenstraw near where the Chapmans would have placed their encampment and ran overland to Venango, as Franklin was then known. It would have cut the distance to Franklin by perhaps a quarter, maybe a third. Had John Chapman stopped to sink a well, he might have beaten Colonel Edwin Drake by six decades. Cornplanter's Path passes right through the middle of Titusville, near the spot where Drake drilled the first commercial oil well in the United States. Settlers had been skimming petroleum from Oil Creek, where Drake drilled, since Revolutionary days.

As with the river path, one is tempted to fill these wooded interior routes with dappled sunlight, scurrying deer, birdsong. Why else imagine them, especially given the cartoon character Johnny Appleseed would become? But on the mid-January day I set out to trace Johnny's footsteps along the Brokenstraw and down the Allegheny to Franklin, things were different; the chirping birds were gone. The temperature that morning stood firm at nineteen degrees. Snow was swirling, adding to a white blanket that had covered fields for a month and would be there for another month to come. At Tionesta and again at Oil City, the Allegheny was frozen from shore to shore.

The point being that the two years during which John Chapman made these looping round-trips between Warren and Franklin held as many January days as July ones, as many miserable, rainy middays as perfect, sunny ones. Buckskin, if that's what he was wearing, is ideal for bucks and does and fawns, but even well-tanned buckskin tends to absorb water like a sponge and can be miserably cold when it's wringing wet. Whatever else he was about on those expeditions, Chapman was tempering himself, learning what it took to survive on his own in the wild, testing the limits of his endurance and finding that, in fact, his endurance was almost without limit, or steadily becoming that way. What a physical pleasure it must have been to learn that about himself. What a confidence builder—he was almost the person the tales he was helping to spread made him out to be!

❦

During these Warren-and-Brokenstraw days John Chapman also seems to have finally hit upon a plan of action more definitive than somehow acquiring a land tract of his own, a revamping that would eventually earn him a slot in the American story far larger than the time and place he was then occupying.

In the spring of 1798, John Chapman "selected a spot for his nursery—for that seemed to be his primary object—near White's on the big Brokenstraw, and sowed his seed," or so Lansing Wetmore wrote in a series of reminiscences published in the *Warren Ledger* in 1854. And there you have it: the first apple nursery of the most famous orchardist in our national history. Or was it?

Like so many of those on whom the "real" Johnny Appleseed story has come to depend, Wetmore presents problems. What to trust? What to cast aside? How to separate out the inflation that so frequently winds through these stories? Wetmore was born in Whitestown, New York, west of Utica, in 1792, and didn't arrive in Warren until 1815. His early history of the region is perforce based on oral tradition, not firsthand knowledge, yet Wetmore was a much-admired man: a lawyer, Warren County's first protho-notary (or chief clerk of the court, with offices in Dan McQuay's old blockhouse), later an associate judge himself, and the father of another prominent lawyer who became presiding judge of Warren and two other counties.

The trust factor also gets tangled up in Wetmore's rotund style and his love of a good story. His reminiscences began as a lecture at the local Lyceum, delivered on March 29, 1853, and later were expanded and printed in the newspaper, and you can still hear the orator in his words, the determination to hold his audience rapt. On that first trip to Warren, John Chapman was still days away—"a hundred miles from human habitation," as Wetmore put it—when he was hit with a snowstorm "full three feet deep." Recalling stories about Indians and snowshoes but without the hickory bows and animal sinews to make them, Chapman set out to craft his own version, fashioned from beech brush and twigs that he heated on a fire until they became pliable. (A fire? In a three-foot snow?) From there, the distinguished jurist charges boldly forward, borne along by gusts of hyperbole.

> The solicitude of the Hebrew mother, Jochebed, while weaving the art of bull rushes which was to bear the body of the infant Moses, on the turbid waters of the Nile, could not surpass that of this bold adventurer. And like her, "with invocations to the living God, he twisted every tender twig together, and with a prayer did every osier weave." It was with him a matter of life and death.

Facts suffer, too. Having heard favorable reports in the Wyoming Valley of the Allegheny Country, on the other side of the state, John starts alone for the west in November 1797—perhaps the only instance of a single adventurer through that solitary wilderness to start "barefoot so late in the season" (when, in fact, Nathaniel accompanied him, the two arrived in Warren at least nine months earlier than Wetmore reports, and who knows what their footwear might have been). Wetmore further has John jumping straight from Pennsylvania to Indiana—his three decades in Ohio don't exist at all—"where for aught that is known he still resides," although Chapman had been dead for almost a decade by the time the judge delivered his lecture.

Yet when Wetmore gets to that first nursery, he grows (for him) strangely quiet. Chapman selected the spot. He sowed his seeds. The nursery was by then "his primary object," and although the spot has "long since washed away," the locals in 1853 still knew it as Apple Tree Bar and knew that the nursery that had once stood there had "furnished the trees for . . . most of the old orchards on the Brokenstraw."

And then comes the clinching detail, the next sentence: "The demand for fruit trees being quite limited, and unable to obtain a livelihood by his favorite pursuit, [Chapman] went to Franklin, where he sowed another nursery, and after a few years left. . . ." Wetmore couldn't have realized it—he clearly knew nothing about Chapman's later years—but here is a large part of Johnny Appleseed's life pattern laid out in bold relief.

John Chapman had come to Warren looking for land. He left it having planted a nursery, but he didn't leave the area entirely. A year later he was back to check on his seedlings. That explains his May 1799 appearance in John Daniels's ledger. Almost certainly, he returned the following May or June, this time without leaving a marker, perhaps to sell what he had grown, maybe only to find the nursery washed away by a spring flood. Sow on a river bar, and you gain the silt but suffer the consequences.

Thus it went for decades to come: the nurseries, always half an eye on land acquisition, and forever that compulsive restlessness. John Chapman had started walking from the southern border of Massachusetts sometime in 1796. He wouldn't stop walking for the next half century, until long after Chapman had become

Appleseed, and the Warren area was no exception. No sooner had John Chapman planted that first recorded nursery than he upped and left it, moving fifty miles downriver to Franklin and pulling Nathaniel along with him. He would do it again and again, within Pennsylvania, between Pennsylvania and Ohio, and finally between Ohio and Indiana, but long before he got to that point Nathaniel had stopped coming along and John, later Johnny, was a solo act.

One generally reliable compilation of the major events of Chapman's life has Nathaniel joining the Moses Cleaveland party that surveyed the Western Reserve of Ohio in 1797. In fact, that seems highly unlikely. The job attributed to him—meat provider to the survey party—doesn't sound like work for someone not yet sixteen and still new to hunting in the wild and trading with local tribes, and we know that Nathaniel was back at John Daniels's trading post by the next July. What's more, the Chapman who traveled with Cleaveland appears to have been a Nathan, not a Nathaniel. Other histories have Nathaniel settling in the vicinity of Marietta, Ohio, as early as 1797, again contradicting the Warren trading-post evidence. Both mis-sightings are likely results of the tendency of early-American Chapmans to pick surnames from the same narrow pool.

However it happened, though, the brothers did part ways before century's end, seldom to be in each other's company again. Maybe Nathaniel was tired of being overshadowed by his older half brother in nearly all matters. Or maybe it was John's inability to stay put. Nathaniel might simply have wanted to live someplace—anyplace—for more than a season or two, and by the century's turn he must have realized that wasn't in his brother's makeup.

5

DOWN TO BUSINESS

The lure of land, of ownership drew John Chapman west—maybe the most American desire of all. More than freedom of speech, of assembly, of religion, Americans have always wanted a piece of the eroded rock they live on.

Property ownership was the great point of distinction between European settlers and Native Americans: The Indians possessed what they could carry, not what they stood and hunted and rode on. That logic largely escaped them. Land ownership was also a breakpoint with the Europe so many of the New World settlers and their ancestors had fled. There, they rented or leased, or simply bowed and survived. In America, every man was a king, or potentially so—sovereign of his acreage, crowned head of the cows in his meadow, prince of the pigs in their wallow. And no place in human history offered more tantalizing opportunities to achieve such dreams. From the post-Revolution land speculation in Kentucky, western Pennsylvania and New York, and the old Northwest Territory, and on through the Civil War–era Homestead Act and the later land rushes into Oklahoma and beyond, America was up for grabs as no country had ever been.

The French historian Alexis de Tocqueville saw this clearly in his 1831–33 tour of the new nation: "In no other country in the world is the love of property more active and more anxious than in the United States," de Tocqueville wrote in *Democracy in America;* "nowhere does the majority display less inclination for those principles which threaten to alter, in whatever matter, the laws of property."

John Chapman was a deep part of all that, almost an exemplar. For land, he dragged his half brother over the mountains. For land, he risked bear and Indian and weathered the killer winters of northwestern Pennsylvania. The fact is, though, Chapman was not well suited to securing what he wanted so dearly. This was another facet of his often self-negating character. Just as he seemed to love an audience but loathe a crowd, so he ached for land but couldn't settle down long enough to claim it.

Franklin, where French Creek meets the Allegheny fifty-six miles south of Warren, is a case in point. Chapman left his first marker there late in 1797, in another trading-post ledger that has long since disappeared. By the next year, he seems to have largely relocated to French Creek, eight miles upstream from the trading post, near the present-day town of Utica, and he was still there as of the April 1801 federal census, one of four John Chapmans in all of Pennsylvania (and one of two on the far side of the Alleghenies) and seemingly living alone by then, since Nathaniel's name is not to be found. (The only Nathaniel Chapman named in the Pennsylvania census was living back on the east side of the state, in Luzerne County, an unlikely spot for Nathaniel unless he was caught by the census taker as he was heading home to Longmeadow.)

That census recorded fewer than 250 "heads of families" in all of Venango County, but the term applied broadly to anyone living on his own. Franklin, the new town, was home to perhaps only five families; the rest of the county's population consisted of trappers, traders, single men of limited or no means, trying to fight a land-holding out of the wilderness and doing whatever they could to survive—people, in short, very much like John Chapman.

In 1804, still mostly in and around Franklin, Chapman tried to turn the odds in his favor, signing two promissory notes. In the first, dated February 1, he agreed to pay a hundred dollars plus interest to the children of Elizabeth and Nathaniel Rudd, his sister—still living back in Massachusetts—and her husband, whom she had married five years earlier. There's no specific mention of how or when the deal was struck, but it must have been prior to the previous September because the two children, John and Elisabeth, to whom he made his promise, both died that month—John, barely four years old, on the twenty-eighth and Elisabeth, still shy of her second birthday, two days later, on the thirtieth—another house of sorrows for another Elizabeth Chapman. (A third child and second son, also John, was born the following September 24, two days before his Uncle John's thirtieth birthday.)

Three days later, John Chapman signed a second note, promising to pay a hundred dollars in land or apple trees, this time to Nathaniel Chapman, although it's impossible to tell at this remove whether the Nathaniel in question was his father, still living back in Longmeadow but on the verge of moving his family west to the vicinity of Marietta, Ohio, or his half brother, who by then appears to have already gone ahead to Marietta to prepare for the coming of the rest of his family.

Either way, John borrowed two hundred dollars from close relatives, who would have been themselves hard-pressed to lend the money, for an unknown purpose. Given that his material needs then and evermore were scant to nonexistent, one can reasonably assume that the money was to go toward a land purchase that had thus far eluded the borrower. Yet even that—if that is indeed what the money was to have been used for—didn't work. Before the year was out, John Chapman would drift out of the Franklin area. No land deed in his name was ever recorded there.

J. H. Newton, author of an 1879 history of Venango County, writes of Chapman: "He was one of those characters, very often found in the new country, always ready to lend a helping hand to his neighbors. He helped others more than himself. He took up land several times, but would soon find himself without any, by reason of some other person 'jumping' his claim. On one occasion he walked several miles on ice, barefooted, merely to show his powers of endurance. He seemed to be as much at home with the red men of the forest, as with his own race."

The passage is beautifully benign and a near-perfect fit with the Appleseed myth that would eventually emerge from this wobble-legged beginning. Still, claim-jumping seems too simple an explanation for Chapman's inability to secure a tract of his own. To be sure, land titles in this far corner of the Pennsylvania wilderness were an absolute mess. Claims were frequently contested—or "jumped"—and in any case at law, then as now, the odds go to those who can afford the best (or best-connected) representation or most successfully demonize the other side, a tactic used frequently against the foreign owners of Holland Land Company. (The nativist movement has been going strong in America since its beginnings.) As de Tocqueville also noted during his 1831–33 tour, virtually every issue in the United States eventually becomes a legal one, but favoritism and legal chicanery aside, the land laws were also written to favor *settlers*—people who would clear the land, build their houses, settle into them, commit for the long term—and that John Chapman was unable to do.

He could, if the stories that survive about him are anywhere near correct, fell a forest almost on his own. He was ingenious at making do on very little. He knew how to clear a field, and plant and protect it. He had the essential tool kit of a pioneer farmer, a backcountry woodsman, and a modern survivalist rolled into one, but he lacked one essential quality: the patience to see the scenario through. Land inspired him, but it also put fire to his feet. Land set him traveling, but it couldn't deliver what he wanted, maybe what he needed.

And, in fact, that restlessness did not always endear Chapman to local historians. Another chronicler of Venango County's earliest settlers, writing a decade after J. H. Newton, recalled a markedly different John Chapman, one "who took up land in different parts of the township, but whose sojourn, owing to his thriftless disposition, was only temporary. He appears to have been impatient of the restraints of civilization, so much so, indeed, that as soon as settlements began to increase he disposed of his few improvements, and with a few other spirits as restless and discontented as himself, he drifted further westward."

That's not to say John Chapman wouldn't continue trying to become a land baron, and indeed by some measures he even succeeded. Between 1814 and 1818, mostly in Richland and Ashland Counties in Ohio, Chapman went on an absolute land-buying-and-leasing spree, but even then, he seems to have been at war with himself. On May 31, 1814, Chapman purchased a ninety-nine-year lease on 160 acres in Washington Township of Richland County. He made only one interest payment on the property, in 1820, and forfeited the land uncontested three years later. That same year he bought another 160 acres, in Madison Township in the same county. That interest payment he did keep up, but eventually the holding whittled down to seventy acres, and that was forfeited after his death for nonpayment.

During the course of his long life, Chapman is estimated to have purchased roughly 1,200 acres of often prime bottom land, plus an assortment of city, town, and village lots. He seems to have never stopped speculating, and as we'll see, he had a keen eye for where to buy and for what lots would be best to build on. But in the end he had little to show for it. To repeat a theme, John Chapman seems to have loved land, but maybe, like the Native Americans, he was never meant to own it.

❦

Apple seeds were another matter. Apple seeds, as John Chapman construed the role of nurseryman, could be planted and, unlike land claims on the frontier, left to germinate and grow into seedlings and beyond. They required attention, yes, but only episodically, and the seeds yielded a crop that could be used as collateral. In fact, that's exactly what Chapman put up when he borrowed a hundred dollars from the indeterminate Nathaniel. The promissory note reads in full: "Franklin, February 4, 1804, for value received I promise to pay Nathaniel Chapman on order the sum of one hundred dollars in land or apple trees with interest till paid as witness my hand. John Chapman." Land was in the mix, too, but if payment was demanded, it was trees he had on hand, not acreage.

The seeds and the seedlings and eventually the whole business model that became his modus operandi fit the schedule of a man compulsively on the move yet always driven to retrace his steps. Who could be surprised, then, that apple seeds and apple tending gave John Chapman his nickname and propelled him through the portals into the American story? The match was perfect, and the fruit ideal.

Here's the odd thing, though: While apples are the one item everyone can absolutely agree on about Johnny Appleseed—he gathered seeds from cider mills, planted the seeds and sold (or gave away) the seedlings, and did all this for more than forty years, following the frontier as it moved westward through Ohio and into eastern Indiana—apples are also in many ways the most controversial part of the man.

Was John Chapman a nurseryman straight and simple, or was he something else, larger and more metaphorical: the nursemaid to western expansion, a frontier Saint Francis, the patron saint of pioneer sinners? Was Chapman the American Apollo or the American Dionysius?

The questions sound overblown, certainly, but the story of apples is always in danger of veering into myth, symbol, even allegory, and dragging apple-men with it. And so it has been with John Chapman. He might have wanted nothing more than to plant a nursery, see his trees grow, and reap whatever profit he could from the exercise; but from those first seedlings forward, he wound his story into a saga that traces back through Germanic and Greek mythology to ancient Egypt and all the way back to the Garden of Eden itself and the biblical story of creation.

The northern bards tell us that when the evil god Loki abducted Idun and the apples she tended for the Aesir gods, mankind went to hell in a, well, apple-basket until Loki could be corralled, the apples returned, and order restored on earth and above. In Greek mythology, another meddling god, Eris, uses a golden apple inscribed "for the fairest one" to sow discord among Hera, Athena, and Aphrodite—a battle of vanities that finally brings on the Trojan War and suffering on a Homeric scale. As far back as Rameses III and 1100 BC, apples were the preferred sacrifice at the Temple of Ammon, in Thebes, although camel bone marrow would do in a pinch. And, of course, apples were the forbidden fruit of the Tree of Knowledge—the bite that introduced sin and death into the world.

Apples have been symbols of fertility, tokens of love, emblems of royal power. The "orb" of the House of Windsor consists of a bejeweled cross astride an apple also girdled in precious stones. The association of apples with good health is ancient. Apples were a treatment for diarrhea going back to at least the sixth century. Roasted—and somewhat counterintuitively—they became a laxative in the fourteenth century. In the sixteenth century, they emerged as a balm for smallpox scars. Robert Burton's *Anatomy of Melancholy*, first published in 1621, advises apples as a specific for the dark vapors. Sir John Mandeville, quite possibly a pseudonym for a fifteenth-century Frenchman, wrote in his travelogues of a race of "little men . . . in farther India" who, though they ate nothing, lived heartily by the smell of apples alone.

In one of the most beautiful tributes to any fruit, the thirteenth-century Franciscan monk Bartholomeus Anglicus, author of an early encyclopedia of botanical observations, celebrates the apple tree's beauty, its great variety and many wholesome qualities thus:

> Malus the Appyll is a tree yt bereth apples and is a grete tree in itself. . . . It is more short than other trees of the wood wyth knottes and rinelyd Rynde. And makyth shadowe wyth thicke bowes and branches: and fayr with dyurs blossomes, and floures of swetnesse and lykynge: with goode fruyte and noble. And is gracious in syght and in taste and vertuous in medecyne . . . some beryth sourysh fruyte and hard, and some right soure and some right swete, with a good savoure and mery.

Not surprisingly, given such praise, apples also have been a gateway to immortality for well more than a millennium. Mortally wounded at the Battle of Camlann, King Arthur is brought back to the Island of Avalon, literally the Island of Apples, and there enjoys eternal life. (In his twelfth-century *History of the Kings of*

Britain, Geoffrey of Monmouth refers to Arthur's final refuge as Insula Avallonis, from *aval,* the Middle Welch for "apple"; in Geoffrey's later *Life of Merlin,* it becomes more specifically Insula Pomorom, the "Isle of Apples.")

Not only is Johnny Appleseed the modern custodian of this rich source material—stories and symbols that trace to the Book of Genesis—but he also stands near the front end of a long historical parade that begins in Almaty, in Kazakhstan, in Central Asia, where the first apple tree is thought to have sprouted into existence in pre-Neolithic times. (The name "Almaty," in fact, comes from the Kazakh for "full of apples.") Birds carried the seed eastward to Europe, maybe as early as birds flew anywhere. Fossilized apples have been found in Swiss lake dwellings that date back to as early as 4000 BC. Land animals, too, got in the act, scattering apple seed in their dung along the Silk Road, beginning perhaps three thousand years ago.

Those earliest apples were small, bitter fruits, much like today's crab apples. (Adam must have *really* wanted to eat of the Tree of Knowledge, unless it was a fig tree, as some contend.) But apples have been under cultivation since well before the Greeks. Cato the Elder noted seven varieties of apples available in third-century BC Rome. Four centuries later, Pliny the Elder recorded thirty-six varieties. It was under the reign of Julius Caesar that apples were introduced to England, and under the reigns of James I and Charles I, in the first half of the seventeenth century, that the apple (or *pomme*) made its way to the New World from the old one just as the potato (or *pomme de terre*) was arriving in the Old World from the new one, as Berton Roueché notes in a lively tour through apple history that appeared in the August 11, 1975, *New Yorker.*

Remarkably, given that the fruit originated in what is now a Muslim/Russian Orthodox republic high up in the Asian

Caucasus, apples would achieve the height of their global popularity in a land halfway around the globe from where they began: America, that shining country on the hill to which, at least in this version, the apple's entire evolutionary history somehow seems to have been pointing.

Henry David Thoreau wrote in "Wild Apples" that the apple

> is the most civilized of all trees. It is as harmless as a dove, as beautiful as a rose, and as valuable as flocks and herds. It has been longer cultivated than any other, and so is more humanized; and who knows but, like the dog, it will at length be no longer traceable to its wild original? It migrates with man, like the dog and horse and cow; first, perchance, from Greece to Italy, thence to England, thence to America; and our Western emigrant is still marching steadily toward the setting sun with the seeds of the apple in his pocket, or perhaps a few young trees strapped to his load.

Thoreau knew nothing about Johnny Appleseed. His essay first appeared posthumously in *The Atlantic Monthly* of November 1862, half a year after his own death and almost a decade before *Harper's New Monthly Magazine* helped rediscover Chapman. Yet the long trail of history Thoreau alludes to, the symbolism, all that apples connote and denote, what they mean and what they suggest would ultimately be placed on the raw-boned shoulders of that very American man who set out from Longmeadow, Massachusetts, in 1796, looking for something else entirely, something far more material than being inducted ultimately into the Mythology Hall of Fame. As Berton Roueché notes, Johnny Appleseed has become to America essentially what Robin Hood is to England, Roland is to France, and the Pied Piper is to Germany—our oldest national folk hero. True, but what a load he has been made to bear!

❦

The problem with folk-hero comparisons like the one above is not Johnny Appleseed but John Chapman. Robin Hood, Roland, and the Pied Piper have at best fuzzy historical analogs—a possible medieval bandit, maybe an eighth-century military governor of Brittany and a thirteenth-century pedophile—but Johnny Appleseed has a very exact one, an early-nineteenth-century apple seed sower named John Chapman, and the two are forever being confused.

As an orchardist, Chapman was almost a commonplace of the frontier. As a business planner and strategist, he was arguably brilliant. Chapman's nursery work was either ingenious or a disaster, depending on interpretation, but when it came to what all business enterprise ultimately comes to—the bottom line—he could have done much better.

Chapman wasn't the first entrepreneur to realize that fruit trees on the frontier filled multiple needs: first, the legal requirement in many cases for an orchard to provide proof of intent to settle, not speculate and move on; second, the emotional hunger in distant lands for something from home, most often a left-behind New England home where rare was the yard without an apple tree or two; third, the nutritional longing if not for apples themselves, then for the cider that apples yielded.

Thoreau was right: Pioneers traveled over the Appalachians with their pockets stuffed with apple seeds. The intrepid might have brought a seedling or two from the old homestead, or scions—twigs from existing trees to graft onto root stock. But winters happened, and drought; and even when there was neither, the saplings and scions had to be kept moist under the most trying transportation conditions. The ones that survived the trip were often stunted—they needed to get over the trauma of transport before they could begin to grow to maturity. Seeds had an easier time of it, but they had to go in the ground, and a crop was years away. A waiting nursery solved so many problems.

By 1790, Ebenezer Zane had established a nursery at Bridgeport, across the Ohio River from Wheeling, Virginia. (The state of West Virginia wasn't carved out of Virginia until the Civil War.) By the end of the decade, he was selling his trees along the route of the famous "trace" that bears his name, some 266 miles of old Indian trail that Zane and his crew cleared from opposite Wheeling across southeastern Ohio to Limestone, Kentucky. The Bentley Sweet, the Ohio Red Streak, the Culp, and the Belmont—varieties largely lost to modern supermarkets but much valued in their day—are credited to Zane's nursery.

Six years later, the Continental Army general Rufus Putnam brought a wagon loaded with as many as fifty varieties of apples from Connecticut, from the orchards of his equally famous brother Israel, and used the stock to establish a nursery on the Muskingum River, a few miles north of Marietta. As cofounder of the Ohio Company, which had purchased 1.5 million acres of Ohio, Rufus Putnam had a vested interest in luring settlers and making them happy, and in his own company's requirement that settlers plant an orchard of at least fifty apple trees in the first year, he had built-in sales momentum.

Others got in the act as well. Across the Ohio River in Hancock County, in the Northern Panhandle of what is now West Virginia, Jacob Nessly—who had migrated west from Lancaster, in Pennsylvania—had fifty cleared acres planted in apples and peaches well before the turn of the century. By 1803, Thomas Worthington had opened a nursery on his own estate near Chillicothe, near the central part of the state. In 1806 another large nursery was established, this one near Cincinnati. By 1813, the Ohio Company was shipping several thousand barrels of apples to markets as far away as New Orleans.

❦

If John Chapman was only one of many nurserymen trying to make a living at the edge of the known world of commerce, his approach to the business couldn't have been more original. Of overhead, he had none so long as he slept outside, as he most often did, and dined on the grains and nuts and berries the fields and forests had to offer. Capital costs were near zero, too: an ax for felling, a scythe for mowing, a grub hoe for planting. The fences he constructed around his nurseries were of brambles, most cleared from the acre or less he had planted, and he must have piled them high to keep the deer out. Modern deer fencing is useless at less than eight feet. Watering was by nature: Chapman left the nurseries to survive on their own. Transportation costs didn't count, since he seemed compelled to walk in any event.

Each fall, Chapman returned to the cider mills he had known in western Pennsylvania and sorted through their redolent discarded pulp for the seeds he would use for the next year's crop. Each spring found him just beyond the edge of the frontier, planting on unclaimed land near some creek or river that he was certain settlers would be following into the interior. And with uncanny accuracy, that's exactly what they did. Other nurserymen sold to the trade as it passed by. John Chapman had his just-in-time inventory waiting when the trade arrived.

Arthur F. Humphrey, a gifted amateur historian, has helped track down the location of the two long-gone cider mills southeast of Pittsburgh that appear to have provided, gratis, the raw materials for Chapman's little business empire: one on the farm of Frederick Medsger along the Youghiogheny River not far south of Interstate 70, in Smithton or more likely Jacob's Creek, roughly thirty miles downriver from Frank Lloyd Wright's famous house at Fallingwater; and the VanKirk cider mill, some five miles due west along the Monongahela River, in the broad ambit of North Belle Vernon. As the crow flies, the two ghost mills and Mansfield, one of several Ohio cities that Chapman briefly settled near, are between 160 and 180 miles apart—a long way to go on foot for supplies even when the seeds were free, but there were always places to stop along the way.

More than a half century ago, biographer Robert Price set out to identify the sites of the nurseries Chapman had established with those Pennsylvania seeds. (Price's criterion was at least one early printed reference.) That list alone ran to thirty-five locations, some as vague as "somewhere on Stony Creek," others as exact as "on the west bank of Rocky Ford, 'on the flats, within the present limits of Mansfield, near where stood the Pittsburgh, Fort Wayne and Chicago Railway Dept.'"

The vast majority, of course, were in Ohio, many at the mouths of creeks, on the edges of marshes, near the headwaters of this stream or that, or on sandbars—like that first one in Warren County—or small islands. "Open places on the loamy lands that border the creeks," is how W. D. Haley put it in the *Harper's New Monthly Magazine* article of November 1871, "rich, secluded spots, hemmed in by giant trees, picturesque now, but fifty years ago, with their wild surroundings and the primal silence, they must have been tenfold more so."

Others have taken up the challenge of identifying parts of orchards or single trees that can still claim some possible kinship with the seedlings Chapman grew and sold. (The average life of an apple tree runs to about thirty-five years, but through grafting, a tree's DNA can survive for untold generations.) Here, though, the myth battles with the man. Who doesn't want to have a tree whose ancestry traces back to the American Robin Hood, the New World Roland?

Purely from a business point of view, the key fact is this: Whatever he sold his seedlings for, and it was measurable in pennies, Chapman realized a 100 percent profit on each item moved, not counting his own sweat equity, which was monumental. Not bad, and remember, this was a volume business: seedlings sold not by the unit but by the dozens, even by the gross. Mighty dollars from little pennies grow. Except in Chapman's case, that didn't quite happen.

The documentation of John Chapman's business assets—nurseries planted, trees on hand at death, etc.—is surprisingly complete for an otherwise shadowy figure out of distant history. What might be thought of as his hidden debits—the young trees he put to charitable causes—are entirely anecdotal, but the stories were told so far and wide across Ohio and Indiana that it's hard not to credit their general accuracy. Chapman was glad to sell his wares, but no one, it seems, went away empty-handed from his nurseries if they lacked the means to pay. Some trees he gave away; others he bartered for bits of clothing. As he got older, and odder, he became increasingly agnostic as to the source of what he wore. The tales are many of his rescuing mistreated horses and paying for the pasturage. As we'll see, the more devoted he became to the Church of the New Jerusalem, the more he was ready to give it almost anything he had—for books, for a campus to build a college, and on and on. He had a missionary zeal, and the true missionary's disregard for dollar signs.

He often paid for pasturing for horses he saw being abused as he traveled the frontier's byways. Chapman might have run the first equine rescue operation in the new nation.

I've come to think of Chapman as a kind of Andrew Carnegie of the frontier. Like Carnegie, he combined many of the characteristics of a hardheaded businessman with the loftier instincts of a philanthropist. But there is one key difference. In his 1889 essay "The Gospel of Wealth," Carnegie, who had made his money in steel, advised readers to spend the first half of their lives accumulating a fortune and the second half giving it away, as he was able to do. Chapman would have agreed in broad terms: Money shouldn't be wasted on frivolous expenses. The existence of need compelled philanthropy, and no one on the frontier seems to have been more ready to give—and give until it should have hurt—than John Chapman. But he missed Carnegie's critical life-cycle division. Chapman didn't delay philanthropy until his wealth had accumulated. He gave his money away in many cases as soon as he had earned it.

❧

Whatever John Chapman's business practices were and whatever their shortcomings might have been, a mythic apple nurseryman ought to be able to grow seedlings that mature into trees that yield mythic apples—the kind we dream about when we dream of apples; the kind, in fact, that are weighing down the boughs in cartoon and storybook treatments of Johnny Appleseed's life and works. John Chapman's apples weren't like that. They were mostly puny, sour little things, more like the wild apples of olden days than the plump ones ripening in Rufus Putnam's orchard, down in Marietta.

That's what happens when a nurseryman grows from seed. Genetically, the seed of an apple is an absolute marvel of diversity. (The exact word in plant-science circles is "heterozygous.") Each little pip contains within itself all the genetic coding for the more than a hundred thousand varieties of apples thus far identified and the innumerable other varieties waiting to be discovered or created. But all that coding also makes apple propagation by seed utterly unreliable.

A seed, for example, produced the first Gala apple tree, but the seeds from a Gala apple have the coding for all those hundred thousand–plus other varieties lurking inside them and thus are so highly unlikely to produce a tree just like the parent that you would be crazy to try it. If you want your tree to produce Gala apples, the only sure route is to graft a branch or a twig—even a lone bud—from a known Gala producer to a bole or only a limb of another apple tree.

That's the first argument against propagating by seed: You don't have any idea what you'll get. The second, more compelling argument is that what you do get by way of fruit is almost certain to be inferior. According to Berton Roueché, maybe one in a hundred seedlings will yield even an edible apple, much less a good one. No one knows for sure why, but if you let apple trees do their own thing—and this applies to many other fruit trees as well—they'll revert toward their wild ancestors. Maybe all those genetic choices simply wear them out.

A third strike against seedlings is the orchards they produce. Not only is the fruit likely to be inferior and varieties all over the place—especially when, like Chapman, you are gathering seed from a cider mill, which lumps all its pomace together—the trees themselves are frequently giants by apple standards and often slow to yield a crop. In the forests of Asia where apples first grew, they had to reach high to find sun among the competing canopy. That same inherent vigor and competitiveness still can shine through when seedlings are left to their own devices—they might grow to thirty or forty feet and take two to three decades to produce a single fruit.

None of this was a secret when John Chapman started his nursery work in earnest. Apples were being grafted and hybridized three millennia ago. Anyone who grew up on a farm in Massachusetts in the closing years of the eighteenth century might not have been as familiar with grafting fruit trees as they were with, say, slopping pigs or milking cows, but they would have been aware of the science of grafting. Chapman was clearly a seeker, a learner. He could have found someone, even in the sparsely populated frontier, to show him technique. And he wouldn't have had to compromise his nomadic lifestyle. Chapman could have planted his nurseries, given the seedlings a few years to grow, then returned and top-worked the young trees by grafting on a scion from a desirable apple variety. The fruit would have certainly been improved, and the time to market halved, since the scion wood was already mature and ready to produce, no matter the age of the rootstock it was being grafted onto.

So why, then, did he do it? Why grow an inferior fruit tree when the technology and the means were at hand to do better?

The standard answer is Chapman's almost animistic refusal to harm any living thing. Animals have souls. Trees feel the grafting knife. In time, that belief would certainly be true of him, and he was probably drifting in that direction already, on the road to conviction. Overnight animists are few. But this more saintly reading of motives might also make a virtue of necessity—in the same way someone might boast that she never repeats gossip because, in fact, no one will feed her gossip to repeat.

Seeds were more portable and compact than scion wood. They fit in a pocket, a shoulder sack, and (like grass seed, for that matter) they could be planted from the dead of winter through early summer. Scion grafting is done in the spring only, when life is flowing back into the rootstock, and back then, grafting would have required beeswax to seal the graft, a pot to melt the wax in, and a fire to warm the pot. The other standard method of apple tree propagation, bud grafting, was limited to the summer months only, and required transporting far more delicate plant life than scion wood. Either form of grafting, though, weighted down a man who liked to travel light. Whatever the spiritual lives of apple trees, however much they might suffer from the grafter's blade, seedlings simply were much better suited to Chapman's transitory, high-volume, pile-'em-high-and-watch-'em-fly business model.

In a May 17, 1943, letter to the editor of the *New York Times*, J. H. Walker of Newark, New Jersey, praised Johnny Appleseed for his Yankee "shrewdness" but also blasted him for a "lack of knowledge" about apple propagation and said that a half century earlier, Johnny had been "damned by many farmers" for cluttering the valleys and fertile fields with orchards that yielded mostly an "inferior scrub stock" of apples. "As an orchardist," the *Times* responded, "Mr. Walker is wholly right. But the first farmers who followed Johnny Appleseed praised him for the scrub apples, which pieced out many a meal of venison and corn pone."

There is, however, another answer—one that goes beyond ignorance, convenience, or belief: Chapman was giving the market what it wanted. This, in essence, is the argument advanced by Michael Pollan in the opening chapter of *The Botany of Desire*, and corroborating evidence abounds.

Looking back over the landscape of olden times, we tend to apply our own standards. We want an apple that is crisp, plump, sweetly tart, whatever our taste desires. The frontiersmen of Ohio saw things differently. Many had orchards. Most knew about grafting, at least in broad terms. By 1806 or so, Ohio farmers would have had multiple apple tree varieties to chose from: those already mentioned plus Early Junes, Carolina Reds, Pryor's Reds, Fall Queens, Milans, and on and on. Yet most of the apples these farmers grew and harvested were the same inferior ones that cluttered the mature limbs of the same ne'er-do-well seedlings that Johnny Appleseed sold, and for one very good reason: The farmers didn't give a hoot for the nutritional value of their apples or for their tastiness, raw or cooked, and they had no intention of using them to "piece out" a meal of venison and pone, as the *Times* editorial suggested. Some of the scrub apples went to making vinegar, to be used as a food preservative and for medicine. All they ever intended to do with the rest of the crop was feed it through the press and ferment the juice. And for that purpose, a pathetic little throwback of an apple was every bit as useful as one an artist might paint and frame, and a lot cheaper and easier to grow.

Not to overstate the case, but life on the edge of civilization in the Old Northwest Territory was often lived through an alcoholic haze. Corn whiskey was doled out free by storekeepers, a bonus with every purchase. Hard cider was as much a part of the dining table as meat or bread. Both lubricated virtually every social event, from house raisings to funerals. One memoirist of the Pennsylvania frontier in the very early 1800s wrote of alcohol that no one "seemed to think there was any harm or danger connected with its use, unless the user got drunk," but "drunk" in this usage pretty much meant passing out.

In their study of New Englanders on the frontier, Virginia E. and Robert W. McCormick estimate that by the early part of the nineteenth century, Ohioans ages fifteen and over were consuming, on average, nine gallons of liquor per year, thirty gallons of hard cider, and a quart of wine. Do the math, and that works out to 3.16 ounces of hard liquor per day, 10.52 ounces of hard cider (and some cider was very hard), and a sip or two of wine daily. And that doesn't include the children, who were frequently given hard cider with their meals, though often of lower alcohol content.

That's why Johnny Appleseed was so welcome on the frontier, Pollan suggests. His seedlings were the front end of the distilling process. Whatever apples he might have carried with him to give out along the way were headed straight for the press and the mash crock—only a few weeks away from being booze in the belly, a buzz in the head, a longer nap for the kiddies.

The tidying up of Johnny Appleseed's story came later, Pollan contends—after the Women's Christian Temperance Union took axes to America's orchards to slay the demon cider and applejack, after apple growers were forced to celebrate the fruit not for its intoxicating values but for its nutritional benefits, its ability, taken once a day, to keep the doctor away—to celebrate the apple, that is (although Pollan doesn't mention this), for being what it had been in the time of King Arthur and before.

Maybe, but all that still begs the question of intent. Was Chapman the frontier bootlegger that Pollan paints him to be—a wilderness pusher; a pacifist Al Capone, not in spats but in cast-off rags—or was he simply following best business practices? Chapman didn't have to look far and wide for a successful model for his own trade. Jacob Nessly up on the hillside on the (now) West Virginia side of the Ohio River had put nearly all of his fifty acres in seedling apples and peaches. He was happily producing the same inferior fruits Chapman's plants produced, and he was making a reputed fortune by doing the distilling himself and turning out apple and peach brandies.

And if Chapman had no primary intent to soothe the beast and befuddle minds, if he was just being the best businessman he had in him, can he ever be the "American Dionysius," as Pollan labels him? Or has Pollan done to Chapman what so many others have done: taken the man and forced a myth to fit him? And not even a complete man at that, because apples and apple tree growing were only the lesser part of John Chapman.

Apples certainly made Chapman famous. They gave him his nickname and committed him to American folklore and mythology. But what animated him, what gave his mind and actions depth and texture, was a dead Swedish metallurgist-turned-mystic and would-be holy man named Emanuel Swedenborg. If Chapman was pushing anything on the American frontier, it was Swedenborg's theology, not hard cider.

6.

A CALLING

In the Christian world, apples are never far from religion. Neither was John Chapman. He needed only to find a theology he could believe in, a system that fit what he already was becoming, and the Ohio-Pennsylvania-Virginia frontier at the start of the nineteenth century offered a full range of possibilities.

Back east, in New England, what became known as the Second Great Awakening was just beginning to take form. After decades of benign neglect, Sunday church crowds swelled, and new congregations flourished. Edward Dorr Griffin of New Hartford, in Litchfield County, Connecticut, wrote in 1799 that he could stand in his front door and "number fifty or sixty contiguous congregations laid down in one field of divine wonders." The next year, 1800, saw a new publication come into existence, the *Connecticut Evangelical Magazine*, to track the movement. Then, in 1801, the revivalist spirit swept through Yale College. Inspired by the preaching of Timothy Dwight, Yale's eighth president, fully a third of the students, most of them already studying theology, stepped forward to be converted and declare themselves evangelicals, and the ranks of the student Moral Society skyrocketed. Like much of the country, Yale had fallen into the embrace of the remote God imagined by the Deists, the perfectly working watchmaker favored by many of the nation's Founding Fathers. Now, God was again nearby and omnipresent. By 1803, one student could write home that "Yale College is a little temple; prayer and praise seem to be the delight of the greater part of the students."

Over the next decade and beyond, religious revivals became a commonplace of New England life, in some places almost continuous. But as Sydney E. Ahlstrom notes in *A Religious History of the American People,* one marked feature of all this religious fervor—and one sharp distinction with the earlier Great Awakening of Jonathan Edwards, George Whitefield, and others—was just how un-fervid it was. People weren't talking in tongues at these revivals or writhing on the floor. Ministers were preaching the Word, not laying on hands to cure the lame and the halt. Hysteria was nowhere to be found, and barely any serious commotion either.

Not so on the frontier. There, at what was then the barbarous far end of America from the proper pews of New England, sin was plentiful, alcohol flowed freely, the bulk of the population were—like John Chapman—young men living rough lives, formal schooling was rare, superstition high, lawmakers far away and law keepers mostly distant, and the revival movement was in full-throated roar. Who could blame the evangelists for taking advantage? The situation was so tempting.

In his study of revivalism on the frontier, Charles A. Johnson cites a July 1800 gathering along the Gasper River in southwestern Kentucky as the official first camp meeting in the United States and maybe the world. The driving force behind the event was a Presbyterian minister named James McGready. Having failed in North Carolina, where his fiery oratory was blamed for "driving people distracted" (his manners, generally described as uncouth, might also have offended Old South sensibilities), McGready migrated to the edge of Kentucky and set up shop where being driven to distraction seemed to be exactly what people had in mind, and "couthness" clearly counted not for a thing.

Services at his own church on the Gasper River had become so well attended that McGready persuaded local woodsmen to clear a campground, sent out flyers announcing a service that would begin Saturday evening and last through the following Tuesday morning, enlisted the aid of a handful of Methodist preachers, and laid on thirteen wagons to carry worshippers and supplies to the grounds. The response was overwhelming. Participants came from as far as a hundred miles away. Many of them spent entire nights in the meetinghouse, forgoing the campground and sleep for the throes of religious experience. In the end, in McGready's own words, "No person seemed to wish to go home—hunger and sleep seemed to affect nobody—eternal things were the vast concern. . . . Little children, young men and women, and old grey-headed people, persons of every description, white and black, were to be found in every part of the multitude . . . crying out for mercy in the most extreme distress."

Even if McGready's assessment errs on the side of self-congratulation, there's no doubt that he had launched a movement that soon spread like wildfire through Kentucky and Tennessee. Both states had been admitted to the Union within the decade—Kentucky in 1792 and Tennessee four years later, in 1796. Both had undergone population explosions in a few scant years, to a combined 325,000-plus residents by the start of the new century, and in both, the revival spirit soared as camp meetings multiplied and grew in numbers and participating clergy. Johnson writes that as many as twenty thousand worshippers attended a meeting at Cabin Creek, in the northern hump of Kentucky, in May 1801. Another meeting, at Indian Creek, a few counties to the west, drew as many as ten thousand congregants. Twenty or more preachers of various denominations—Methodists, Baptists, and Presbyterians—would work the crowd into a frenzy, joined by lay preachers rising up out of the crowd to deliver their own sermons or sometimes simply too drunk to know what they were saying because on the frontier of that day, God, man, and whiskey intermingled freely.

❧

Almost with its earliest successes in Kentucky, the camp meeting revivalists began looking northward, across the Ohio River to the Northwest Territory. The first known gathering on the Ohio side of the river, at Eagle Creek in what is now Adams County, took place on June 5, 1801—less than a year after McGready had built the template for the movement, and with much the same result. One of the organizers would later describe participants "praying, shouting, jerking, barking or rolling, dreaming, prophesying, and looking as through a glass at the infinite glories of Mount Zion."

The Eagle Creek meeting was, in the main, a Presbyterian undertaking, and the Presbyterians generally had Ohio covered on two fronts: to the southeast, via Kentucky, and from the northeast, via Erie, Pennsylvania, where a presbytery—or church administrative body—was established in 1801 to provide for the spiritual needs of the tide of settlers about to burst into what would soon become Ohio. Together, the Presbyterians might have executed a pincer movement and claimed the needy souls of a whole generation of pioneers in the Northwest Territory. But word of the barking and rolling, the jerking and shouting that the camp meetings had occasioned was beginning to filter back east, to the chagrin of church leaders.

Disciplinary action ensued, followed (almost inevitably) by schisms. Stonites—disciples of one of the early Kentucky Presbyterian revivalists, Barton Stone—went one way. Campbellites—followers of another disaffected frontier Presbyterian, Thomas Campbell—headed off in another direction, eventually helping to spawn two modern-day Christian movements: the Disciples of Christ and the Churches of Christ.

Into the breach left by the retreat and splintering of Presbyterianism on the edge of the wilderness stepped the Methodists and the Baptists, less sensitive about camp meeting demonstrativeness. Methodists west of the Alleghenies grew more than tenfold in the first twelve years of the new century, to 29,000 white members and almost 1,700 African-Americans. Those numbers would continue to explode through the next two decades, until total membership was on the order of 175,000. Baptists experienced a similar growth. In Kentucky, their numbers doubled in the first three years of the century alone, to more than 10,000. By 1820, about one in every eighteen Kentuckians professed to be Baptist—almost 32,000 people.

Those numbers were almost predictable. The Trans-Allegheny West was growing, and religion with it. But everyone knew that the other side of the Ohio River would soon hold a large prize, and just about any denomination with a message to deliver and a theological wrinkle to hang it on was trying to get in on the game, or was at least drawn to the challenge. Out of the German church strongholds of eastern Pennsylvania, particularly Lancaster, came the Brethren movement to minister to the needs of the German communities of the frontier. By 1810, the United Brethren in Christ had established a conference in Miami, Ohio, almost to the Indiana border.

Late to the party and also somewhat hobbled by its own respectability, the Congregationalist Church joined forces with the Presbyterians (in a deal brokered by Jonathan Edwards's son) to find a foothold in the Old Northwest. Under the terms of the Plan of Union of 1801, settlers of either persuasion were free to form joint congregations and employ a minister of either denomination.

The plan worked in part, but given that Ohio was already being peopled with a virtual diaspora out of Congregational New England, the union probably should have worked better.

Further out at the margins of the mainstream—and in some cases well beyond them—a whole new horizon of possibilities was forming for religious seekers. Mysticism and pantheism were in the air, maybe inspired by the spirit gods of Native Americans soon to be driven into the still-deeper wilderness by western expansion. By the 1780s, the German physician Franz Anton Mesmer (think "mesmerize") had helped open the door to an unknown inner world of the pysche with his experiments in hypnotism, which he referred to as "animal magnetism." Almost simultaneously, the Universalist movement was taking root in and around Boston, with its promise that grace was open to all—that Christ's death had redeemed not only Christian believers but the entirety of humankind.

Borne on such wings of change, utopian movements flourished—the Oneida Community in New York, Brook Farm in Massachusetts, Robert Owen's "Great Truth" community at the beautifully named New Harmony, Indiana. America itself, after all, was a utopian experiment, the "ideal" writ large in governance. So, too, flourished a whole generation of millennialists, convinced that when Christ did come again, it would be to America—the New Jerusalem of the promised thousand-year kingdom. Vermont farmer William Miller, eight years John Chapman's junior, read the Book of Daniel and divined that Judgment Day and the Second Coming would arrive within a thirteen-month window beginning in March 1843, a heralding heeded by fifty thousand or more followers. When that window closed without event, a Miller disciple, Samuel Snow, recalculated and fingered the next Yom Kippur, the Jewish Day of Atonement, set for October 22, 1844. That date passed as well, and the Millerites fell into the Great

Disappointment instead of millennial bliss, but the movement would soon resurface as the Seventh-day Adventists. Meanwhile, between the two Millerite miscalculations, on June 27, 1844, Joseph Smith was murdered by a mob in Carthage, Illinois, while awaiting trial, with his Latter Day Saints only halfway to their eventual home in Deseret.

Much of the superstructure of modern religious fundamentalism was being constructed and field tested on the ever-receding American frontier. The place was alive with God, bubbling with new permutations and combinations of faith and interpretation and theology, many of which have survived and prospered into our own time. Of all the survivors, almost none is more obscure today, yet more representative of nearly everything that was going on in those early decades of the nineteenth century, than the Church of the New Jerusalem, which traced its origins not to an American divine but to a Swedish scientist and man of letters.

❦

Emanuel Swedenborg was born in Stockholm on January 29, 1688, the son of a Lutheran bishop, and educated at Uppsala University. Afterward, he spent five years touring England, France, Holland, and Germany, gobbling up everything he could learn about mathematics and astronomy, and then returned to Stockholm and set about demonstrating that he was quite likely the most learned man in Sweden and one of the great minds of eighteenth-century Europe. As "assessor extraordinary" to the Royal College of Mines, he spent three decades improving and modernizing mining practices in Sweden, but that was only his day job. On the side, he published learned papers and books that spanned a vast scientific terrain: the first work on algebra in Swedish, studies of the movement of atoms that presage modern nuclear physics, groundbreaking neural work showing the connection between the various areas of the cerebral cortex and motor regions of the body, other neural work that dissected cerebrospinal fluid, and on and on.

Swedenborg's range was enormous. He could have made a lasting mark in any one of perhaps half a dozen fields. But by his fifties what had come to occupy his mind most was God, the infinite, the spiritual life, and the spirit world. The defining moment—the one that would reset the compass of his life—arrived in April 1745, late in the evening, in a private dining room of a London chophouse.

> I was hungry and ate with a hearty appetite. Toward the end of the meal a kind of fog came over my eyes: everything darkened, and I saw how the floor was covered with horrible crawling animals, snakes, frogs. I was astonished, because I was in full possession of my reason. At length the darkness prevailed, and then suddenly passed over. I saw a man sitting in one corner of the room. Being quite alone, I was terrified when he spoke to me, saying: Don't eat so much! Again everything became dark, but the light returned, and I found myself alone in the room. . . . I went home, but that night the man again showed himself to me. He said he was God Almighty, and that he had chosen me to explain the spiritual contents of Holy Writ, and that he would himself inspire me with what I had to write about them. . . . And from that day onward I gave up all concern with worldly writing, and devoted my work to spiritual matters.

As Swedenborg's spiritual powers strengthened, stories of his "second sight" became legend: the time he turned pale just as he was sitting to dinner in Gottenberg and said that a great fire had broken out in Stockholm, some three hundred miles away. Two hours later, he announced with relief that the fire was now under control but "had almost reached my doorstep," and another two days after that a letter arrived confirming the fire and the fact that it had nearly engulfed Swedenborg's home. On another occasion, he startled the queen of Sweden by describing to her in detail the contents of the last letter she had written to her deceased brother. "No one but God knows this secret!" the queen is said to have exclaimed, but that was the point: Swedenborg, in fact, *knew* it from God, or the next closest thing.

As with Joseph Smith and the Book of Mormon, Swedenborg had been led to secret truths. Smith got there via the stone tablets that he discovered buried upon a hill in New York State and through the magic spectacles that allowed him to translate the tablets. Swedenborg cut to the chase. In his dreams and in the spirit visitations that became more and more common in his middle years and beyond, Swedenborg was in direct communication with angels who were themselves only one remove from God.

Swedenborg didn't have to guess as to the nature of heaven. He had seen it, exactly. Heaven "is divided into two kingdoms, regionally into three heavens, and locally into countless communities." There is no speech in heaven as we conceive of it; rather "everyone in heaven speaks from his thought, for they have thought-speech there, or vocal thought." Not only do angels have homes, but Swedenborg had been with them in their houses. "Their dwellings are just like the dwellings of earth which we call homes, except that they are more beautiful. They have rooms, suites, and bedrooms, all in abundance. They have courtyards, and are surrounded by gardens, flowerbeds, and lawns. . . . This has happened to me when I was fully awake, when my inner sight was opened."

Nor did Swedenborg have to speculate on the nature of hell, for that also had been revealed to him. In the spiritual world, everything that was most pronounced about us in the natural one becomes more so, and we vastly surpass our earlier condition, for better or worse. If we acted out of a particular "good" in life, in death that goodness becomes unspeakably beautiful. If we acted out of a particular "evil" in life, then in death "an absolutely incredible malice displays itself. There are thousands of things that erupt from this malice, among them some things such that they are beyond description in the vocabulary of any language." And the worst of them all erupts from the evil of self-love. Until we free ourselves of that, we cannot serve our neighbors as God intended.

Swedenborg, of course, wasn't alone in having visions, talking with angels, claiming to have (and even displaying) second sight. Others before him had described heaven in detail; others had offered their own interpretations of hell. John Milton's *Paradise Lost* and Dante's *Inferno* come readily to mind. But no one else created such a robust body of literature about what he had seen and experienced. Beginning in the late 1740s, he set down his biblical interpretations, theological teachings, and divine revelations in six different works, one in eight volumes and another in four, as well as filling a dream journal that has kept generations of Freudians and Jungians occupied. The last of Swedenborg's titles—*The True Christian Religion*—was published in Amsterdam in 1771, one year before his death, in March 1772, at age eighty-two.

That was part of Swedenborg's appeal: the sheer volume of commentary. The other was the way he approached his subject. Swedenborg was a mystic with a bench scientist's instincts and habits. He didn't merely describe heaven in broad terms; he mapped it. Nor did he talk in general terms about the relationship between the spiritual and physical worlds. He laid out an entire theory of correspondences between the two. At the tail end of the Age of Reason, Swedenborg was a scientist Romantics could believe in. At the advent of the Romantic Epoch, he was both empiricist and dreamer. Swedenborg had seen into the Great Beyond and left lab notes behind. Intellectual Europe and America could hardly resist him.

The London-based Swedenborg Society lists thirty writers, philosophers, thinkers, and intellectuals across three centuries who, it says, were clearly influenced by Swedenborg. Among them: Charles Baudelaire; William Blake, who broke with Swedenborg after a long infatuation but was clearly attracted to his imagery; Jorge Luis Borges; Thomas Carlyle, to whom Swedenborg was "one of the spiritual suns that will shine brighter as the years go on"; Johann Wolfgang von Goethe; Henry James, Sr., the father to both William, the founder of modern psychology, and Henry Jr., the novelist; Carl Jung, who once wrote, "I admire Swedenborg as a great scientist and a great mystic at the same time"; Immanuel Kant, who like Blake attacked Swedenborg after first being drawn to him; Czesław Miłosz, the 1980 Nobel laureate in literature; Arthur Schopenhauer; the playwright August Strindberg, Swedenborg's fellow countryman; and William Butler Yeats.

Walt Whitman believed that Swedenborg would quite likely "make the deepest and broadest mark upon the religions of future ages here, of any man that ever walked the earth." Emerson praised Swedenborg as "the most imaginative of men, yet writing with the precision of a mathematician." Honoré de Balzac, the great French novelist, announced in an 1837 letter that "Swedenborgianism" was his religion. (The "g" turns soft in "Swedenborg" whenever a suffix is added to the name.)

Whether Swedenborg himself had any desire to found a religion, or even a denomination, is highly doubtful. In death, though, he had no say in the matter. Practically from the time Swedenborg drew his last breath, his admirers began to transform his writings into theological doctrine and Swedenborg himself into the agent of the Second Coming, which had arrived not on the pounding hooves of the Four Horsemen of the Apocalypse but rather in the inner truths of the Bible that had been made known to the Swedish mystic.

In his home country, forty-six clergymen of the Church of Sweden declared themselves believers in the gospel of the New Age as it had been revealed to Swedenborg. In the diocese of Skara, where Swedenborg's father had once been bishop, 60 percent of all clergy said the same. Back in Manchester, England, the rector John Clowes set about translating Swedenborg and preaching his radical gospel in his own Anglican church, and a young London printer, Robert Hindmarsh, formed with a few friends a reading circle to better understand such dense works as the eight-volume *Arcana Coelestia* and *Heaven and Hell,* which had just been made available in English.

In a 1917 address to the Annual Convention of the New Jerusalem Church, in Philadelphia, the Reverend H. Clinton Hay picked up the story of the church's founding from there:

> Still later, to secure publicity, [the reading-circle members] took chambers at the Inner Temple, Fleet Street, and advertised in the newspapers, inviting all readers of Swedenborg to come and help in extending a knowledge of his writings. This brought James Glen, a Scotchman who was on his way to settle at Demerara, South America [now Guyana]. He related how the captain of a ship in which he had sailed back from a previous voyage to South America had presented a copy of *Heaven and Hell* to him, which had filled him with astonishment, first at the nature of the information given, and second at the goodness of the divine providence in opening his mind to such a flood of spiritual truth.
>
> So Mr. Glen sailed for America, full of gratitude and happiness, to become the pioneer missionary of the Lord in his Second Coming to the new world of freedom—of democracy—and in this special sense, perhaps, the "new earth" prepared to receive the New Jerusalem now descending from God out of heaven.

On June 5, 1784, at Bell's auction room and book store [in Philadelphia], he gave the first public proclamation of the New Church in America, if not in the world.

Thus, the Church of the New Jerusalem arrived in what the Puritans and a succession of prophets of the First and Second Great Awakenings had already declared was the New Jerusalem on Earth—America, the Shining City on the Hill. What's more, the Church had found its way by chance near to the elite core of the new nation. Francis Bailey, the renowned "Printer of the Revolution," attended that first meeting at Bell's Auction House, and would soon take on the task of reprinting Swedenborg's works in America. His 1792 edition of *True Christian Religion* contains a list of subscribers who helped with the expense, including Bailey's fellow printer, near neighbor, and good friend Benjamin Franklin as well as Robert Morris, the land baron and financier.

According to Reverend Hay, a copy of *True Christian Religion* was sent to George Washington, who is said to have read it closely in the final months of his life. Swedenborg's works also apparently found their way to Washington's early patron Thomas, the 6th Lord Fairfax, holder of a vast land grant known as the Northern Neck Proprietary—almost six million acres, 12 percent of the Colony of Virginia—and to his nephew, Ferdinand, and Ferdinand's son, Wilson M. C. Fairfax, who in 1803 became the first New Churchmen in the nation's capital. (Lord Fairfax, if he was a "full receiver," as Hay contends, must have come across Swedenborg on his own, because he died almost three years before James Glen reached Philadelphia. Ferdinand's and his son's conversions should have made for interesting family discussions, since Ferdinand's father, Bryan, later the 8th Lord Fairfax, was the Episcopal bishop of Alexandria.)

Another Virginia plantation owner, Robert Carter of Nomini

Hall, not only accepted Swedenborg's teachings but, in 1791, freed his more than five hundred slaves after receiving "the truth," although, in this case, the "truth" was doled out in portions: A maximum of thirty slaves were freed annually, so that the last were manumitted in 1812, eight years after Carter's death. Robert Carter himself moved to Baltimore, where he helped establish the first New Church temple in America, dedicated in January 1800. The first pastor of that church, John Hargrove, twice preached before President Thomas Jefferson and both houses of the U.S. Congress. The second of those sermons, preached on Christmas Day 1804, must have surprised at least a few listeners. Hargrove's subject was the Second Coming of Christ—a new "general advent, *'in the spirit'*"—which by New Church doctrine had arrived forty-seven years earlier, when Swedenborg was at last fully gifted "with the *spiritual sense* of [God's] holy word."

The Church spread north as well. At Harvard, a young divinity student named Sampson Reed stumbled over a three-volume set of *Arcana Coelestia* with Swedenborg's handwritten notes in the margins and delivered an oration on the subject that deeply affected an even younger Ralph Waldo Emerson. (Reed was twenty-one at the time; his famous listener, eighteen.) Emerson would go on to become, at least for a time, one of Swedenborg's chief New World enthusiasts. Reed meanwhile helped launch the Boston Society branch of the New Church and devoted much of the wealth he amassed as a wholesale druggist to promoting the Church and Swedenborg.

Most important for these purposes, Swedenborg's doctrines and the church built on them also spread west, following the frontier across the Alleghenies into western Pennsylvania, chasing America's destiny. James Glen, the Scotsman who introduced the New Church to the New World, had sailed for South America before a crate of Swedenborg's books, shipped from London, arrived for him in Philadelphia. Francis Bailey bought the books at public auction and brought them home, where they appear to have been devoured by his adopted daughter Hester (known as Hetty) Barclay.

By 1785, Hetty and her father had started a reading circle in their Philadelphia home and print shop at 116 High Street, today's Market Street. Four years later, in 1789, Hetty followed the Pennsylvania Trail west to Bedford, halfway across the state, where she moved in with an older brother and formed what is generally regarded as the first New Church reading circle on the western frontier, although by then the frontier was already reestablishing itself on the far side of the Alleghenies. (Five years after Hetty arrived in Bedford, George Washington would march thirteen thousand troops there to put down the tax-inspired Whiskey Rebellion.)

Meanwhile, back in Philadelphia, John Young, who also had been present at James Glen's first talk and was a fellow member of the Bailey household reading circle, was courting Francis Bailey's other adopted daughter, Maria Barclay, Hetty's niece perhaps or maybe only her cousin. John and Maria were married in November 1794 at the Old Swedes' Church in Philadelphia and soon moved west themselves, all the way across the Alleghenies to Greensburg, some thirty miles east of Pittsburgh. As Hetty had done, the Youngs established their own reading circle to discuss and promote Swedenborg's teachings. And it appears to have been there, in Greensburg, either at John Young's white wooden house at Second and Main Streets or at his nearby country cottage, "Skara Glen," that John Chapman first seriously encountered Emanuel Swedenborg, some time not long after the start of the new century.

❦

If one is looking for a miracle in Johnny Appleseed's life, this might be it, for the odds of Swedenborgianism's finding him, or his finding it, would seem to be roughly those of finding a theological needle in a haystack. For starters, the fit could not have been more odd, at least on the surface. John Chapman was the son of a perpetually failing farmer. His academic credentials were nil. Thus far, he had been unsuccessful in securing property of his own, and his nursery business, such as it was in those early years, was unlikely to produce much more than a subsistence income.

The New Church that Chapman found in western Pennsylvania was rooted in almost his polar opposite. Francis Bailey, the foster father and father-in-law of the two women and a man who were helping carry the Church west, was a person of considerable substance and wealth. He and his wife, Eleanor, would have their likenesses painted by Charles Willson Peale, then the most celebrated portraitist in the nation. John Young wasn't far behind. He had arrived in America in the early 1780s almost empty-pocketed after paying off his brother's gambling debts, but his father had been a highly successful cloth merchant back in Glasgow, and Young himself had clerked in the Edinburgh offices of Sir Walter Scott's father before leaving for America. In Philadelphia, Young quickly found work in the law offices of Stephen Du Ponceau and must have prospered there, because he and his new wife had their wedding portraits painted by none other than Gilbert Stuart—two of the more than one thousand portraits Stuart executed of the leading political and social figures of the day.

The message, too, was hardly in the Christian mainstream, although with Chapman that might have been a plus, and anything but simple. But the sheer math of the two connecting is daunting enough. Other churches seeking to establish themselves on the edge of the frontier measured their growth in ecstatic camp meetings of hundreds, even thousands. The New Church calculated its growth mostly in the single persons who had joined church reading circles.

The *Annals of the New Church* for 1806 recorded "about twenty receivers of the Heavenly doctrines" in all of Philadelphia, where the movement had begun in America two decades earlier. New Churchmen were apparently so rare in Ohio that the *Annals* for that year took note of the fact that one of them, Adam Hurdus, newly arrived with family in Cincinnati, "soon afterwards becomes acquainted" with another, living twenty-seven miles away in Lebanon. By 1808, Adam Hurdus had built an organ, the first in Ohio, and was conducting New Church worship in his home. In Philadelphia, maybe a dozen men, but no women, were meeting in a reading circle. Boston had welcomed one new member.

So it goes through the *Annals:* drips and drabs in a time of religious explosion. By 1811, the Cincinnati society had grown to perhaps eighteen members. New York City finally had regular Sunday services, though for precious few. Six years later, by the time of its first American General Convention, the Church tallied a total of 360 members living in nine states. This was either growth by inches or death by small wounds, depending on expectations, but there was one ecstatic moment for the Trans-Allegheny New Church.

In October 1806, John Hargrove, the Baltimore-based pastor, undertook an evangelistic tour of western Pennsylvania. In Bedford, where the late Hetty Barclay (she died in 1796), the Espy family, and others had helped establish a New Church stronghold, Hargrove baptized "between 30 and 40 persons children and parents, from infancy up to the venerable age of 79," he wrote in a letter dated December 20, 1806, describing his mission. From there, Hargrove traveled across the Alleghenies, a trip that clearly left an impression: "Paul, himself, perhaps, was never in more *'perils by land,'* than I was while going over the mountains in the stage . . . and yet received no hurt." Safe on the other side, he was met in Greensburg by John Young, "one of the oldest, most learned, and most respectable receivers of our doctrines in the United States." Hargrove stayed with Young several days, during which time he preached at the courthouse. Then the Baltimore minister swung thirty miles southwest to Brownsville, on the banks of the Monongahela River, where he "baptized near 40 souls, old and young."

❧

Was John Chapman among those fresh New Churchmen welcomed at Brownsville? Hargrove's own handwritten accounts of the baptisms and marriages he presided over proved to be a powerful tease. The index shows a John Chapman on page 34, exactly where the baptisms of 1806 are listed, but this was John Christopher Chapman, son of W. Christopher Chapman, baptized on February 2, 1806. Farther down the same page is Hargrove's notation that the "78 souls I baptized" during his western Pennsylvania trip are recorded elsewhere, in a volume of his papers that appears to have gone missing at all the usual repositories.

It is, in short, impossible to say for sure if Chapman was ever officially taken into the Church and, if so, whether it was under John Hargrove's hand in that mass baptism in the Monongahela. But the date does feel right. It was in 1806 that Chapman finally committed for good to Ohio—the year he was famously sighted drifting down the Ohio River in his makeshift catamaran, bags packed with seed. Something had happened to give his life added direction and purpose. A religious experience—one already felt or powerfully in the making—fits with what is known of the rest of his years. And Brownsville, in addition to being near Greensburg, was also not far downriver from the VanKirk cider mill, where Chapman gathered seeds, and within striking distance of his other supplier, Frederick Medsger's cider mill along the Youghiogheny River. And in late October or early November, when the baptisms took place, Chapman would have been returning to either or both mills to store up seed for the next year's plantings.

The seemingly unlikely connection between John Chapman and John Young could have come obliquely through Hetty Barclay. If the Chapman brothers took the Pennsylvania Trail, they would have passed through Bedford, where the New Church texts were much consulted. Maybe the Chapmans got a first introduction to Swedenborg there and were then referred to Young, across the mountains almost all the way to Fort Pitt. But the tie might also have been the common interest of just about everyone at the threshold of the Old Northwest: land. John Chapman wanted it. He had tried to secure it. But even if he could have settled down long enough to homestead, titles were a mess in western Pennsylvania—the legacy of inept legislation and sometimes competing claims with Virginia—and as a freshly appointed judge, John Young's principal duty was to sort through the chaos and bring the rule of real-estate law to the Pennsylvania frontier. It was a big challenge. By all accounts, Judge Young was up to the task. He died in Greensburg in 1840, at age seventy-eight, a much-honored and admired man.

One tradition holds that Chapman was entrusted with a letter sent about 1798 from General James O'Hara, commander at Fort Pitt, to Young. This fits nicely with the Disney version of Johnny Appleseed's life, which has him happily farming a small holding near Pittsburgh until he musters the gumption to follow the tide of settlers westward into Ohio. Why not be a happy and trustworthy courier as well?

To be sure, there's not a lick of physical evidence to support the notion and some considerable evidence to contradict it. O'Hara had commanded at Fort Pitt, but he had resigned his commission in May 1796 and by 1798 was hard at work constructing the first glassworks in Pittsburgh. Chapman for his part never appears to have happily farmed anywhere, and two-plus years later, early in

1801, the census takers recorded him as a resident of Venango County, eighty-five miles up the Allegheny River.

Pull enough threads together, though, and a highly circumstantial case can be made. O'Hara's Pittsburgh glassworks preceded the far more successful Pittsburgh Plate Glass Company, now PPG Industries, which made a vast fortune for John Pitcairn, who became a Swedenborgian in middle age, part of a Pittsburgh circle of New Churchmen that included William Carnegie, father of the great industrialist Andrew. What's more, Pitcairn continues long after his death in 1916 to be a main benefactor of the General Convention of the New Church. A Church college and the ornate and lovely New Church Cathedral are both located on the Pitcairn family estate at Bryn Athyn, in the northern suburbs of Philadelphia.

So maybe it was the letter—and fate's hand through it—that brought the two Johns, Chapman and Young, together. But apples seem just as reasonable. Not long into the new century, Chapman's pattern was clearly established: seedling nurseries, cider mills, the itchy-footed roaming. As few as their numbers were, many of the New Churchmen in western Pennsylvania were landed. They needed orchards, and seedlings start orchards. Commercial contacts could have led to theological discussions, the contacts and discussions to more contacts, and on and on. The connective tissue is thin, but here, too, highly circumstantial evidence leads in sometimes heady directions.

For example: Blennerhassett Island, in the Ohio River a few miles downstream from Parkersburg, West Virginia. In 1798, Harman Blennerhassett, an adventurous and wealthy Irish aristocrat, and his wife, Margaret, settled on the island and proceeded to build perhaps the most spectacular mansion west of the Appalachians. Done, like Washington's Mount Vernon, in the Palladian style and appointed with alabaster chandeliers swinging from silver chains, the house encompassed some seven thousand square feet and was surrounded by vast lawns and a formal flower garden of over two acres.

The West Virginia Division of Natural Resources, which administers the island as a historical state park (the mansion burned to the ground in 1811), states flatly in its promotional literature that Johnny Appleseed was one of several famous visitors to the island—a select group that also includes George Rogers Clark, Henry Clay, and King Charles X of France. The Appleseed claim, in turn, appears to be based on local tradition, which holds that Chapman was invited to the island in the spring of 1806 by Margaret Blennerhassett, perhaps because she had become a New Church reader, and there set out an orchard that was destroyed by flooding a year later.

If the tradition is accurate—and the island was locally famous for its apple production—John Chapman would have landed there at one of the stranger moments in American history, because inside that elegant mansion, Harman Blennerhassett and Aaron Burr were supposedly plotting together to raise an army and establish a separate American empire, somewhere in the Southwest. Word leaked; treason charges were brought by an old Burr enemy, President Thomas Jefferson; and Burr fled the island before year's end. Captured in the Mississippi Territory, he was returned to Richmond, put on trial, and eventually acquitted, largely on the grounds that his treason was not sufficiently "overt."

Harman Blennerhassett also fled the island, along with his wife and family, but was captured and held in prison until Aaron Burr's acquittal. Neither he nor his wife ever returned to their mansion, which allegedly had been plundered by the Virginia militiamen who came to arrest him. Had Chapman's apple tree nursery not been washed away by a flood, it would have grown toward maturity on a ghost island.

Did John Chapman have any idea what was happening as he planted the orchard, *if* he planted an orchard? It would have been hard even for a deeply distracted man to miss the activity. Blenner-hassett and Burr were doing more than plotting. They might not have raised an army, but they were warehousing men and arms on the island. Maybe when Chapman was seen later that year pad-dling his catamaran down the Ohio, he was on the lam, skedad-dling into the wilderness until things blew over!

Pursue this line of reasoning still further and it's even possible to lend some credence to the highly suspect theory that the Chap-mans had made it as far south as the mouth of the Potomac River in Virginia on the first leg of their journey out of Longmeadow. Following the Potomac upriver would have brought them to Al-exandria and the beginnings of the new national capital. There, they might have happened upon Ferdinand Fairfax and his son, Wilson, both of whom had developed an infatuation with Swe-denborg. Ferdinand by then had inherited Belvoir, the Fairfax es-tate along the Potomac. The Belvoir mansion had burned down (a continuing theme in these tenuous Swedenborgian connections!), but Ferdinand and Wilson might have invited John Chapman and his brother to visit the orchards there. Thomas Lord Fairfax had been among the first people in the New World to import apple trees from England. Perhaps they even toured the "fruit garden" that George Washington had planted at Mount Vernon. The two estates were close by, and Ferdinand was a frequent visitor.

It's a terrible stretch, of course, but how spectacular if the penni-less, land-starved John Chapman was first introduced to Sweden-borg and apple growing by the close kin of a titled lord who had owned in his prime an eighth of the entire Virginia colony, and even indirectly by the Father of Our Country!

❦

Apples, God, the New Jerusalem, the ever-restless John Chap-man—let your imagination run and don't look too hard for signposts along the way, and the combination can take you almost anywhere. That's why Chapman translated so easily to myth. So little held him to actual history. But what is certain in all this welter of guessing, educated or otherwise, is that Chapman's New Church ties would shape his life profoundly and forevermore. This was a singular faith for a singular man.

In his 1917 oration on the founding of the New Church in America, Reverend Hay exhorted his listeners not to forget

> "Johnny Appleseed"—John Chapman—who visited the new settlements of Ohio in 1801, sowing apple seeds and New Church truths at the same time by the wayside, for the benefit of coming generations. The latter kind of seed being somewhat scarce with him, he would break the bindings of such books as *Heaven & Hell*, and leave the successive chapters at successive houses, and move them along at his successive visits, greeting his readers as he approached with the cry, "Here is news right fresh from heaven for you."

This, in fact, is the standard version of Chapman's evangelizing, but the implication almost always is that the news fresh from heaven he was delivering was scriptural—the Beatitudes on the eve of his own death, the Sermon on the Mount, a sampling of the standard parables. That wasn't Swedenborg. Swedenborg dismissed the Holy Ghost, denied the Trinity, announced in no uncertain terms that Christ was not distinct from God but was God himself on earth. There is but one God in whom *is* a trinity. Original sin, that scourge of Puritanism, exists not at all in New Church theology. The first eleven chapters of Genesis—the biblical account of creation, of the Garden of Eden and the generations to follow Adam—are in New Church terminology a "different history." The evils that haunt us are hereditary, not original;

we have to repent of them—shun them to be unburdened. In that way, we judge ourselves in life and carry the verdict with us into the next world.

Swedenborg wasn't ignorant of the Bible. Far from it. He dissected Scripture as few before or since have. Indeed, it was Swedenborg who discovered that the Book of Revelation is "all about the establishment of the New Church," as the Reverend Kurt

Johnny read "aloud the strange Gospel to the astonished family around the hearthstone . . . with a glow of enthusiasm such as to affect even those who looked upon him as half-witted or a heretic."

Horigan Asplundh put it in a May 2009 sermon delivered at the Bryn Athyn Cathedral. That's how it was with Swedenborg: His writings were the third book of the Bible, without which the other two—the Testaments Old and New—were not only incomplete but incompletely understood.

Heaven and Hell, which Reverend Hay cites, is divided into three parts: "Heaven," "The World of Spirits," and "Hell"—sixty-three chapters in all. If Chapman was indeed leaving a chapter at each cabin he passed by, or at least each household who would accept one, he was operating an extraordinary frontier lending library—a footmobile before the bookmobile was invented—and spreading an extraordinary message across the edge of the wilderness.

The three heavens of Chapter 5, for example, so distinct from one another that "anyone who ascends from a lower heaven is gripped by a tension to the point of pain. He cannot see people there, much less talk with that. And anyone who descends from a higher heaven loses his wisdom, stammers, and falls prey to despair."

Or the fact (Chapter 48) that one enters the spirit world, after death, with

> every outward and inward sense he enjoyed in the world. As before, he sees; as before, he hears and speaks, he smells and tastes; as before he feels the pressure when he is touched. He still yearns, wishes, craves, thinks, ponders, is moved, loves, and intends as before. . . . He even carries his natural memory with him. For he keeps all the things he has heard, seen, read, learned, or thought in the world from earliest infancy right to the last moment in his life.

(Keeping all memory, one should add, is not always a blessing in Swedenborg's spirit world.)

Or finally (Chapter 56) that hell and heaven are mirror images of each other—the same number of communities, three hells to match the three heavens, both ruled by God in equal measure—and that it is the perfect balance between these two, the balance of the false against the true, the evil against the good, that in Swedenborg's words "puts man in a freedom for thinking and intending . . . to let in or accept what is evil and what is false . . . or what is good and true."

This was John Chapman's truth. This was where his restless wandering and searching had led him. Land, apples, and Swedenborg's God were his own Holy Trinity.

7.

IN COUNTRY

Newell Dwight Hillis's 1904 novel *The Quest of John Chapman: The Story of a Forgotten Hero* opens on a beautiful May morning in the spring of 1788. The fictional town of Redham, Massachusetts—not far from Ipswich, on Essex Bay north of Boston, where John Chapman's paternal ancestors first made landfall in the New World—buzzes with excitement. Wagons are packed high with belongings. A restless crowd of townsfolk is milling about, waiting for the journey to Ohio Country to begin. "These are the New Pilgrims," the author tells us, "and to-day will witness the first swarming of the New England hive."

Hillis's novel, in fact, is based on an historical event. On April 7, 1788, forty-eight New Englanders arrived at the confluence of the Ohio and Muskingum Rivers on a tiny flotilla of ships, including a flatboat they had named the *Mayflower*. At the mouth of the Muskingum, they reenacted the Pilgrim landing at Plymouth 168 years earlier and thus officially founded Marietta, the vanguard of white settlement in the Old Northwest. The four dozen pioneers, all male, included three carpenters and two blacksmiths, essential for building the new town; a number of patriots of the Revolution, most notably the future orchardist Rufus Putnam, who was to be superintendent of the new colony; and Congregationalist minister Manasseh Cutler, chief organizer of the expedition for the Ohio

Company, which hoped to make Marietta the portal to the 1.5 million acres of the territory it had purchased from Congress and a major gateway to westward expansion generally.

History, though, is only the backdrop for Hillis's tale. In the foreground is a feud between Redham's two leading citizens, once best friends: Colonel William Durand, a hero of the Revolutionary War, and Dr. John Chapman, the local Congregational minister and a disciple of Jonathan Edwards. The feud, over theological matters, has divided the town, but no one has suffered more than the children of the principals: Dorothy, the Colonel's daughter, who is to be one of the swarming Pilgrims; and John, the minister's son (and future Johnny Appleseed), who has been forbidden to go along.

Early on, we see young John Chapman pining for the girl about to get away: "Look at that boy yonder on the steps—the handsomest boy that ever walked into a lecture hall! God save him from pride! And that girl yonder with the red coat and fur! She is the single spot toward which John's eyes are always turned. Yes, yes, yes!"

Hillis was the longtime pastor of Brooklyn's Plymouth Church of the Pilgrims, where Henry Ward Beecher once held forth, and a stern public moralist who once called for sterilization of all Germans after World War I. And he tends to suffocate his melodrama with moral lessons and literary license: Chapman, for example, becomes in time a master grafter of apple trees; he turns his plant husbandry to grapes in North Carolina and peaches in Michigan. What's more, no one ever suggested that in real life John Chapman was the handsomest man alive. Suffice it here to say that while our young fictional hero will go to Ohio in search of Dorothy, he will find her dead of a broken heart and instead end up devoting his life to kind acts and good deeds spread broadly across the map of America.

On the subject of Ohio, though, and the hold it had on the New

England imagination, Hillis gets it just right, especially in the person of the shady Captain Picquet, "at once Spaniard and Indian," who had been hired to lead these late-eighteenth-century Pilgrims westward:

"If Heaven has smiled upon this region east of the Alleghanies," he tells Colonel Durand, "then, in overflowing benevolence, the skies have laughed outright upon the lands west of the Alleghanies. Oh! It is a goodly land, with rich soil and heavy forests; a land where the wild bees fill all the hollow trees with honey . . ."

"All our young men seem to be turning their thoughts toward the Ohio River," the colonel interrupts him.

"Well, sir," Picquet replies, "can you rightfully blame them?" Ohio "is the garden of the world. The Eden that long ago was lost must have been located in our valley of sunshine."

Perhaps, but there was one large problem in attaining this fresh Garden of Eden of 1788, and a crusty old judge watching the gathering in Redham puts it succinctly when he criticizes the migration's leaders for sending these New Pilgrims "beyond the Alleghanies and put[ting] a thousand miles of forest and half a million Indians between these children and the far-off home-land."

The mountains of Pennsylvania were obstacle enough, but to the judge, to his listeners, to everyone involved, those half a million Native Americans were by far the greater challenge involved, even if Hillis's number is wildly exaggerated.

The Iroquois had long claimed the Ohio Country, but in practical terms, by the mid-seventeenth century, it had come under the control of the Shawness, the Wyandots, and the Delaware. A Shawnee town at the mouth of the Scioto River, along the Ohio in the southern tip of the territory, included some sixty houses when a French party visited it in 1749. By then, the Wyandots were ranging south and east out of their new home near present-day Detroit, into the Maumee and Sandusky river valleys, to hunt and trap furs. At the same time, the Delawares were establishing villages along the Tuscarawas River, in the eastern part of the country, near teeming elk herds. Later, they would be joined on the Tuscarawas by the so-called Christian Delawares, Indian converts led west by Moravian missionaries out of the German strongholds of eastern Pennsylvania. Lesser representations of Ottawa, Mingo, and Miami dotted the territory.

To a greater or lesser degree all these tribes had been forced into Ohio by settlement elsewhere. The Shawnees and Delawares had been pushed west, out of the Delaware River Valley and New Jersey. The Wyandots, originally Huron, had wandered in from Canada. Now, the vise was tightening again. White traders helped accustom them to modern implements—rifles and powder, woolen blankets, iron hoes—that they could afford only by over-hunting their own lands for furs and skins to trade. (One Moravian missionary wrote that Delaware men were shooting as many as 150 deer each fall, an unsustainable quantity even among a vast herd.) Cheap whiskey—the Pennsylvania legislature set the price at five dollars a cask and prohibited traders from charging more—weakened morale and led to muddled bargains in which Native Americans gave far too much away for far too little.

In broad terms, of course, this is a truncated history of the culture clash that defined the entire American frontier, all the way across the continent. Tribes changed. Over-hunted deer became over-hunted buffalo and bison and, later, over-fished rivers and streams. But always the push was westward. Ohio Country, though, offered some unique wrinkles of its own. French and British intrigue, for example. The French saw the Ohio tribes as their protection against British incursion into the lands farther west, claimed for the French crown. The British, always desirous of eradicating France's influence in the New World, sought to lure the territory's Indians to King George's side by, among other tactics, discounting the price on what had become essential supplies—loss leaders, in effect—and hinting at an Indian sovereignty over the lands that was never to be.

In the French and Indian War—the almost inevitable outcome of such intriguing—most of Ohio's tribes placed a bad bet, siding with the French, only to have France cede its claims to British control at the 1763 Treaty of Paris, including Indian lands the French had never conquered and thus had no real right to give away. That same year, Pontiac's War, named for the great Ottawa chieftain, swept through Ohio Country, to much drama but little effect. Within two decades, the Revolution had replaced British control with American authority. By then, though, Ohio's native tribes were facing a far more undeniable force than any national government: the ineluctable dynamics of an expanding population hungry for land. This, too, would happen all along the frontier as America lurched, stumbled, and sometimes raced to the Pacific, but at the Ohio River, those forces dammed up and became magnified as they would never be again.

Virginians needed nearly a century and a half after the founding of Jamestown to cross the Blue Ridge Mountains in any number, led by that possible Swedenborgian Lord Fairfax, who established his land office at Greenway Court in Clarke County in 1751, and hired a young George Washington to survey and plat the western reaches of his epic holdings. Only forty years later, Virginia's mostly Scotch-Irish "Butternuts"—named after the color of their homespun apparel—had piled by the thousands into the state's chimney, what would become West Virginia in the Civil War.

South of Ohio Country, Kentucky had first been opened to settlement in 1750, when physician and explorer Thomas Walker discovered the only natural passage through the Appalachians, the Cumberland Gap, at the conjunction of Virginia, Tennessee, and Kentucky. Twenty-five years later, the Transylvania Company hired none other than Daniel Boone to lead a party to widen the trail, and another fifteen years after that, in 1790, the first wagons rolled into Kentucky. Over the next decade, the state would see its population swell almost threefold, to over 220,000. Boone wasn't the only Kentuckian longing for elbow room, and for many of them, Ohio was just a river's breadth away.

And so it went due east and northeast as well. New England's economy was in steep transition, a good time to move on. In the midst of an economic boom, Pennsylvania and the Middle Atlantic states were pushing transportation routes ever westward. The Northwest Ordinance of 1787 had given the Ohio Country the veneer of a governmental structure. Only one thing stood in the way of such manifest destiny—the Ohio tribes—and they didn't stand a chance, at least in the long run.

In the last week of September 1790, General Josiah Harmar led a force of 1,453 troops (including only 320 regulars) out of Fort Washington, at Cincinnati, and up the Great Miami River Valley, headed for Kekionga, the main enclave of the Miami tribe, just to the west of what is now the Indiana border. Harmar's goal was to crush tribal resistance in Ohio Country once and for all. Instead, a month later, Harmar's career lay in ruin, his army routed by a combined force of Miamis, Shawnees, and Potawatomis under the command of Little Turtle.

The following fall, General Arthur St. Clair, the first governor of the Northwest Territory, led a second force to Kekionga, with strikingly similar results. As Harmar had, St. Clair walked his army into a trap laid by Little Turtle, with logistic help from the French. (Almost three decades after the Treaty of Paris, the French were still meddling in the New World.) As with Harmar, too, St. Clair saw his career destroyed in consequence. Far from stilling the Indian threat in Ohio, the two failed expeditions stoked it. Packet boats between Pittsburgh and Cincinnati came under such regular attack that owners took pains to assure passengers that vessels were equipped with "convenient port holes for firing out of."

The third expedition against the Miamis, two years later, proved the charm. Better equipped, better trained, better provided for, and under the leadership of a more able and determined general—the Revolutionary War hero "Mad Anthony" Wayne—the American forces defeated the combined Indian army at the Battle of Fallen Timbers, effectively ending tribal resistance in Ohio Country. Soon, Kekionga would be known by a new name, honoring the conquering general: Fort Wayne.

The treaty conference that followed in June 1795 at Fort Greenville and the Greenville Treaty Line that emerged from that—pushing Indians into the least fertile north-central and northwestern tier of the territory—were largely formalities. The New Eden finally was up for grabs.

❦

Ohio was no longer purely virgin land when John Chapman's presence was first noted there, at the very start of the nineteenth century. Statehood was only a few years away. Marietta was already in its second decade. Land hustlers, the heralds of civilization all across the American continent, had held the most accessible parts of the territory squarely in their sites for better than a decade.

By early 1791, the Paris-based Scioto Company had sold more than a hundred thousand acres of Ohio to French settlers, reeling them in with promises of "a climate wholesome and delightful, frost even in winter entirely unknown . . . and venison in plenty, the pursuit of which is uninterrupted by wolves, foxes, lions, or tigers." Six hundred–plus settlers traveled to America that year only to learn that while the company had reserved a huge tract of land from Congress—4.5 million acres, much of the southeast quadrant of the state—it had (a) never paid for or obtained title to the land, (b) thus didn't own a hectare of it, and (c) in any event had sold settlers land that properly belonged to the Ohio Company of Associates. With the help of the Ohio Company, a small party of the French did finally make it to what is now Gallipolis, almost a hundred miles downstream from Marietta, but promises of a mild climate notwithstanding, the Ohio River froze solid that first year, and the mostly artisan settlers were, in the words of William Dean Howells, "masters of trades utterly useless in that wild country . . . carvers and gilders, cloakmakers, wigmakers, and hairdressers." (The Scioto Company land agent who sold the French on this mad scheme and then ran off with their money had the delightfully ironic name of William Playfair.)

For its part, the Ohio Company was fronted by respectable patriots: Rufus Putnam; Manasseh Cutler, who had been a major stockholder in the Scioto Company; Winthrop Sargent, Harvard graduate, war hero, and later the first governor of Mississippi Territory, who like Cutler segued easily from the Scioto to the Ohio Company; Samuel Holden Parsons, tied to the first Great Awakening both by his preacher father and by his wife, who was descended from the Mather clan; and others. As might be expected of such a group, the company was cloaked in high purpose, caught well by Cutler in a sermon he preached shortly after that first New Pilgrim landfall:

> Under the conduct of a Kind Providence, we see settlements forming in the American wilderness, deserts turning into fruitful fields, and the delightful habitations of civilized and christianized men. . . . We this day literally see the fulfillment of the prophecy in our text gradually advancing, incense offered to the most high God in this place, which was lately the dreary abode of savage barbarity. . . . Here may the Gospel be preached to the latest period of time; the arts and sciences be planted; the seeds

132

of virtue, happiness, and glory be firmly rooted and grown to full maturity.

But this was, after all, real estate, and the Ohio associates were determined to sell it. Maps commissioned by Cutler foreshortened the distance between portages to rivers that flowed into Lake Erie. In his writings, he praised Ohio's soil and climate as perfect for "the Indian tea, Japan varnish tree, and European grapes." As a lobbyist before Congress on behalf of both the Scioto and Ohio companies, Cutler seems to have been almost without peer.

If the bloom was off the rose, though, the Ohio of 1801 was still about as fresh as such a ripe prize could be. Today's Ohio population hubs barely existed, if they did at all. Cincinnati was a hamlet of maybe eight hundred, a year away from gaining its first village charter. Cleveland had been surveyed for the first time in 1796. Four years later, its semipermanent population is estimated to have stood at . . . three. An early attempt to found a village at current-day Columbus had been washed away by flood: in 1800, the future capital and state's largest city was most notable for its undisturbed ancient Indian burial mounds. What would become Toledo was then Fort Industry—basically a stockade.

In all, the soon-to-be state counted a little over 42,000 inhabitants in the census of 1800, including 198 freed blacks—roughly one person for every square mile of land. New York City's combined boroughs had a population 40 percent greater on a land mass less than 1 percent that of Ohio. Philadelphia claimed about 10,000 more residents than all the territory.

Many of the state's new residents arrived from Pittsburgh on flat-bottomed "Kentucky boats"—fifty to a hundred feet long, fifteen to twenty-five feet wide, square at the ends—that were rowed or poled down the Ohio River when drifting wouldn't do. (The boats also ran a square sail if an advantageous wind could be found.) Ferries also plied the river, out of Wheeling and between Kentucky and fledgling Cincinnati. R. Douglas Hurt writes in *The Ohio Frontier* that Robert Benham's Cincinnati ferry charged six cents a person, eighteen cents for man and horse, and an even dollar for team and wagon. That works out to about seventy-two cents per individual passenger and twelve dollars for a team and wagon in today's money, a bargain but not as great as one might suppose.

Once across the river, settlers had the option of following Ebenezer Zane's Trace into the interior of the territory, and many German immigrants seem to have done just that. From the very earliest years of the century, Lancaster, which Zane established at the crossing of the Hockhocking River, had store signs in English and German, much like the Pennsylvania city of the same name, and by 1807 this new Lancaster also had its own German-language newspaper.

Most new settlers, though, chose at least temporarily the far bank of the Ohio River and its proximity to the river trade. As of 1800, better than one in every thirty territorials lived in a thin 104-mile strip between Letart Falls and the mouth of the Scioto River—sixty-plus miles downriver from Marietta at its northern end and a hundred miles upriver from Cincinnati at its southern tip, often within sight of the Virginia (now West Virginia) and Kentucky they had left behind. During his 1807–1809 journey down the Ohio River, Fortescue Cuming spent a night near Letart Falls and took note of the recreational habits of the local population:

> They have frequent meetings for the purposes of gambling, fighting, and drinking. They make bets to the amount of all they possess. They fight for the most trifling provocations, or even sometimes without any, but merely to try each others [*sic*]

prowess, which they are fond of vaunting. Their hands, teeth, knees, head and feet are their weapons, not only boxing with their fists . . . but also tearing, kicking, scratching, biting, gouging each others [*sic*] eyes out by a dexterous use of a thumb and finger, and doing their utmost to kill each other, even when rolling over one another on the ground.

One man told Cuming about commiserating, after one such recent brawl, with a combatant who was missing the better part of his nose. " 'Don't pity me,' said the noseless hero, 'pity that fellow there,' pointing with one hand to another who had lost an eye, and shewing the eye which he held triumphantly in the other."

❧

From the very beginning of his time in Ohio, Chapman cut a different path. As with the territory's other pioneers, he made the rivers—the Ohio and Muskingum, most notably—his highways, either by shore or on water, and the creeks and Indian trails his off-ramps and arterial routes. But Chapman pushed deeper into the interior than all but a few others. Between his explorations in country and his seasonal returns to the cider mills of Pennsylvania, he almost certainly traversed more of early Ohio than anyone else alive. And for a loner traveling into and out of the heart of this wilderness darkness, he left a surprising amount of markers.

Oddly enough, given Johnny Appleseed's fame as a walker and paddler, a number of accounts of his earliest time in the Ohio backcountry have him on horseback, saddlebags packed with product. In 1801, for example, he is said to have shown up mounted at Wellsburg, on the Virginia side of the Ohio River, then crossed at the ford at Cox Ripple, a little below Steubenville, and planted a nursery on the old Indian camping grounds at Mingo Flats. Later, still traveling by horse, he apparently laid

Lake Erie

•Cleveland

PENNSYLVANIA

HURON

ASHLAND
•Ashland

RICHLAND   WAYNE   Present Route U.S. 30

•Mansfield

•Perrysville   Tuscarawas River

                        CARROLL

                    O H I O   JEFFERSON

KNOX   Walhonding River   Steubenville•
Mount Vernon   Wellsburg•

Kokosing River
(a.k.a. Owl Creek)   •Coshocton
                    COSHOCTON

LICKING
                                                  Wheeling•
Newark•   Licking River

                                        BELMONT

        N

              Muskingum River

W   E   •Dexter City

        S   Ohio River

                                •Parkersburg   VIRGINIA
                    Marietta•

0   5   10 15 miles

0   10   20 kilometers

        Counties with known or suspected orchards
        and nurseries planted by Chapman

        Counties where Chapman leased or purchased land

——— Likely route of Chapman's western migration, beginning circa 1803 out a nursery on Big Stillwater Creek near Freeport, in Belmont County, and perhaps another near Newark, in the Licking Valley, on the farm of Isaac Stadden.

It was during this same trip that Chapman is thought to have delivered his first semi-recorded thoughts on orchards and apple propagation. "They are starting one up the river on the Virginia side and talking of grafting," he is supposed to have said in reference to Jacob Nessly's fledgling groves of apple and peach trees back across the river, near Wellsburg. "They can improve the apple in that way but that is only a device of man, and it is wicked to cut up trees that way. The correct method is to select good seeds and plant them in good ground and God only can improve the apples."

The story dovetails nicely with Chapman's animism and the deep religious streak that would soon have him diving headlong into Swedenborg and the correspondences between the physical and spiritual worlds, and it stokes the myth that would eventually grow up around Johnny Appleseed. But the quote feels suspect nonetheless. Seeds gathered from mill pulp are whatever they are, good or bad, but hardly select. And Nessly was doing exactly what his supposed critic was doing: growing almost all his trees from seed, and then distilling the inferior fruit into brandies. Nessly didn't give a fig for improving fruit either, so long as the mash broke down into alcohol.

The horse, too, if not questionable, at least becomes absent in other accounts from what seems to be this same trip. To John Cuppy, James Downing, George Foulk, and Isaac Miller—all Indian scouts in the "Seven Ranges" area of eastern Ohio—Chapman appeared on foot and almost like an apparition, stepping out of the woods to warn that hostile Delawares were roaming the neighborhood. By the time Chapman arrived at the farthest reach of his 1801 journey—seventy-five miles into the wilds of Ohio

Territory, at Owl Creek—the horse had disappeared altogether, and just about any trace of civilization with it. The Owl Creek area would be one of Chapman's key bases of operations for half a decade to come, and it was then about as raw as a place could be.

When Chapman first planted nurseries there, probably about 1803 (because the trees were ready for sale by 1806), his only neighbors would have been a half-crazed squatter named Andy Craig and, farther upstream, living in the wild with his wife and what would eventually become twelve children, John Stilley, thought to be the area's first white settler. In his 1862 history of Knox County, A. Banning Norton tells us that Craig lived with "a great, raw-boned woman" whom he had lured away from her own husband in Wheeling, back across the Ohio in Virginia. Craig's motives in doing so baffled a fellow frontiersman, who years later told Norton: "I'd as soon slept with a man as her. . . . Why he should have taken her into the wilderness for a sleeping companion I can't see."

Apart from the oddities of his own domestic arrangement, Craig seems to have been a magnet for trouble. Two escaped slaves who had taken Indian squaws as wives were idling near his little log hut on Owl Creek when trackers finally caught up with them. One of the ex-slaves, a mulatto, was tackled by his former master's son as he tried to cross the creek. In the brawl that ensued, the master's son, Tumlinson, was killed and the mulatto captured, lashed to the son's horse, and led off back to Virginia. A day and a night later, he was found shot to death and still tied to a tree. Had Chapman been at Craig's, or nearby, while all this unfolded? Maybe. The best estimate is that the murders and mayhem occurred between 1800 and 1803, and one early history of the region suggests that Chapman might have actually lived briefly with Craig and his big, raw-boned "sleeping companion" when he first arrived on Owl Creek. But if he wasn't in the vicinity, Chapman certainly would have known what happened. Craig told everybody, and he had ready evidence: Tumlinson's bones had been uncovered. In 1805, Craig apparently ran across the slave who did escape, living with his squaw among the Indians on the plains near Sandusky, on the shores of Lake Erie, another eighty miles between himself and the next pack of Virginia trackers.

John Stilley's story is no less violent and considerably more exotic. Orphaned as a child in western Pennsylvania when his father was massacred by Indians in 1774, he was taken in by a brother-in-law only to be abducted five years later, along with his adoptive family, by the Wyandot tribe. The others were given up at Detroit after the Revolution, but Stilley was accepted into the Wyandots and lived with them until persuaded to leave by the same brother-in-law. He settled first in Kentucky, where he became an honored Indian fighter. Then he moved on to where Chapman would have found him, land he had first seen as a boy of six or seven, on the back of an Indian mount. It had been Wyandot hunting grounds then and was still barely more than that, although the Delawares roamed the land now. On the other side of Owl Creek from where John Chapman planted his nurseries, Indian land stretched for miles upon miles.

In the off-year election of 1806, when the Owl Creek settlers finally had a chance to cast a vote, fifteen eligible males wandered out of the forest from near and far to cast their ballots, among them the future Johnny Appleseed. What a sight they must have been, and what a triumph for frontier democracy.

❧

In a way, what is most remarkable about these accounts from the early Ohio frontier are not the particulars of John Chapman's comings and goings so much as the fact that among such singular people, in such a wild place, he still managed to stand out as if he had been painted neon purple. In Warren and Venango Counties back in Pennsylvania, Chapman had been remembered as an industrious young man, always ready to lend a hand, or, alternatively, as a restless discontent, in both interpretations driven by a desire to acquire land. Here, in the central interior of Ohio at the start of the new century, the landless Chapman still longed for acreage and with good cause: As of 1803, U.S. military lands in the state not already claimed by Revolutionary War veterans were offered up for sale under what amounted to extraordinary terms: tracts as small as a quarter section, or 160 acres, and no state taxes for five years. But now, in addition to his land obsession, Chapman had become, in A. Banning Norton's memorable phrase, "the oddest character in all our history."

Norton, to be sure, was writing in 1862. Unlike Chapman's earliest chroniclers, he knew his subject had become Johnny Appleseed, although the myth was still in its formative years. Memory also is almost never wholly accurate, especially the longer it sits, and Norton's sources, the ones who knew Chapman when he was in his late twenties and early thirties, were themselves nearing or beyond eighty when the author interviewed them. Still, the portrait that emerges is so sharply drawn that it's hard not to credit it, at least in part.

Chapman, Norton writes, was "of medium height, quick and restless and uneasy in his motions, and exceedingly uncouth in dress. In truth, he cared not what he wore, nor who before him might have worn the garment upon his back." His garments were cast-offs, often traded for seedlings; footwear was nonexistent. On his head, Chapman might wear "an animal's skin, a cloth, or tin case." For a time, Norton writes, Chapman favored an "old military chapeau" given him by a passing officer:

Thus accoutred he came suddenly upon a dutchman, who had just moved into the country, and scared him most to death. . . . The sides were ripped, and as it flopped in the wind—on a head covered with long black hair, a face with a long beard and dark black eyes peering out from the vast undergrowth, and a body enveloped in a coffee sack, with a hole through which he had run his head, it was enough to frighten any honest dutchman almost out of his wits.

Virtually all the stories that would come to dominate the Appleseed canon can be found in Norton's description of Chapman's years in Knox County: his excessive generosity, the kindness to every living creature, eccentricities towering enough to scare an honest Dutchman half to death. But Norton's description also has a balance and roundness to it that becomes increasingly rare as the myths take hold and begin to strangle Chapman's humanity. John Chapman wasn't just "an artless child of nature," Norton writes; he was also a "man of much intelligence . . . hooted at and derided by the scoffers and jibers of the country, and yet did he in his lifetime perform far more of good than they all did." Flesh and blood, in short, but with all his oddities and his weaknesses and strengths of character somehow magnified to the nth degree—exactly as happens in Swedenborg's afterworld. How *could* Chapman have been easily forgotten?

❦

Whatever lured them to the Ohio territory and wherever they settled into it, the common lot of just about every one of John Chapman's contemporaries was hardship. New settlers almost always had to contend with a season or two of cramps and diarrhea as they accommodated themselves to the fresh microbes of a new home, but that was the least of it. Disease seems to have been almost everywhere in the Ohio of those days—malaria, "bad air," "putrid throat" (scarlet fever), "hooping" cough, catarrhal fevers, and on and on—and medical help was mostly a chimera.

In 1793, tiny Cincinnati and its surroundings were hit by an outbreak of smallpox. As of 1800, the entire Western Reserve, three million acres of northern Ohio, had a single trained physician, but he seems to have been more interested in dairy farming and cheese making than in the healing arts. In 1807, yellow fever ravaged Marietta, leaving fifty people dead. That same autumn, influenza swept all across the frontier. As late as 1820, better than half the 165,000 people then living within a fifty-mile radius of Columbus were miserably ill with who knows what. (The number 165,000 is amazing in its own right, considering almost *no one* had been living within that same radius only two decades earlier.)

Douglas Hurt writes that as many as 25 percent of newborns on the early Ohio frontier never made it past their first birthday. Another one in four died before age twenty-one. Girls could marry with parental consent at age fourteen; boys, at age seventeen, by which time they were halfway through their lives, at least as measured by mortality tables. Males in those early years in Ohio had a life expectancy of thirty-four years; females, thirty-six years—only slightly worse than the estimated national averages for 1800, but on the frontier these settlers and pioneers and woodsmen had to work so much harder to achieve their allotted years.

What were they thinking of, these strangers to a strange land? One measure of what they expected are the things they brought with them. Inventories of the estates of two settlers, Abner Pinney and Levi Buttles, who arrived in 1804 in Worthington, now in the northern suburbs of Columbus, are filled with the practical—steel traps, iron wedges, weaver's reeds, hooks, hogs, kettles, flat irons—but they also hint at the comfortable life both men and their families had left behind and were pointing to again: a silver watch, a wooden clock, fourteen linen sheets, fourteen pillowcases, silver shoe buckles, plated knee buckles, japanned tumblers, pewter teapots, a dictionary, Bibles, *Robinson Crusoe,* Shakespeare's *Edward, the Black Prince,* and so on.

Both Pinney and Buttles had emigrated from the Farmington River Valley of Connecticut, west of Hartford. Both were members of a new Scioto Company, organized in 1802 to "make a settlement in the Territory of the United States Northwest of the Ohio and between the Muskingum and the Greater Miami Rivers." Like many of the New Englanders who came west, they were people of at least moderate means—the silver watch was worth $13 at probate, the wooden clock $18, almost $250 in current value. Both Pinney and Buttles would have chipped in the $2 taken from all Scioto Company subscribers to fund the purchase of books to fill a library that, in fact, was already waiting when the bulk of the new settlers arrived at Worthington; and neither had much chance to enjoy a single bit of it—the town, the books, any part of what they had helped to create.

Abner Pinney was all but dead on arrival in Worthington— the first to be interred in the new graveyard. Levi Buttles lasted until the following June, but he had lingered at death's door from March on, after being caught without shelter in a late snowstorm. For the Buttles family, visions of the New Eden had already been dampened. They spent their first winter in Ohio in a one-room cabin with a dirt floor, along with the three or four hired laborers that Levi had paid to accompany them. For his fourteen-year-old son, Arora, Levi's death was an almost unbearable burden on top of all else the family had suffered: "He would go to the edge of the woods," his sister later recalled, "and seat himself on a log and bury his face in his hands, and moan for hours. He thought he was out of sight and hearing of any one, but they all heard him and it almost broke their hearts."

Others in that little community suffered almost as much. Ruhamah Mays, who followed the original Worthington settlers west the next spring, wrote back east to a friend, complaining of the absence of any cleared roads as they neared their destination: "We had to cut and tug three days in the wilderness & see no human being nor scarce any water." Later, temporarily ensconced with Levi Buttles's survivors in their slightly enlarged dwelling, Ruhamah sent back a home-economics dispatch from the front:

> Pork is easy made but no cellars to put it in, the best of beef but no cider. We have a barrel of whiskey stands in one corner of one of our front rooms. We have the best of wheat flour & I think the indian meal preferable to that in new england but we have no place to store it only in bags & we are over run with mice . . .

And these, mind you, are the almost-positive accounts. The mice were horrible, yes, but Ruhamah Mays went on to say that there didn't seem to be a rat in all of Ohio. Imagine the misery of those who couldn't find any silver lining in the clouds overhead.

In an article on Abner Pinney, the Buttleses, and others for the journal *Old-Time New England*, Robert and Virginia McCormick write that the travails of Worthington's settlers confirm Frederick Jackson Turner's thesis that conquering the frontier "required each successive migration to return to primitive living conditions." That's often the pace of progress—two steps forward, one step back; two forward, one back—and it was as true of John Chapman as it was of the frontier experience as a whole.

However crowded the Longmeadow house might have been, it was a roof overhead. However stressed the larder back in southern Massachusetts, there most often was a cow in the barnyard and a new crop to bring in. By going in-country in Ohio at the start of the new century, Chapman slipped backwards like just about everyone else, but unlike so many others, he never seemed to want to get back to where he had once been.

Shelter disappeared, along with prepared meals, and so Chapman learned to live alone in the great outdoors and dine on what the woods and fields and creek banks had to offer. Clothing cost money, of which he had little, so he bartered for what he wore and whittled his raiment down to only what bare decency and extreme climate required. Other settlers pined for the comforts of their old lives and longed for the days of milk and honey ahead. Reduced to almost nothing, John Chapman made an aesthetic of nothing, a virtue of his hardships.

Maybe that is ultimately why he grew so close to Native Americans at a time when whites and Indians were always on the edge of breaking into gory conflict. Yes, Chapman was a medicine man of sorts. He understood plants and their properties. Catnip (for the stomach, nervous conditions, and colds), fennel (indigestion, gout, lupus), horehound (coughs, colds, and as a tonic), mullein (congestion, sore throat), pennyroyal (disorders of the ovaries, as an aid in childbirth), rattlesnake root (snakebites, dysentery), and other herbs were all part of his portable apothecary. Chapman also seems to have been something of an animal whisperer. One tale has him nursing a wounded wolf cub and later traveling the backwoods trails with his wolf pet, now full-grown. Native Americans must have been struck by his oneness with nature, so rare in the American wilderness of his day, as well as his sheer fearlessness, to go unarmed among all the dangers of the wilderness, Indians included.

A century later, the ornate verses of his admirers would seize on these same qualities and elevate Appleseed to a kind of nature deity in Indian eyes. But perhaps the deepest bond between Chapman and Ohio's Native Americans was more simple than that: Possessions of and for their own sake meant not a thing to

Chapman. He was an artist of minimalism. The Indians, A. Banning Norton writes, "could read his character at a glance. All was revealed by his eye, clear as the sunlight of God. He was without selfishness. He sought not to intrigue with or cheat them. . . . He put confidence in their honor, and they never would do him wrong."

Admirable, yes, by our modern lights. And loosey-goosey as well. But Chapman's wasn't a life being made up on the fly. He wasn't going solely where his bliss led him, even though one senses that his bliss was ever mounting. There was a plan. There was even what we would today call synergy. And by 1805 on Owl Creek, in this same Licking Valley, among this same rogue's gallery of characters, it had all started to come together.

8.

THE PLAN

John Chapman's special genius—one might as easily write his "special compulsion"—was to find the exact seam between past and future, between encroaching civilization and resistant wilderness. By the middle of the first decade of the nineteenth century, Mount Vernon, in Knox County, 115 miles in country from the Ohio River at Steubenville, was such a place, precariously balanced between the New Eden that drew settlers to Ohio and the New America they were creating.

When the first frontiersmen pushed into the area in any numbers around the turn of the century, this part of Ohio had been a flora and fauna wonderland. Wild grapevines on the bottomlands grew as thick as a man's body and yielded "immense quantities of fruit," N. N. Hill writes in his 1881 history of the area. Huckleberries were everywhere, along with raspberries, blackberries, even cranberries. Paw-paws—large, sweet, and delicate to the touch—grew in great, shrub-like clumps.

The earliest pioneers remembered a small herd of buffalo wandering into the area about 1803 and causing great excitement. Panthers still prowled the margins, sometimes heard but rarely seen, although several were killed in the first decade or so of white settlement. Bears were almost a plague—they feasted on the settlers' pigs—while wolves "were found in great abundance," so much so that the Ohio legislature very early on set a bounty of four dollars per adult wolf scalp (better than fifty dollars today) and two dollars for immature ones. Not surprisingly, many a pioneer made wolf slaughter and scalping his primary employment. Deer were so plentiful that venison was the hamburger and hot dog of the frontier table. Passenger pigeons, though, seemed to dwarf in numbers every other living thing.

"I have visited two pigeon roosts and have heard of a third," a Marietta minister wrote to a friend in June 1803. "Those I have seen are astonishing. One is supposed to cover a thousand acres; the other is still larger. The destruction of timber and brush on such large tracts of land by these small animals is almost incredible. How many millions of them must have assembled to effect it, especially as it was done in the course of a few weeks."

Pike as long as five feet could be found in the streams. Snakes— black rattlers and copperheads among them—seem to have been common as dirt, along with scorpions, spiders of (according to Hill) extraordinary size, gnats, hornets, yellow jackets, and enough other discomforts to give this New Eden a slightly dark edge. But even then, in 1805, Wonderland was losing some of its wonder.

Elk, plentiful in the area before the settlers, were never seen there again. That small group of buffalo was the last natural herd recorded anywhere nearby, at least up to the time Hill wrote. Panthers disappeared altogether from the county by 1812. Wolves lingered but with their numbers and threat greatly diminished. Clearly, the legislature had found an appropriate price point with its scalp bounty. When the frontier was first broached in any quantity, bald eagles were much sighted; by the time Hill recorded pioneer memories, the national symbol had become a rare wonder. By midcentury, pike of the size Hill described had long ago disappeared from area waters.

All that was just to the east of Mount Vernon, where settlement was coming from—the rolling hills and valleys cut by the Ko-kosing, the Walhonding, the Mohican, the Tuscarawas, and the Muskingum Rivers. To the west, where settlement was going, the topography was flatter and the land still mostly Indian fields and hunting grounds, as it had been for centuries upon centuries. Native Americans had been ranging over this part of central Ohio since the mound builders of antiquity, and they were still very much in evidence.

The first Europeans to pass up these valleys and into Knox County could have encountered a half dozen tribal leaders whose names were still familiar to virtually every white in the Northwest Territory at the start of the nineteenth century. Among them: Gelelemend, also known as Killbuck, the grandson of the principal Delaware chief, Netawatwees, and himself a chief until he was forced from power, turned against his own tribe, and helped American forces attack and destroy the Delaware capital at Coshocton village in the early 1780s; and the mercurial Captain Pipe, another Delaware, who in 1778 joined Killbuck and White Eyes in signing the first-ever treaty between the Continental Congress and Native Americans. (The peace was short-lived. Four years later, Captain Pipe helped to defeat the Crawford Expedition against Ohio's northern tribes and seems to have personally approved of the execution—by burning at the stake—of its leader, Colonel William Crawford.)

At the fork of the Muskingum River, where it branches into its Tuscarawas and Walhonding tributaries, the Moravian missionary David Zeisberger and others had established the Christian Delaware village of Lichtenau, an early-American melting pot that allowed Zeisberger to turn out more than a dozen manuscripts on Delaware grammar, vocabulary, and phrases, as well as Delaware-language hymnals and liturgies, and sermons preached in the Delaware tongue. (The slaughter of some of Zeisberger's

Delaware "Christians" seems to have brought on Captain Pipe's blood frenzy.)

In his remarkable 1750–51 journal of his travels in Ohio, Captain Christopher Gist tells of passing through a long succession of tiny Indian "towns"—four Delaware families here, maybe a dozen Wyandots there—carrying greetings from George III, the "great King over the Water," and from the colonial governors of Pennsylvania and Virginia, the Indians' "brothers." English traders, Gist writes, were dotted among the villages, in constant danger on all sides but mostly from the French and their Indian allies.

Christmas Day 1750 finds Gist at the site of present-day Coshocton, forty miles down the Walhonding from Mount Vernon. At first, the few whites on hand refuse to join him in prayers, being not inclined "to hear any good," but finally a blacksmith comes forward and a few well-disposed Wyandots, and the service gets under way, during which Gist makes an eloquent plea for freedom of religious worship.

The next morning brings a Wyandot experience of an entirely different order and magnitude:

> A Woman, who had been a long time a Prisoner, and brought into the Town on Christmas Eve, was put to death in the following manner; They carried her without the Town and let her loose, and when she attempted to run away, the Persons appointed for that purpose pursued her, & struck her on her Ear, on the right side of her head, which beat her Flat on her face on the Ground; then they struck her several times thro the Back with a Dart, to the heart, Scalped her, and threw her scalp in the air, and another cut off her head.

Two weeks later, on January 12, 1751, Gist attends a council at the Wyandot "King's House," intending to press the British cause, but "the meeting being a little disordered with Liquor, no Business could be done." Another three days on, still heading up the Walhonding to what would become Mount Vernon and beyond, Gist walks into a tiny place known as White Woman's Town. (This part of the Walhonding was also known as White Woman Creek.) "This White Woman," he tells us, "was taken away from New England when she was not above Ten years old, by the French Indians; She is now upwards of fifty, and has an Indian Husband and several children—Her name is Mary Harris, she still remembers they used to be very religious in New England, and wonders how the White Men can be so wicked as she has seen them in these woods."

Mary Harris, though, turned out to have a wicked streak of her own. A few years later, her Indian husband would seek to introduce a second wife into the household. Mary's disapproval must have been titanic because a few days after Number Two moved in, Mary stove in her husband's skull with a hatchet. It was the newcomer who fled, though, fearing she would be blamed, as indeed she was—captured, blamed, beaten, and scalped much as the Wyandot prisoner had been—although the poor woman did ultimately gain a kind of immortality, because the tiny Indian village where she was executed is still known today as Newcomerstown.

So it goes throughout Gist's journal and indeed throughout the entire interface of cultures then taking place across the Northwest Territory: the mundane and comical; the grandiose, grotesque, and melancholic; and occasionally the truly bizarre. The nineteenth- and twentieth-century Ohio novelist William Dean Howells (*The Rise of Silas Lapham*) tells a story about two of the Frenchmen lured to Ohio territory by the Scioto Company chicanery who were later making their way down the Ohio by flatboat: "[These] two philosophers . . . believed so firmly in the natural innocence and goodness of men, that they invited some Indians aboard their boat and were at once tomahawked." In another of Howells's real-life "Stories of Ohio," a Colonel Robert Elliott is shot by an Indian, who then jumps on him with a scalping knife. "But at a touch the poor man's wig came off in his hand," Howells writes. The Indian "lifted it and was heard to say with an oath, 'Lie!' while he stared at his trophy in bewilderment."

Far more touching is Howells's account of eleven-year-old O. M. Spencer, who was taken captive near Cincinnati in 1792, carried to a Shawnee village on the Maumee River, and finally released only through the intervention of George Washington himself. The boy "was at last returned to his friends by canoe to Detroit, by sailing vessel to Erie, by land to Albany, by water to New York, and by land through Pennsylvania to Cincinnati. He was two years in getting back to his friends"—but what tales he had to relate!

As always in these stories, one wonders at the capacity for endurance by these settlers, young and old, but what is maybe most telling about Christopher Gist's journal are the instructions he was given at the outset of his journey by "the Honorable Robert Dinwiddie, Esquire, Governor and Commander of Virginia," on behalf of both the Crown and an even earlier Ohio Company, hungry as all of them were for Indian lands:

> You are to go out as soon as possible to the Westward of the great Mountains, and carry with you such a Number of men as You think necessary, in Order to Search out and discover the Lands upon the river Ohio, & other adjoining Branches of the Mississippi down as low as the great Falls thereof; You are particulatly [sic] to observe the Ways and Passes thro all the Mountains you cross, & take an exact account of the Soil, Quality and Product of the Land, and the Wideness and Deepness of the Rivers, & the several Falls belonging to them, together with the

courses and Bearings of the Rivers & Mountains as near as you conveniently can: You are to observe what Nations of Indians inhabit there, their strength & Numbers, who they trade with, & what comodities [*sic*] they deal in.... You are to take an exact and particular Journal of all Your Proceedings, and make a true Report thereof to the Company.

Gist's job, in short, was to walk amiably among the Native Americans of Ohio, secure their support for Great Britain and their souls when possible for the Church of England, take note of which tribes leaned toward France despite his efforts, measure (for appropriation) the land beneath the Indians' feet as he did so, and make an exact record of his progress. Given that he managed all that and came back alive, Gist must have been extraordinarily gifted.

By 1805, many of the Native Americans and their affairs that had so occupied the earliest frontiersmen were significantly tamed if not settled matters. Killbuck had been converted by the Moravians in 1788 and was living peacefully in Goshen, Ohio, under the name he had adopted from the man who had saved his life during the French and Indian War: William Henry. Captain Pipe and part of the dwindling remains of the Delaware tribe had moved to the northern reaches of the new state and would soon depart Ohio for good, for Indiana and westward from there. Murder and mayhem between whites and Indians wasn't done—and indeed a flare-up of bloody tensions during the War of 1812 would help propel Johnny Appleseed into mythology—but relations were, as they say in the diplomatic world, normalized. Indeed, they were almost ritualized. By the earliest years of the new century, Indians were regularly carrying stacks of skins and pelts into the trading post at Mount Vernon, arranging themselves on the floor, and waiting patiently as their senior leader pointed to an item he wanted, established a barter price, peeled off the requisite amount (two raccoon furs, one buckskin, etc.), and moved on to the next item. Then it would be the turn of the next most senior leader, and so on. Common currency and a bar code scanner could have saved everyone months and months of their lives.

❦

Mount Vernon, along Owl Creek (now known as Kokosing River, after an Indian word for "owl"), is a near-perfect expression of the middle world that central Ohio found itself inhabiting only a few years into statehood. The town was founded in 1805 by a trio of settlers led by Ben Butler, who had arrived at century's turn and would live in the area until his death in 1872, a few months after his ninety-third birthday. No sooner had the town been laid out than a doctor—a man named Henderson, from Baltimore—appeared on the scene. Unfortunately for his practice, Henderson's very first medical recommendation, that he inoculate Butler's infant son (Joseph, born October 1806, the first white child in the settlement) against smallpox, was ill-received by the father.

"I didn't then know exactly what inoculating meant," Butler would later recall, "but I was mad, and I threatened to put my knife into him and scared him so that he would not attempt to 'noculate any more in that town. He stayed around for a time, until he ran away with a woman."

Two years later, in 1808, what little Mount Vernon had to show for itself was almost completely destroyed by a tornado that ripped the roofs off nearly all the structures, killed most of the livestock, sent the horses that survived scattering every which way, felled hundreds of ancient white oaks, and even flattened Andy Craig's lean-to up the Owl Creek. The tornado, one historian noted, was "the most extraordinary event of those early times." Yet Mount Vernon did survive, both as a precarious outpost at the edge of the frontier and as an arrow pointed straight at the heart of the Indian lands beyond, and John Chapman was very much a part of it all.

❦

The original July 1805 map of Mount Vernon offers a snapshot of the Yankee businessman inherent in John Chapman. The town has been divided into more than two hundred lots. At the northeast corner stands a completed brickyard. On the southwest end a mill, with finished millrace, is shown to be in operation, as is a nearby tan yard. A graveyard has been marked out, as yet undug, and three hotels, as yet unbuilt. Other lots are designated for gunsmiths and blacksmiths, although those also are still in the planning stages. Indeed, among all the grand schemes, only half a dozen houses have been completed, including the log cabin that served as both town tavern and Ben Butler's home. Mount Vernon was mostly a dream waiting to happen.

Just east of the town, by far the largest tract of land shown on the map, is one of John Chapman's orchards. Just west, between the millrace and Owl Creek, is another, smaller but on the prime bottomland that Chapman favored for his work. These are the nurseries that he had been planting since at least 1803, the ones that began yielding salable seedlings about 1806, but Chapman's interests wouldn't end there. In 1809, for fifty dollars, he bought two of the town's most select building sites, along the planned main "Market Street" and just far enough up from the creek to be out of the flood plain.

There's no evidence that Chapman ever intended to build on either lot, but building, occupying, living in, settling down were never issues with Chapman. That wasn't what he was in it for. At the macro level, Chapman's primitive orchards were signposts in the wilderness, telling where white civilization would next arrive, while his speculation was part of the first cold hand of capitalism laid on a virgin land. At the micro level, though, the synergy between land and apples was much more personal.

Chapman's seedling nurseries a few years beyond the edge of the frontier assured product to sell when settlers arrived. His real-estate dabbling with whatever profits he could hold on to from his nurseries (in light of his philanthropic nature) gave him the potential to reap further riches as the settlements grew and demand for property mounted—like a slowly maturing bond. And the coming of settlers, the forming of communities, and the trips back and forth to western Pennsylvania to renew his seed supply provided what amounted to a circuit-preacher's golden opportunity to spread the glorious truths that God had delivered to Emanuel Swedenborg. Inchoate or not, intentional or constructed from convenience or out of the dawning reality of his own life and ways, this *was* the Plan, and for the next decade, John Chapman pursued it with a single-minded intention.

❦

Geology splits Ohio almost exactly in half, roughly along a diagonal, southwest-to-northeast axis. At the bottom of the state, the Allegheny escarpment—the western edge of the Appalachians—begins east of Myersville, in Adams County, and meanders northeast toward the center of the state, past Chillicothe, until it approaches Newark. Then, with outcroppings, it heads almost exactly due north for fifty miles—west of Newark, Mount Vernon, and Mansfield—before turning northeast again toward Ashland and beyond.

The glaciers of the Ice Age helped created this divide, and what the glaciers left behind, early settlers honored. Mount Vernon, as we've seen, began to gain a permanent white population about 1800 and was incorporated in 1805. The town of Delaware, just thirty-four miles due west off the escarpment in the watershed of the

Scioto River, wasn't settled until 1808 and didn't incorporate until 1816. Newark, due south of Mount Vernon at the forks of the Licking River, has a similar history and an almost exact analog. Newark dates from 1802, founded by a small party led by General William Schenck, who named the village (originally New Ark) for his New Jersey hometown. Columbus, also thirty-four miles due west off the escarpment, wasn't founded for another ten years, in 1812, and then only because the legislature had decided to plunk a capital down in the dead center of the state. Due north of Mount Vernon at a fork of the Mohican River, Mansfield dates back to 1808, while Marion, thirty-seven miles to the west, wasn't platted out until 1822, and Shelby, no more than a day's walk northwest, waited until 1818.

Multiple factors explain the time lag. The river systems that carried the early settlers into eastern central Ohio turn northerly as they approach the end of the Appalachians, finding more valleys to run through instead of tumbling down the escarpment. The earliest road into the area, Zane's Trace, went the other direction: shooting due west from Wheeling to the town Ebenezer Zane named for himself—Zanesville—and then following the edge of the escarpment southwest through Lancaster and Chillicothe to the Ohio River (again), and across it (by ferry) to Maysville, Kentucky. Indian pressures, too, weren't to be ignored. The Greenville Treaty Line of 1795—the practical result of Wayne's victory at the Battle of Fallen Timbers—had pushed Ohio's tribes mostly into the northwest quadrant of the state, but Native Americans continued to occupy the plains below the escarpment, and they still had at least semi-legal claim to land not far from Mansfield.

The bottom line is that for these and still more reasons, the forces of civilization, of western expansion and manifest destiny, paused for a breather when they got to the western edge of the Allegheny escarpment, and John Chapman adjusted accordingly. For a decade, since Longmeadow, his movement had trended ever westward. Now he began to wear a north-south path between Newark, Mount Vernon, and Mansfield, and to what would become Ashland, and up the many streams and creeks that branched off along the way.

Of all the cities on Chapman's circuit, Newark seems to have been the one that most needed the soul-edifier in him, his purifying news right fresh from heaven. By the terms of the day, Newark was almost civilized, tied back to the east in a way that none of the villages to the north could claim. Zane's Trace might have ignored Newark, but in 1805–1806 the U.S. Congress passed "An Act to Regulate the Laying Out and Making a Road from Cumberland, in the State of Maryland, to the State of Ohio"—what became the National Road, today's U.S. 40—and that road took off straight as an arrow from Zanesville to Newark and eventually from there to Columbus, Indianapolis, Terre Haute, and beyond, much to the envy of many of Newark's northern neighbors. In 1808 Knox Countians petitioned the state legislature for roads, complaining that settlers there couldn't "receive letters or any kind of intelligence or any private conveyance nearer than Newark or Zanesville." But access to roads and transportation and the sophistication that presumably comes with both doesn't seem to have improved the moral character of the local population. Chapman once cited early Newark as an earthly demonstration of the hell that Swedenborg describes so graphically in books like *Heaven and Hell:*

> In general their faces are frightful, lifeless as corpses. Some are black, some like fiery little torches, some swollen by pimples, distorted veins, and sores. Many have no visible face, but only something hairy or bony instead; with some, only the teeth stand out. Their bodies are grotesque, and their speech apparently arises from anger or hatred or revenge because each one talks out of his own false nature and has a voice quality that

stems from his evil nature. In short, all of them are reflections of their own hells.

Maybe Newark wasn't that bad—how could it have been?—but Chapman knew both the early town and his Swedenborgian texts well, and if the village even tended toward the hell that the Swede had visited in his waking and sleeping dreams, it must have been a fearsome place.

❦

Mount Vernon was not without its own rough characters, none more so than James Craig, who was living in the town as of 1807 and probably for several years before. (James Craig was almost certainly related to Andy Craig, who was still living outside town with his apparently monstrously unattractive common-law wife.) James Craig had one of the earliest businesses in town—he sold refreshments and corn whiskey out of his cabin, and consumed liberally of his own products—but he made his true mark as a two-fisted brawler.

Knox County historian A. Banning Norton describes Craig memorably as "grit to the backbone . . . It became almost an every-day occurrence with him to have a fight; and, if no new comer appeared to give his fighting life variety, he would, 'just to keep his hand in,' scrape up a fight with his neighbors or have a quarrel with his wife—all for the love of the thing." The highlight of Craig's fighting life appears to be the day he had four separate, almost-to-the-death brawls with the same man: Joe Walker, "also a game chicken," according to Norton. But this is a highlight reel that continued well into Craig's old age, by which time the judicial system had long since established itself in Mount Vernon and taken a dim view of his frequent public fisticuffs. Indeed, when Craig was indicted for brawling for what proved to be the last time, he is supposed to have told the judge to go easy on him because he was "one of the best customers the court had."

Still, if the Mount Vernonians weren't much different in kind than their neighbors to the south in godless Newark, they seem to have had more of a sense of humor, or maybe just cunning. In a scene that calls to mind the 1998 Irish film *Waking Ned Devine,* Robert Price recounts a bit of 1808 japery in which Mount Vernon managed to outduel Clinton, only a mile and a half away, to become the Knox County seat. First, Ben Butler, Joe Walker, and other Mount Vernon supporters cleaned up their own act on the eve of an inspection by the state commissioners—managing, in Price's word, "to put on altogether a splendid show of gracious, respectable hospitality and business decorum." Simultaneously, just to ice the cake, the same town fathers also plied a less respectable contingent of the immediate population with whiskey—the Craigs come to mind—and sent them off to Clinton to greet the commissioners' arrival there with "a disgustingly boisterous and disreputable exhibition of human depravity."

Maybe Johnny Appleseed himself was part of the charade and of the celebration afterward back in Mount Vernon—great bonfires lit, live trees blown to smithereens with gunpowder charges, corn whiskey flowing like water. One would like to think so. Chapman didn't mind a little nip, and he could read Swedenborg or act the madman with almost equal facility. All we know for certain is that Chapman waited less than a year after Mount Vernon had won the competition to purchase those two prime town lots, real estate bound to ripen in value once the county seat established itself and commerce grew.

We know, too, that when it came to his own business, John Chapman was ecumenical in the extreme. Whether his customers were saints or sinners, Mount Vernon rubes or Newark cosmopolitans, Butternuts pushing in from Virginia or New England Congregationalists following the same tortured trail he had across the Pennsylvania ranges, Chapman was waiting, with product to sell, and, as always, his overhead was virtually zero.

Chapman's approach to the nursery business couldn't have been more original. Of overhead, he had none so long as he slept outside, as he most often did, and dined on the grains and nuts and berries the fields and forests had to offer.

❧

In his *Centennial History of Licking County*, Isaac Smucker writes that John Chapman launched but a single nursery in the county, on what at the start of the twentieth century was known as the Scotland Farm, about three miles northeast of Newark, and that it was pretty much a failure. "It was neglected, the enclosure was broken down and the young apple-trees were browsed upon by animals, so that few of them were ever transplanted." Other accounts credit Chapman with a kind of primal nursery, planted in 1801 on the farm of Isaac Stadden, from which all the early orchards of the county sprung, but that, too, is in question. Years later, Isaac Stadden's widow, Catharine—whom Smucker describes as "a first-class Pioneer woman, very liberally endowed with intellect and memory"—would dismiss Chapman as a Johnny-come-lately to the local orchard scene. Catharine herself had brought the first apple trees when she and her husband moved into the area from western Pennsylvania in 1800, or so she contended, and those had been added to not by Johnny Appleseed but by an "experienced horticulturist" and "more practical man" with the easily confused name of Johnny Goldthwaite.

(Smucker, it should be noted, is a name that continues to be associated with Chapman. Jerome Monroe Smucker, the Ohioan who launched the J. M. Smucker jam-and-jelly empire, always said that his first products came from the fruit of trees begun in Johnny Appleseed's nurseries, but those trees had come of age in Orrville, eighty miles north-northeast of Newark. In what might be regarded almost as a crazy coincidence, *Family Business* magazine in 2009 ranked the J. M. Smucker Company as the ninety-first largest family-owned enterprise in America. Number ninety-two was the Asplundh Tree Expert Company family, descendants of three Swedish-American brothers and among the most generous supporters of the Swedenborg-based Church of the New Jerusalem.)

Still other Licking County historians and memoirists more generous than Catherine Stadden or less exacting than Isaac Smucker credit Chapman with multiple nurseries in the county: northeast of Granville, east of Hanover, west of Granville, near Fallsburg, and St. Albans Township. William Stanbery, who arrived in Newark from New York City in 1809 and went on to become the county's most distinguished lawyer and a three-term U.S. congressman, recalled being told that Chapman had first arrived in Newark in 1801 leading a horse with leather saddlebags packed with apple seeds. Stanbery also remembered Chapman's calling on him during the lawyer's first year in town and spending the night at his request—although Chapman insisted on sleeping in a nearby grove, rather than under Stanbery's roof. (William Stanbery lived to be eighty-four; Catharine Stadden, to the ripe age of ninety-one. Merely associating with Chapman, for good or ill, seems to have added decades to people's lives!) As always, too, there were individual trees in the county said to have been touched somehow—almost anyhow—by Johnny Appleseed's hands.

In Knox and Coshocton Counties, the record is more certain if hardly assured. By 1810, Chapman was selling trees from a nursery on the south bank of Owl Creek, tucked into the corner of the four-thousand-acre holding of Robert Giffin, who built a cabin for his wife and four children near where the nursery had taken root. Although Chapman's plot was tiny—no more than seventy-five feet square—it supplied trees for first orchards all across the region, according to early historians. At just about the same time, he had apple trees maturing in a much larger orchard—perhaps an acre—along the fork of the Mohican River, within hailing distance of a cabin built and occupied by John Butler. This nursery, too, took up a small corner of another four-thousand-acre estate, but the owner in this instance was an absent land speculator who never knew the uses to which Johnny Appleseed was putting his property. Tradition has it that Chapman had filled this clearing with three bushels of seed, a preposterous number if he actually drilled a hole and planted each one, as opposed to simply broadcasting the seed across the surface of the ground. Three bushels of medium-size apples totals about three hundred individual apples; three bushels of apple *seed* might total a million seeds in all. But it never does to underestimate the man's tenacity.

Still other plantings could be found in an area known as Indian Field, on the north bank of Owl Creek; on something then called Nursery Island, at some unidentified spot in the Mohican River, on the present-day Knox-Coshocton county line; and in Newcastle Township, at the far west of Coshocton County. The locations are numerous, but the identifying characteristics are almost always the same: nearby water, silt, untended or unclaimed land, and the stretching fingers of transportation routes into the mostly unknown.

Farther north, in what would become Richland and Ashland Counties, Chapman is said to have secured a small plot for a nursery on the farm of Alexander Finley, near Taylortown, in 1809. By 1811 or perhaps 1812, he had another "very fine" nursery up and running a mile and a half west of Mifflin. Still other nurseries could be found in Green Township, on bottom land near Leidigh's Mill in Orange Township, elsewhere in Richland County, and perhaps even to the west in Crawford County, at the very edge of the Allegheny escarpment.

In all, this chain of nurseries must have extended for several hundred miles, not as the crow flies but as travel was done back at the start of the nineteenth century, mostly by foot, up and down river and stream and creek valleys, following the paths that nature had been carving out for eons. Occasionally, Chapman would entrust a nursery to the care of a nearby farmer. Most often, though, he tended to the seedlings himself—a circuit-walking nurseryman, just as he was a circuit-walking evangelist.

Several accounts contend that Chapman was careful to prune his apple trees so that they would be symmetrical, and illustrators, too, tend to favor rounded and well-balanced trees whenever they tackle Johnny Appleseed in an orchard. Pruning, though, would seem to run against the grain of Chapman's frequent admonitions against grafting. Does a tree feel the pruner's knife less than the grafter's blade? If it is God's will that an apple tree should grow from seed and yield whatever fruit its dominant genes may dictate—sour, sweet; large, small—why is it not also God's will and nature's plan that a tree should take whatever shape or form the seed might ultimately determine? Splitting such theological hairs is utterly unlike Chapman, or Appleseed. Yet H. S. Knapp's 1863 history of Ashland County uses as its frontispiece a sketch of Johnny Appleseed done from memory by a woman who had seen Chapman multiple times in her youth, and there in his right hand is, undeniably, a pruning knife.

Documentary evidence of Chapman's nursery-business dealings is scattered at best, almost entirely in the form of written orders for x amount of trees to be claimed at y date for z consideration, generally measurable in single-digit dollars. This order relating to his large orchard in Knox County is typical:

> October 1812, for value received I promise to pay or cause to be paid to Benjamin Burrell one hundred and fifty trees at my nursery near John Butlers in the month of March such as they are when called for. John Chapman.

Sometime between 1817 and 1820, he left a similar promissory note behind: "Due John Oliver one hundred and fifty trees when he goes for them to some of my Nurseryes on Mohecan waters," probably in the vicinity of Perrysville, southeast of Mansfield. About the same time and place, Chapman wrote to Martin Mason, asking him "please to let Evan Rice or bearer have thirty eight apples trees and you will oblige your friend." At the going rate, 150 trees might have amounted to $6 total; 38 trees would have fetched maybe $1.50, hardly worth the paperwork even back then *if* Chapman hadn't been running a volume business, a Dollar Store approach to nursery work.

Of Chapman's real-estate dealings along this rough north-south axis of central Ohio, the record is far more complete, preserved in the folios and libres of county deed books and in the ledgers of the military land districts that predated the counties. Between 1809 and 1818, John Chapman would take ninety-nine-year leases on five separate 160-acre tracts in three different counties: Richland, Ashland, and Wayne, just to the east of Ashland, where J. M. Smucker would eventually set up his jelly factory. Details vary—in one case he had a partner in the lease; in two other cases the leases were first taken by others, then assigned to Chapman—but collectively the properties were valued at $1,600 (about $16,000 in current dollars) and seem to have entailed annual interest payments of $19.20 per property, exactly 6 percent, which Chapman failed to meet on multiple occasions. (These had originally been federal lands reserved for schools. The land couldn't be sold—education might still triumph over speculation—but it could be leased for ninety-nine years.)

There were also the two village lots that Chapman had purchased in Mount Vernon in 1809, at $25 each, one of which he eventually sold, nineteen years later, for $30, a clean 20 percent profit, and another lot in Mansfield, number 265, which he purchased on June 1, 1818, from Henry Wilcoxen for $120 and unloaded five months later on Jesse Edgington for an unknown sum. (The Mount Vernon lot, it should be mentioned, was sold to Jesse B. Thomas, who had just completed his second term as a U.S. senator from Illinois and was resettling in Ohio.)

In retrospect, all this buying, selling, and leasing—the lots flipped, the interest payments committed to and not made—can seem almost frantic. "Getting and spending, we lay waste our powers," William Wordsworth wrote in 1806, just as Chapman was launching the Plan. But the next line of that famous passage highlights the difference between Chapman's free-wheeling and dealing and the soul-deadening commercialism Wordsworth was writing about: "Little we see in Nature that is ours." Everything in nature belonged to Chapman, and he seems to have belonged in turn to everything natural that surrounded him. The symbiosis was complete.

In fact, for a man who had been almost constantly on the move for more than a decade, this interplay of the nursery business and land speculation amounted almost to a settling in, what passed for domesticity in an untamed life.

❦

Always, too, there was the preaching: Chapman's ministry of word, deed, and example. Rosella Rice, who knew Chapman in her childhood, recalled: "Almost the first thing he would do when he entered a house, and was weary, was to lie down on the floor, with his knapsack for a pillow, and his head toward the light of a door or window, when he would say, 'Will you have some fresh news right from Heaven?' and carefully take out his old worn books, a Testament, and two or three others, the exponents of the beautiful religion that Johnny so zealously lived out—the Swedenborgian doctrine."

One early account tells us Chapman kept his scraps of precious text dry in that saucepan hat he is often said to have worn. Others suggest that the texts themselves had almost talismanic qualities. "His Swedenborgian books were, as before stated, ever-present companions," H. S. Knapp writes in his Ashland County history. "Mr. Josiah Thomas inquired of Johnny whether, in traveling on bare feet through forests abounding in venomous snakes, he did not entertain fears of being bitten. 'This book,' replied the old man, 'is an infallible protection against all danger, here and hereafter.'"

The most famous of all the "religious" Appleseed anecdotes took place in the Mansfield town square about 1829. There, a fiery fundamentalist preacher named Adam Payne was holding forth on the sin of pride when he suddenly called out to the crowd: "Where now is your barefooted pilgrim [or 'primitive Christian' in some versions; there are many variations] on his way to Heaven?" And with that, the almost always barefoot John Chapman stepped forward, held up a foot for inspection, and proclaimed, "Here he is."

To Reverend Payne, Chapman must have appeared at that very moment almost as an apparition. He would have been dressed in his usual assortment of patchwork rags, and little enough of those; his hair and beard, long, scraggly, unkempt perhaps even by frontier standards; those dark eyes almost like glowing embers, as they are so frequently described. That was what nature had given him, but his self-nurture was entirely compatible. Chapman's diet, in fact, was straight out of the John the Baptist cookbook: honey, berries, fruit, some cornmeal for mush, milk whenever it was available. (Chapman seems to have had a special passion for milk.) Locusts, a favorite snack of John the Baptist, would have taxed Chapman's animism, but in many other ways, the two channeled each other. It was almost as if Chapman were trying out for the part of "primitive Christian." And how he seems to have relished the role, almost to the point of method acting!

In his Coshocton County history, N. N. Hill cites correspondence

from a C. S. Coffinberry, a Michigan resident "who was well acquainted with [John Chapman]," as follows:

> John Chapman was a regularly constituted minister of the
> Church of the New Jerusalem, according to the revelations of
> Emanuel Swedenborg. He was also constituted a missionary of
> that faith under the authority of the regular association in the
> city of Boston. The writer has seen and examined his credentials
> as to the latter of these.

In fact, no such credentials ever appear to have been issued, and
Chapman was often indifferent to documentation, especially in
his land dealings. Proof, though, hardly mattered. Certified or not,
Chapman's deep religious convictions explained everything about
him to the people of central Ohio. His celibacy, for example. Like
Swedenborg (or as Swedenborg was understood), Chapman was
in frequent "spiritual intercourse" with departed spirits—in Chapman's instance, two spirits of "the female gender, who consoled
him with the news that they were to be his wives in the future
state, should he keep himself from all entangling alliances in this."
Religion also allowed Chapman to get away on occasion with
being something of a common scold, even maybe a royal pain in
the neck. Willard Hickox of Mansfield remembered Chapman
stopping by a pioneer cabin and there discovering

> near the doorway a bucket of "slops" which the housewife had
> probably designed for the pigs, and upon the surface of which
> were floating some fragments of bread. He at once employed
> himself in removing these pieces from the bucket, and while
> thus engaged, the woman of the house appeared. He greeted her
> with a gentle rebuke of her extravagance—urging upon her the
> sinfulness of waste—and that it was wickedness, and an abuse

of the gifts of a merciful God, to suffer the smallest quantity of anything which was designed to minister to the wants of mankind to be diverted from its purpose.

And, of course, religion explained as well the almost endless anecdotes about Chapman's generosity in hard times to just about one and all: the shoes he gave up in the dead of winter so others wouldn't have to go barefoot in the snow, the trees "sold" for scraps of clothing, the abused horses he paid to have boarded in kinder circumstances. "Not once in a century is such a life of self-sacrifice for the good of others known," N. N. Hill wrote in 1881. And indeed, Chapman does seem to have had a heart without bottom, except perhaps when it came to his own family.

❦

Nathaniel and Lucy Cooley Chapman and the youngest half dozen of their many children followed John Chapman west in 1805, relocating from Longmeadow to a settlement known as Duck Creek, fifteen miles up the Muskingum River from Marietta in Washington County. The new home was only eighty-five miles as the crow flies from Mount Vernon—almost a casual stroll for the ever-strolling John Chapman. A decade would have passed since father and son had last seen each other, and the need at Duck Creek must have been great and growing. Father Nathaniel died there in 1807, two years after arriving, still farming rented land as he had his entire civilian life. Lucy and her two youngest children, Davis and Sally, born in 1800 and 1803, remained as of the 1810 census. Who knows where or with whom Jonathan, only twelve and by some accounts a deaf-mute, and Mary, age fourteen, had wandered to or been placed by then, but the family finances must have been perilous.

Given such circumstances and what we know of John Chapman's

charitable impulses and religious bent, one might assume that he would have rushed to be with his dying father or at least stepped in afterward to help support his stepmother and half siblings. Perhaps he did, but apart from later hagiographies, which sometimes go so far as to have Chapman meticulously building a new home for Nathaniel and Lucy, no hard evidence supports either assumption. Rather than hastening to his family in its time of need, Chapman appears to have kept on doing exactly what he had been about since at least the mid-1790s: distancing himself from them.

Few people, if any, were better known in central Ohio in the opening decades of the nineteenth century than John Chapman, and few, if any, were more parsimonious with the details of their own past. Every county produced at least one mid- to late-nineteenth-century history of its early years, and Chapman is featured in virtually all of them, but not in Williams's 1881 *History of Washington County,* and John Chapman was a man very hard to miss.

In nearly all those early histories, too, the authors remark on how little is known about his background or cite misleading facts as accepted truths. N. N. Hill, for example, uses the same C. S. Coffinberry who had witnessed supposedly documentary evidence of Chapman's ministerial credentials to fill in the background of Chapman's early years: "As early as 1780, he was seen in the autumn, for two or three successive years, along the banks of the Potomac, in eastern Virginia"—roughly, that is, when John Chapman was turning six years old.

Chapman's half brother Nathaniel, with whom he had first ventured forth from Massachusetts, was in Ohio by at least 1805 and in fact managed to leave a distinct trail in accounts of that time, but he almost completely disappears from the narrative of his older brother's life. The one exception is Chapman's half sister Persis, almost two decades his junior. She married a man named

William Broom and settled first in Perrysville and then in Mansfield, on what is now West Fourth Street, and later moved to the Fort Wayne area, just about the time Chapman started frequenting the eastern edge of Indiana. Chapman stayed on occasion with the Brooms in all three places, and, as later estate records would show, William Broom clearly worked for his brother-in-law for a time, to the extent that Chapman ever had employees. But Persis is at best a shadow in Chapman's history.

One family story holds that about 1842 or 1843, John Chapman made a last, sentimental journey to the Duck Creek area to visit the half brother and half sisters who remained there, after which he returned to Fort Wayne "older and very tired," according to Frank Chapman, himself descended from one of the stepsiblings. It makes for a nice rounding off—a valedictory trip for the soon-to-die wanderer—but this last trip is also suspect for the same reason, an attempt to smooth off the edges on sometimes rough relationships. The fact is that, with the exception of Persis and Nathaniel (and then only early in life), Chapman's brothers and sisters by his father and Lucy Cooley's marriage aren't even shades of shadows in his story, although almost to a person they lived within the general ambit of his travels.

Why? Well, the absence of business opportunities might have played a role. *Williams History* assures as that the Duck Creek area was not considered prime soil. What's more, the area was generally well settled, and downriver in Marietta people expected more of apples than Chapman's genetically random seeds were apt to produce. Israel and Rufus Putnam's Connecticut apple tree scions had been sent across the Alleghenies packed in beeswax and were already spoiling local gourmands with as many as two dozen varieties of apples widely admired back in New England for their flavor.

Religion could have played a role, too. The Freewill Baptists and

Methodists both had a strong foothold in Duck Creek. Camp meetings, Williams writes, "were immemorial to the oldest inhabitants." For a student of Swedenborg and the New Church, all that barking and eye rolling and endless exhortation must have been a burden to bear.

Or simple incompatibility could explain it all. Persis Broom and her husband might have been useful to her stepbrother, but as one chronicler wrote, Persis "was not at all like him; a very ordinary woman, talkative, and free in her frequent, *'says she's'* and *'says I's.'*" As for Nathaniel, the mark he left was not one likely to enthrall the gentle humanitarian in his ex–traveling companion. One account has Nathaniel claiming to have killed the last bear in Washington County. Another has him part of a mob that took fatal revenge on a half-breed named Silverheels whom half brother John had befriended almost a decade earlier. And Persis and Nathaniel, after all, were only stepsiblings; Lucy, only a stepmother. People drift apart; personality gaps often widen over time.

Or maybe it was those two promissory notes for a hundred dollars each that Chapman had signed back in 1804—one to his full sister, Elizabeth, and her husband, and the other to either his father or his half brother Nathaniel. There's no way of knowing if the notes ever came due and, if they did, whether brother-son John made good on his promise. A hundred dollars in 1804 equals roughly fifteen hundred today. Families have fractured over less.

But none of those answers, one suspects, is really sufficient to the cause. True, Chapman was famously indifferent to money, but his personal motto clearly was much like the central tenet of the Hippocratic Oath: First, do no harm. As for being embarrassed by his stepfamily or ill at ease with them, he was often antsy in too much company, but he didn't have a snooty bone in his body. Something deeper seems to have been going on, some fundamental act of reinvention. Ever since he'd left Longmeadow, John Chapman had been in the process of becoming someone else. In central Ohio, perhaps, he realized that he would never get there without willing his own past out of existence. As Chapman, he was man; as Appleseed, he was myth in its larval stage. Did Chapman ever really think along these lines, in any conscious way? That seems unlikely, maybe even impossible. But history was about to choose for him.

9

MAN TO MYTH

From the very moment he entered the historical record as anything more than a duly recorded birth, John Chapman was veering toward myth. He could fell trees like a human tornado; endure cold like an Inuit, or maybe a penguin; survive weeks, even months, on a handful of seeds and berries. Chapman's hand was the one always ready to be lent. He was stoic as a pillar saint in the face of danger and travail. The celluloid Homers of the Walt Disney Studios would ultimately adorn Chapman with chirping bluebirds and misty-eyed wolves, but hyperbole, out of which myth is built, followed John Chapman like a loyal dog, almost to the point of embarrassment.

Part of this, of course, is the work of later chroniclers, who rarely resisted embellishment when they got around to the future Johnny Appleseed. Part is attributable to Chapman's own self-mythologizing: He seems to have been perfectly willing to spread a tall tale about himself. But the larger part emerged from deep within Chapman's own character. He was bursting with uniqueness—one of those people almost impossible to recall without a heavy dose of excess.

One of Chapman's most florid memoirists, the mid-nineteenth-century poet and novelist Rosella Rice, was a central Ohioan through and through. She was born about 1830 in Perrysville, in the southern part of Ashland County, familiar territory to Chapman, and she stayed on in the county her entire life. Rice's father was one of the area's first pioneers. An uncle claimed to have been among those who had spotted Chapman on the Ohio River in that 1806 foray, paddling his lashed-together canoes. Rice absorbed Chapman lore around the family hearth and witnessed him with her own eyes when she was still a girl and he a nomad of sixty years and more.

But Rice was also no stranger to pouring it on. The dedication of her 1863 novel *Mabel: Or, Heart Histories* might serve as a model for the often overblown prose of the era: "To my parents: the dear father, whose pure life is like a beacon to my darkened pathway; whose life and sympathy have blest and cheered me; and to my mother and step-mother, who rest from their labors, angel-crowned, in heaven." And when it came to Chapman, her restraints were few.

"Among his many eccentricities," Rice recalled, "was one of bearing pain like an undaunted Indian warrior. He gloried in suffering. Very often he would thrust pins and needles into his flesh without a tremor or a quiver; and if he had a cut or a sore, the first thing he did was to sear it with a red hot iron, and then treat it as a burn."

Rice remembered, too, Chapman's "strange, deep eloquence at times . . . Sometimes in speaking of fruit, his eyes would sparkle, and his countenance grow animated and really beautiful, and if he was at table his knife and fork would be forgotten. In describing apples, we could see them just as he, the word-painter, pictured them—large, lush, creamy-tinted ones, or rich, fragrant, and yellow, with a peachy tint on the sunshiny side, or crimson red, with the cool juice ready to burst through the tender rind."

So many were Chapman's sterling qualities, according to Rice, that it never occurred to her or her friends to do what the young have done with major oddballs since the beginning of time: make fun of the man, have sport at his expense, scream and run in the other direction when they saw him coming. "No matter how oddly he was dressed or how funny he looked, we children never laughed at him, because our parents all loved and revered him as a good old man, a friend, and a benefactor."

Other memoirists only a generation removed from those who would have known Chapman in the flesh sketch what amounts to a New World Saint Francis, a poignant counterpoint to the realities of life on a dangerous and rapacious frontier.

"He never killed anything, not even for the purpose of obtaining food," A. J. Baughman said at a November 1900 celebration in Mansfield. Chapman's "mission was one of peace and good will and he never carried a weapon, not even for self defense," according to Baughman's primary source, Dr. William Bushnell, who had known the future myth in the flesh and "best understood this peculiar character." "The Indians regarded him as a great 'Medicine Man,' and his life seemed to be a charmed one, as neither savage man nor wild beast would harm him. Chapman was not a mendicant. He was never in indigent circumstances, for he sold thousands of nursery trees every year. Had he been avaricious, his estate, instead of being worth a few thousand might have been tens of thousands at his death."

In his 1863 history of Ashland County, less than two decades after Chapman's death, H. S. Knapp (citing Henry Howe's earlier history of Ohio as his source) strikes similar saintly notes. Knapp takes us, for instance, to that "cool autumnal night" when Chapman/Appleseed doused his campfire rather than see mosquitoes lured to their death: "God forbid that I should build a fire for my comfort, that should be the means of destroying any of his creatures." He sits us by a second campfire on another, much colder night when our hero famously slept on the snow rather than disturb the bear and her cubs that were already occupying the hollow log he had marked for his own bed. Finally, Knapp walks us through the morning on the prairie when Chapman was bitten by a rattlesnake. "Some time after, a friend inquired of him about the matter. He drew a long sigh and replied, 'Poor fellow! he only just touched me, when I, in an ungodly passion, put the heel of my scythe in him and went home. Some time after I went there for my scythe, and there lay the poor fellow dead.'"

Chapman, Knapp assures us, "declined, repeatedly, invitations to take food with the elder members of the family at the first table. . . . It was not until he became fully assured that there would be an abundant supply of food for the little children who had remained in waiting, that he would partake the proffered hospitality."

Chapman's honesty, his thoughtfulness to man and child and beast, appears to have been almost superhuman. Indeed, it might be unbearable—the self-abnegation, his constant sacrifice. How much goodness can we take? Yet in *Historical Collections of Ohio*, Henry Howe writes in his entry on Perrysville that Chapman was a "constant snuff consumer and had beautiful teeth," and then adds the shocking news, which must have been common knowledge all over town, that this presumed lifelong celibate, betrothed of two spirit-world virgins, "was smitten here with Miss Nancy Tannehill and proposed, but was just one too late: she was already engaged." Not to mention the snuff stuck in the gaps between her would-be suitor's beautiful teeth and the tobacco-juice dribble that certainly would have stained some part of Chapman's straggly beard a nicotine yellow. John Chapman, it turns out, was human after all.

Thus Chapman/Appleseed might have stayed for the remainder of his years—poised between his nursery work, land speculation,

and ministry, on the one hand; and on the other, his many, inevitably exaggerated excesses of character. (Poised, that is, between
Chapman and Appleseed, a fence-sitter for the ages!) But Chapman was already leaning toward myth, and the War of 1812 would
push him that way for good.

❦

Like John Chapman and Emanuel Swedenborg, the War of 1812
has mostly disappeared into the mists of time, obscured by the
glow of grander conflicts. The Revolution gave us the Minutemen and Bunker Hill, Washington and Lafayette, Saratoga and
Yorktown, independence. The Civil War brought together Lincoln,
Lee, and Grant; the Emancipation Proclamation; a nation divided
against itself; horrible body counts. The First World War took us
global; the Second had two fronts, perfect villains in Hitler and
Mussolini, and a sneak attack at Pearl Harbor that nearly knocked
America out before the fight began. Vietnam divided the nation
once again. But only once in the history of America has an enemy
occupied the symbolic heart of the country, torched the U.S. Capitol, burned the White House and the Treasury building next door,
and forced the president to flee to safety: the War of 1812—on
August 24–25, 1814, to be exact.

A very rough timeline of this vastly ignored war goes as follows
(without getting into deeper causes and entangling foreign alliances):

- *November 1810.* Voters elect a new Congress heavily tilted
  toward "war hawks" intolerant of the British treatment of the
  United States.

- *March 1811.* At President James Madison's behest, Congress
  enacts a trade embargo against Great Britain.

- *November 1811.* At Tippecanoe River in Indiana Territory, General William Henry Harrison and his thousand-man army defeat a coalition of Indian tribes led by Tecumseh and his brother, known as the Prophet. The defeat and continued western expansion help align Tecumseh and other Indian leaders with British forces in the fight to come.

- *June 18, 1812.* The U.S. Senate votes 19–13 to declare war against Great Britain.

- *August 16, 1812.* In the first major battle of the new war, American general William Hull surrenders his army of 2,200 men to British forces at Detroit. Not a single shot is fired.

- *October 1812.* The second major engagement of the war goes little better for American forces. At the Battle of Queenston Heights, across the Niagara River in Canada, General Stephen Van Rensselaer is forced to surrender his nine hundred soldiers when New York state militia refuse to follow him across the border.

- *December 1812.* Madison gains a second term when he defeats Federalist antiwar candidate De Witt Clinton 128 votes to 89 votes in the Electoral College.

- *September 10, 1813.* After a ferocious ten-hour battle, Captain Oliver Hazard Perry and his squadron of ten ships defeat a six-vessel British force on Lake Erie. Perry's dispatch to his superiors becomes a classic: "We have met the enemy and they are ours."

- *October 5, 1813.* Free at last to cross Lake Erie unopposed, future president William Henry Harrison crushes British forces and their Indian allies at the Battle of the Thames, near Chatham in Ontario. Tecumseh is killed in the fighting.

- *August 24–25, 1814.* While peace talks are under way at Ghent, in Belgium, British forces occupy Washington, DC, and torch many public buildings. Only a violent storm the next day prevents the destruction from being far worse.

- *September 11, 1814.* Though outnumbered three to one, Americans defeat an eleven-thousand-man British army at Lake Champlain in New York. Five days later, a British attack on Baltimore is repulsed by artillery fire from Fort McHenry. Witnessing the battle inspires Francis Scott Key to pen "The Star-Spangled Banner."

- *December 24, 1814.* The strangely misnamed War of 1812 officially ends with the signing of the Treaty of Ghent.

- *January 8, 1815.* Unaware a treaty has been signed, another future president, General Andrew Jackson, hands the United States its greatest victory of the war and one of its most lopsided triumphs ever, at the Battle of New Orleans. British casualties total more than two thousand. American wounded amount to fewer than two dozen. With the rout, Jackson becomes a national hero.

It was during roughly the second quadrant of that time line— shortly after Hull's surrender at Detroit and a year before Perry secured Lake Erie—that John Chapman entered the fray and the myth of Johnny Appleseed began to take deep root. The debacle in Detroit and British control of Lake Erie, pre-Perry, meant that the towns and villages of central Ohio were essentially unprotected from the north. The British were expected any day. Ohio's own tribes were rumored to be flooding toward Canada to join the attack. For better than a decade and a half, ever since Wayne's victory at the Battle of Fallen Timbers, Ohio's whites and Indians had been keeping an uneasy peace. Now, war cries, real or imagined, were heard again, and nerves grew frayed to and beyond the breaking point.

In one moment of near-calamitous mistaken identity, Chapman himself was almost shot by a fellow settler and close acquaintance who thought his friend was an Indian sneaking through the woods. In fact, what the settler mistook for a red Native American legging was a venison ham hanging from the belt of the ever-generous Chapman, who was bringing it to his would-be assailant. What irony if the frontier's most notable vegetarian and ardent philanthropist had had his life cut short over a gift of deer haunch!

Another case of mistaken identity had more extensive repercussions. Inveterate roamer that he was, Chapman was hired by a few settlers along the northern reaches of his circuit to journey to the mouth of the Huron River, on Lake Erie, and carry back any intelligence about British and Indian activity. On what must have been only his first or second such reconnoitering, in late August of 1812 within weeks of Hull's capitulation, Chapman returned with startling news.

"Flee for your lives," one settler recalled Chapman's shouting through the woods. "The Canadians and Indians are landing at Huron!" And flee they did—with cattle and whatever household goods they could carry, through darkness and rain, sometimes cutting a path through the underbrush as they went, across the rain-swollen Huron to Mansfield and, when that didn't seem sufficient distance between them and the pursuing Redcoats and savages, farther south, toward Fredericktown, only five miles short of the garrison at Mount Vernon. The panicked settlers were halfway there—one man wearing only an overcoat and carrying his pantaloons with him, according to A. Banning Norton—when a horseman overtook them with fresh intelligence.

Chapman hadn't been the only one to hear the news. Word

had reached Cleveland as well that nine British ships carrying a hundred fighting men each were headed across the lake, and indeed the nine ships had now made landfall and were exactly as reported . . . except the nine hundred soldiers were Americans, paroled back across enemy lines under the terms of Hull's surrender.

❦

One might think that, having cried wolf once, Chapman would have been less heeded when his voice was raised a second time in alarm, but in this instance—only a few weeks later—the threat was local, the danger imminent, and the resulting violence both real and tragic. As is almost always the case with these bloody frontier clashes between new and Native Americans, cause and effect are intricately entwined, and the innocent, the guilty, the star-crossed and damned often hard to pick apart.

The "known" facts are these: In early September 1812, a Colonel Kratzer, who headed up the militia stationed in Mount Vernon, determined to remove the area Indian population to the southwest corner of the state, far from British influence, and accordingly, a small detachment of militia under Kratzer's command proceeded to the Delaware village at Greentown, near Perrysville, a tribal center that had grown to as many as 150 dwellings. In preparation, though, they first stopped at the cabin of James Copus, a local preacher, about 2.5 miles from their destination. Recalling events years later, Wesley Copus, the third youngest of the preacher's seven children, picks up the story from there:

> Mr. Copus and [Kratzer] entered into a long conversation respecting the justness of his mission. Mr. Copus had on two or three occasions preached to these people, and enjoyed their full confidence; and since he had been with them, a period of nearly three years, he had seen no signs of hostility in any of them. All

these considerations were laid before the officer, but to no purpose.

The officer told Mr. Copus that his mission was not one of
blood; but that he merely intended to persuade them to throw
themselves under the protection of the United States government; and that he only wanted him [Mr. Copus] to use his
influence in a peaceable manner to press the importance of a
peaceable surrender to the government, and their rights, lives,
and property should be protected.

With this understanding, Mr. Copus consented to accompany the officer to the village. Accordingly, taking his little son
Wesley . . . they and the officer and his soldiers left the cabin
and proceeded to the village, where a council was held and the
agreement made, in which it was stated that their village should
be protected during their absence, or until they were permitted
to return. . . .

After the Indians had been gone some distance from their
village, the soldiers left behind to guard their goods until they
could be conveyed away, set fire to the village and burned it to
the ground. On casting their eyes behind them, the banished vil-
lagers saw, to their horror and astonishment, the smoke of their
ruined wigwams.

Worse was to follow. Among the Indians removed from Greentown that day was a twelve-year-old Wyandot girl who had the
misfortune to be visiting friends when the soldiers arrived and was
herded off with them. At Mansfield, their first stop, her father—
Toby, well-regarded among the locals—came to see her, and the
two took advantage of a lapse in the guards' attention to slip out
of the temporary camp where the Indians were being held. A mile
outside of town, though, they were discovered by two soldiers who
fired upon them, then raced back to camp to tell Colonel Kratzer

of the escape. Unharmed, the daughter made it through the woods and back to her Wyandot village, but Toby had been hit and lay nearly dead in a creek when the soldiers returned with a search party. That's when the horror began.

One of the soldiers, who had recently lost a brother in an Indian ambush, took Toby's own hatchet and buried it in the Indian's skull. Then the two men cut off Toby's head, scalped it, and stuck the head on a pole, where it remained for days. According to witnesses, the soldiers proceeded to fill Toby's scalp with whiskey and pass it between themselves and their comrades, drinking freely.

The almost inevitable revenge followed several days later when Levi Jones, a Mansfield trading-post merchant, was ambushed by Indians—shot, stabbed, and scalped—just outside the village, next to one of Chapman's nurseries. Two other locals, Wallace and Reed, went missing at the same time and were presumed murdered as well. (In fact, the two had simply wandered off and would wander back in again.) And with that panic set in once more.

What little local militia there was had gone with the Mount Vernon soldiers to escort the Greentown Delawares southwest across the state. A war party was roaming, with much to be riled about. There was also the continuing danger of a British and Indian force sweeping in from Lake Erie. Mansfield's few families could be gathered in the blockhouse on the village square, but farther south, all the towns and tiny settlements and isolated cabins clear to Mount Vernon, where more soldiers remained at the garrison, were essentially unprotected. The stage was set, in short, for John Chapman to become the Paul Revere of the frontier, and he didn't disappoint.

The story gets told in various ways, but A. J. Baughman caught the details and feel of just about all of them in his 1900 centennial history of Mansfield:

As an attack was considered imminent, a consultation was held and it was decided to send a messenger to Captain Douglas, at Mt. Vernon, for assistance. But who would undertake the hazardous journey? It was evening, and the rays of the sunset had faded away and the stars were beginning to shine in the darkening sky, and the trip . . . must be made in the night over a new cut road through a wilderness—through a forest infested with wild beasts and hostile Indians.

A volunteer was asked for and a tall, lank man said demurely: "I'll go." He was bareheaded, barefooted and was unarmed. His manner was meek and you had to look the second time into his clear, blue eyes to fully fathom the courage and determination shown in their depths. There was an expression in his countenance such as limners try to portray in their pictures of saints. It is scarcely necessary to state that the volunteer was "Johnny Appleseed" for many of you have heard your fathers tell how unostentatiously "Johnny" stood as "a watchman on the walls of Jezreel," to guard and protect the settlers from their savage foes.

One early settler told N. N. Hill years later that he could still recall Chapman's dramatic arrival at his own family's clearing in the woods. "Although I was but a child, I can remember as if it were but yesterday, the warning cry of Johnny Appleseed, as he stood before my father's log cabin door on that night. I remember the precise language, the clear, loud voice, the deliberate exclamations, and the fearful thrill it awoke in my bosom. 'Fly! Fly! For your lives! The Indians are murdering and scalping at Mansfield!' These were his words. My father sprang to the door, but the messenger was gone, and midnight silence reigned without."

Another settler recalled a more complex warning, and a more terrifying one. Chapman, he remembered, "visited every cabin and delivered this message: 'The Spirit of the Lord is upon me, and he hath anointed me to blow the trumpet in the wilderness, and sound an alarm in the forest; for, behold, the tribes of the heathen are round about your doors, a devouring flame followeth after them.'" He could feel even now, the man said, "the thrill that was caused by this prophetic announcement of the wild-looking herald of danger . . . on a moonlight midnight with his piercing voice."

Just about every version agrees that Chapman made the trip bareheaded and barefooted, and that he set off just at sunset, but by what means and in what time frame the trip was made are open to interpretation. Had there been a horse available for the purpose—and it's hard to believe there wasn't—surely Chapman would have jumped on it and set off on his mission that way, just as Paul Revere had, maybe even with a lantern to light his way. Historian A. Banning Norton has him doing just that. But most accounts by those with any actual proximity to the events in question insist not only that Chapman made the trip on foot but that he made it all the way to Mount Vernon before morning, and some accounts contend even that he made it to Mount Vernon and back to Mansfield again, troops following in his wake, before sunrise. And therein indeed lies the very stuff of myth, because, by happy coincidence, the distance between Mansfield and Mount Vernon is almost exactly twenty-six miles—the same distance as Philippides' famous fifth-century BC run from Marathon to Athens to announce a Greek victory over the Persians.

Olympic-quality marathoners at the peak of their training, running on prepared surfaces and wearing shoes made of space-age materials, can complete a twenty-six-mile run in a little over two hours. Could Chapman have covered the same distance in, say, twice that time—through darkened woods, veering this way and that to specific cabins? Perhaps. Could he have made the journey round-trip? Ultramarathoner Takahiro Sunada has run a hundred kilometers (roughly sixty miles) in just over six hours. Chapman didn't do that, but sunset to sunrise gave him maybe an eleven-hour window. Chapman was still shy of his thirty-eighth birthday, in excellent condition for long-range travel. By virtue of his own incessant meandering, he knew the way better than any person alive, and having warned everyone of the danger on the way down to Mount Vernon, he could have sped directly back, with the soldiers trailing him. So yes, this, too, is within the realm of the conceivable.

Still, the time stretches credulity. The distance is inherently suspicious. (Remember, too, that Philippides dropped dead in his tracks as soon as he had announced the Greek victory.) And Chapman's message, especially the long version, and the saintly demeanor with which he stepped forward to accept the task seem designed to serve mythopoeic ends more than historical ones. (Just try shouting out "The Spirit of the Lord is upon me etc." a hundred times or more without breaking stride.) Besides, in practical terms, his race to Mount Vernon and back didn't really do all that much good.

The Indians, still outraged, lay low until the Mansfield-area settlers drifted back from the blockhouse, then struck again. The first to die were Frederick Zeimer and his family, and a neighbor, Martin Ruffner, who had come to warn the Zeimers and been caught in front of their cabin when the Indians attacked. Zeimer had already angered the Indians by tying clapboards to the tails of their horses caught grazing in his field. Now, he, his wife, and his daughter, Kate, age sixteen or so, paid the price. Kate was the last to die, a tomahawk in her brain, according to the confession of the Indian who killed her and was later released with the understanding that he would disappear into the far, far west of the New World.

After that, the Indians came hunting for the one man who was probably as innocent of deceit (Chapman excepted) as anyone involved in the whole sorry episode: the minister who had persuaded the Indians to leave in the first place, James Copus. Copus, in fact, had feared revenge and brought a small contingent of soldiers home from the blockhouse with him, but after spending an undisturbed night in his barn, the soldiers dropped their guard in the morning and left their rifles leaning against the cabin wall while they went off to a nearby spring to wash up. That's when "45 painted savages" commenced their attack. Again, Wesley Copus, who watched his father die that day, picks up the story:

Two of the soldiers were caught, in running about eighty yards, and murdered on the spot; a third being fleet, distanced his pursuers, who, finding it impossible to overtake him, fired upon him; one ball passed through his bowels, and another through his foot. He ran about half a mile [where] he was found, about eight weeks afterward, his body resting against a tree, with his handkerchief stuffed in his bowels. . . .

As soon as the attack was made upon the soldiers at the spring, the firing commenced upon the cabin. Mr. Copus, on hearing the alarm, sprung from his bed, and, seizing his rifle, partially opened the door . . . when he received a fatal wound. A rifle ball passed through the center of his bosom, and, staggering backward, he fell across the table, exclaiming, "Soldiers, I am a dead man, but do not be discouraged; fight like men, and save yourselves and my family." He said no more; his affrighted wife and daughter helped him upon his bed, from which but a moment before he had arisen in health, but upon which he was now carried a dying man. He breathed his last about one hour afterward. . . .

The battle lasted from daylight till about ten o'clock a.m., when the savages, finding that they could not succeed in their undertaking, raised the retreating yell, and gathering up their dead and wounded—nine in number—retreated from the cabin, firing upon a flock of sheep, which, during that eventful morning, had huddled together upon the brow of the hill, looking down in strange bewilderment upon this scene of bloodshed. The poor affrighted animals tumbled down that hill one after the other, until they lay in one heap at the bottom.

As with so many Chapman/Appleseed stories, it's the final detail in this story that makes it read so true: the children who refused to make fun of this odd, odd man; the snuff habit; that sad, sad mound of dead sheep at the bottom of the hill. No wonder John Chapman disappeared into his Appleseed persona. The two were living so close together, at the outer edge of civilization.

❧

The compelling irony of John Chapman is that just as he was being propelled into myth, he was in many ways at his most intensely and recognizably human. The dozen years after his daring all-night race were spent buying, selling, leasing, planning, and business scheming. Chapman was flipping properties, extending his nurseries north into the Fire Lands, almost to Lake Erie itself, and west, beginning his migration toward Indiana. These were the years of near (or at least relative) domesticity, maybe the years of a broken heart if Henry Howe is right about the girl who got away in Perrysville, and certainly the time of his most successful proselytizing and most ardent church work.

A May 15, 1821, letter from Daniel Thunn to Margaret Bailey mentions that Chapman "proposed to make a Deed over to the New Church for a Quarter Section of Land and take payment in Books of the New Church." This was part of an abiding wish of the mostly self-educated Chapman: that his church might build a college on land he himself had arranged for. The following year, he was among thirty-nine Mansfield-area New Churchmen to endorse a petition seeking a license of ordination for Silas Ensign so that he might "preach the Gospel of Jesus in this place and the surrounding neighborhood." The number of signees, more than three dozen for a church that counted its growth often in single digits, suggests just how successful Chapman was in helping the New Church to grow in and around Mansfield: He had been the sole Swedenborg professor when Ensign, then a Methodist minister, arrived in town. The fact that Chapman was the very last of the thirty-nine to sign might also suggest how hard he could be to track down, even for good causes.

Multiple letters of the era sent back and forth between New Church members refer to Chapman as a frequent correspondent, especially in his desire for more of Swedenborg's writings to distribute among the cabins of the frontier. An April 16, 1821, letter to the Reverend John Clowes in England from William Schlatter, a leading light of the American branch of the church, refers to Chapman as "a singular man," but adds: "our friend Mr. Conly who was conversed with him in Ohio states him to be intelligent and says the great object of his life appears to be to promote the doctrines."

Clearly, the Plan was fully in effect and working as well as it ever would, or could. Chapman was Businessman, Nurseryman, Churchman—as Main Street as a barefoot man in tatters could ever be. But as the War of 1812 had already shown, there was something in John Chapman that couldn't resist courting the mythologist's hand, and in 1817, the New Church raised him halfway to heaven for it. On January 14 of that year—four months before the First General Convention of the New Jerusalem in the United States of America convened in Philadelphia—the Society for Printing, Publishing and Circulating the Writings of Emanuel Swedenborg, based in Manchester, England, issued a report on the church's progress in the New World that included this "curious anecdote":

> There is in the western country a very extraordinary missionary of the New Jerusalem. A man has appeared who seems to be almost independent of corporeal wants and sufferings. He goes barefooted, can sleep anywhere, in house or out of house, and live upon the coarsest and most scanty fare. He has actually thawed ice with his bare feet. He procures what books he can of the New Church Swedenborg, travels into the remote settlements, and lends them wherever he can find readers, and sometimes divides a book into two or three parts for more extensive distribution and usefulness. This man for years past has been in the employment of bringing into cultivation, in numberless places in the wilderness, small patches (two or three acres) of ground, and then sowing apple seeds and rearing nurseries.
>
> These become valuable as the settlements approximate, and the profits of the whole are intended for the purpose of enabling him to print all the writings of Emanuel Swedenborg, and distribute them through the western settlements of the United States.

The author of the report is unknown, but the Cincinnati preacher Adam Hurdus, a native of Manchester, is a likely suspect. Hurdus's hidden hand—or perhaps William Schlatter's—might also have been at work five years later, in 1822, when attendees at the Fifth General Convention, also in Philadelphia, heard a further report about this "extraordinary missionary's" work: "Having no family, and inured to hardships of every kind, his operations are unceasing. He is now employed in traversing the district between Detroit and the closer settlements of Ohio. What shall be the reward of such an individual, where, as we are told in holy writ, 'They that turn many to righteousness shall shine as the stars forever.'"

A year earlier, in the same letter that makes mention of Chapman's desire to trade land for books, Daniel Thunn refers to him as "the Appleseed man you certainly must have heard of." Eighteen months later, in a November 18, 1822, letter, a Reverend Holly of Abingdon, Virginia, writes of Chapman and Ohio that "they call him John Appleseed out there"—the first written mention of the name that would also be recorded as Appleseed John and would eventually settle into the familiar Johnny Appleseed.

Chapman's run through the night had revealed his mythic possibilities. The Manchester report had placed him almost in the spirit world with which Swedenborg himself was so familiar. (Chapman had "appeared" in the western country; he was all but incorporeal in his absence of wants and sufferings.) And now he had a name to go with his new identity. It remained only for the corporeal itself to disappear—for John Chapman to get out of the way of his own destiny.

10

THE LAST FRONTIER

~

John Chapman and Meriwether Lewis—the "Lewis" of Lewis and Clark, the famed explorers—were almost exact contemporaries, born thirty-nine days apart. (Lewis was the senior of the two.) William Clark, Lewis's partner, was older than both by a scant four years, and, superficially at least, there is much to link the three men. All were boys at the birth of the nation. All went west at roughly the same time—Lewis and Clark in 1803, Chapman probably seven years earlier. The three conquered the wilderness; befriended and were befriended by Native Americans; made their way by luck and skill and, yes, undaunted courage; and left their marks indelibly in the history of the Northwest. But, of course, these were two different Northwests, unfolding on completely different time scales.

Fly west over the Dakotas, Montana, Idaho, and across eastern Oregon and Washington, and it's still easy to imagine the land below you as a frontier wilderness. This is the setting for Lewis and Clark's great trek along the Missouri River, through the Rockies, and down the Columbia River to the Pacific Ocean. And from 35,000 feet, the human imprint remains today remarkably small.

Euro-American history accreted slowly in this part of the country. Washburn, North Dakota, where Lewis and Clark built Fort Mandan and spent the winter of 1804–1805, was nothing more than a few cabins as late as 1869. Great Falls, Montana, where the expedition had to portage eighteen miles around a series of five cascades, sat deserted for eight decades afterward. Astoria, at the mouth of the Columbia River, which the explorers reached in mid-November 1805, soon became an outpost of John Jacob Astor's fur-trading empire, but the city itself wasn't incorporated until 1876, the launch of an unfulfilled dream to create the crown jewel of the Northwest.

The history of what was once known as the Northwest Territory—John Chapman's world—was written at a different pace and scale, across different terrain. As we've seen, population pressures moving out of the east turned Indian hunting grounds into clearings, and clearings into villages and established towns in a matter of decades. Plentiful rivers made transportation easier. After the rugged trip across the Alleghenies of Pennsylvania, the hills and ridges and narrow valleys of eastern Ohio must have seemed almost welcoming.

When the Northwest Ordinance was enacted in 1787, the land it covered was defined mostly by forts: Fort Pitt, formerly known as Fort Duquesne and then just becoming Pittsburgh, at the territory's eastern portal; Fort Detroit, on land that the Indians, French, and British had all occupied in living memory; and Fort Dearborn, now Chicago, at the bottom of Lake Michigan. Fort Washington, later Cincinnati, was two years away from being built on the Territory's southern border. By the time of the Civil War, nearly seventy-five years later, the forts had become full-blown cities. Detroit's population stood at 46,000 in 1860. Pittsburgh, soon to boom as a Union armaments manufacturer, counted 50,000 residents, up from 1,565 at the start of the century; Chicago's population was nearly 110,000, a more than fourfold increase in ten years alone. Cincinnati, the last of the ring of forts to be established, topped them all. A village of 2,500 people in 1810, it had ballooned into American's seventh largest city fifty years later, with more than 161,000 residents.

For Johnny Appleseed, this relatively rapid fill-in of what had been a no-man's-land at the onset of his mythic ascension amounted to almost pure oxygen. Myths need people to grow; they require oral and written traditions to pass them on. People on deserted islands unknown and unnoticed by the world can accomplish superhuman tasks; they might even become legends in their own mind. But to make the leap to a public holding requires, by definition, public awareness.

For John Chapman, encroaching civilization was surely less of a blessing. His pure oxygen was the crease between advancing settlement and retreating wilderness, and by his early fifties, that crease and the landscape that accompanied it were becoming harder and harder to find.

For thirty years, Chapman's home had been the trailing western side of the Appalachians. Warren and Venango Counties in northwestern Pennsylvania, where he and his half brother Nathaniel first appeared on the frontier; the cider mills in the southwestern part of the state, along the Monongahela and Youghiogheny Rivers, where Chapman returned annually to replenish his seed supply; the watershed of the Muskingum River and its tributaries in eastern Ohio, where he established his nursery business and built himself a life and a widespread reputation are all of a topographic piece: rolling hills cut by rivers, creeks, and streams, with almost always a patch of bottom land—or more than a patch—just right for a man who liked to launch his nurseries in that rich silt. Even today, when Pennsylvania and Ohio are the sixth and seventh most populous American states, you can still drive the back roads of Appleseed Country and spot hundreds of locations that the real Appleseed, John Chapman, might once have eyed for his business or simply admired for the coming together of so many elements that inspired his work and mission. Indeed, if the boundaries of the eastern American states had been determined by natural features and not by land grants and other considerations, the western half of Pennsylvania and the eastern half of Ohio would be a single political entity, with its eastern border along the Susquehanna and Juniata Rivers; the Ohio River as its central highway; and a western border down the far side of the Allegheny escarpment, halfway between Newark and Columbus, Mount Vernon and Marion, Mansfield and Bucyrus.

John Chapman didn't discover this territory or lead the future into it, as Lewis and Clark led the way into the Pacific Northwest. He didn't blaze trails for later settlers to follow à la Daniel Boone. Unlike Davy Crockett—or the famous ballad version of Crockett—he wasn't "ahead of us all, meetin' the test" (although, to continue the lyrics, he might have been "followin' his legend into the West"). But Chapman's entire adult life had been spent here. He was of this land's essence, and the land was of his essence, and for three decades the match was near perfect. How much so gets captured sweetly in the 1873 reminiscences of E. Vandorn, one of two brothers who about 1819 were summoned by Chapman to help him raise a small log cabin on land he was then clearing southwest of Mansfield, near Lexington.

"I was to go where a man lived by the name of Harding," Vandorn recalled, "and then follow a line of blazed trees, marked for some four miles in the wilderness, to his camp." (The Harding in question was Amos, great-grandfather of President Warren G. Harding.)

> In the dusk of the evening we saw smoke curling up amongst the tree tops, and directly we saw Johnny standing close to a fire kindled by the side of a large log, an old tree which had been torn up by the roots.

I never shall forget how pleased he appeared to be when we came up to him in the wilderness, four miles from a living soul but Indians, among bears, wolves, catamounts, serpents, owls and porcupines, yet apparently content and happy. . . .

After sitting down and chatting for a while, Johnny poked in the ashes with a stick and dragged out some potatoes, saying, "This is the way I live in the wilderness."

One of the brothers then remarks, "Well, you appear to be as happy as a king." And Chapman replies, "Yes, I could not enjoy myself better anywhere—I can lay on my back, look up at the stars and it seems almost as though I can see the angels praising God, for he has made all things for good." And so, indeed, it must have seemed. Chapman had company when he wanted it, and solitude when he didn't. He could call on the strong-armed boys from the cabins he visited when a job was too big for him alone, spread the glorious truths revealed to Emanuel Swedenborg through torn-apart texts and via his own relentless testimony, and plant his apple seeds and sell the seedlings to newcomers for whom orchards were a source of food and drink, and a sign and promise of permanency. And then, as was bound to happen, this wonderfully harmonious balance between person, place, and a precise moment in history began to break down.

The river and creeks and streams that Chapman had followed into the Ohio interior began to play out, as did the terrain the rivers carved. The Licking, the Walhonding, the Tuscarawas, the Kokosing, the Mohican and its two forks—all the branches and fingers of the Muskingum system, Chapman's highways and by-ways—they all trace backward to their sources in the multicounty area where Chapman had been living since the very earliest years of the nineteenth century. Civilization had arrived along those waterways, with no small help from the man who had seedling and sermons waiting for settlers as they arrived. But now the logjam of factors that had paused westward advancement along that spine of central Ohio was breaking apart.

The 1817 Treaty of Maumee Rapids ran to twenty-one articles and had been attested to by the signatures (all *X*s) of no fewer than ninety-three Native American dignitaries from seven different tribes, but the practical effect was simple: The Greenville Treaty of twenty-two years earlier was dead and gone. New land was opening up for white settlement. The remaining tribes would soon be pushed farther back, all but out of the state except for scattered reservations. The Panic of 1819—the bursting of a speculative bubble that traced back to the War of 1812—slowed the inevitable. Land prices collapsed. Buyers disappeared. Unemployment reached stratospheric heights, as high as 75 percent in Philadelphia. But panics by definition are cyclical, and by the mid-1820s, the great east-to-west migration that would define American life for a century and a half to come was again up and running.

When Chapman first arrived in what would become Newark, Mount Vernon, and Mansfield, the nearby white population was generally measurable in the single digits. All of Licking County was thought to have only three white families in 1801, the likely date of Chapman's first tentative venture into the Ohio wilderness—including the Indian fighter John Larabee, who was living in a cabin built inside a huge hollowed-out sycamore tree. By 1830, the population of Ohio was booming: almost a million residents, ready to double over the next twenty years. Indiana, by contrast, counted a third as many people in a land area only one-seventh smaller than its neighbor to the east.

The bottom line is that if Chapman wanted to stay in the crease between wilderness and settlement where he had so long been, and where the Plan had worked so well, he had to move on, too.

And therein resided the problem and the irony. Chapman had led the way for the encroaching civilization—even helped feed the settlers—that now threatened to displace him. To his west, below the escarpment, the land flattens out into a featureless terrain that was often marshy and sometimes malarial before drainage ditches and retention ponds turned it into almost continuous farm acreage, all the way to the Indiana border and well beyond. To the northwest, in the watershed of Lake Erie, the land rolls more, but here, too, the terrain ultimately deflates, scoured by glaciers in the last great Ice Age.

For Chapman, the choice was essentially between past and future: Stay where he was, accept the reality that the American edge had arrived on his doorstep and was now moving beyond it, and deal with the consequences. Or uproot himself and get out in front of settlement once again. No great surprise, he chose the latter. This time, though, things were different.

❦

A six-foot obelisk monument in Mansfield's South Park reads: "In Memory of John Chapman, Best Known as Johnny Appleseed, Pioneer Apple Nurseryman of Richland County from 1810 to 1830." Robert Price sets the effective date of Chapman's departure from this part of central Ohio seven years earlier, citing county land records as evidence. Chapman was through by then with those ninety-nine-year leases on 160-acre tracts, with their crippling interest payments. On June 25, 1823, he purchased the first of a long string of smaller parcels—2.5 acres, in this instance, in Ashland County for forty dollars cash—that were clearly meant for nursery work and nothing more. Maybe, then, 1823, not 1830, is the valedictory date, but it seems best to split the difference between the two. Chapman might have made the psychological break with his "big-land" central Ohio schemes as

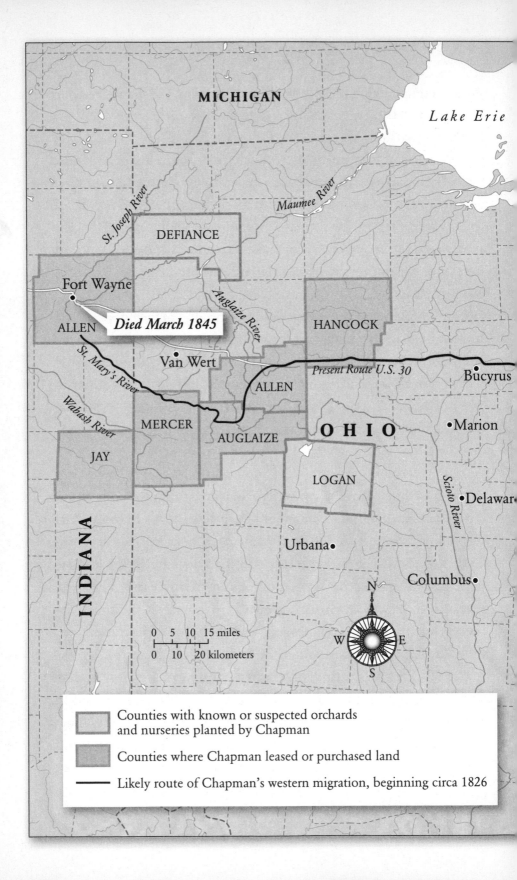

MICHIGAN

Lake Erie

Maumee River

St. Joseph River

DEFIANCE

Fort Wayne

Died March 1845

ALLEN

Auglaize River

HANCOCK

Van Wert

St. Mary's River

ALLEN

Bucyrus

Wabash River

MERCER

AUGLAIZE

Present Route U.S. 30

O H I O

•Marion

JAY

LOGAN

Scioto River

•Delaware

INDIANA

Urbana•

Columbus•

N

0   5   10   15 miles

0   10   20 kilometers

W   E

S

Counties with known or suspected orchards
and nurseries planted by Chapman

Counties where Chapman leased or purchased land

—— Likely route of Chapman's western migration, beginning circa 1826 early as 1823, as Price suggests, but physically, Chapman took another half decade to really give up on the land and places he had come to know so well.

The 1823 property was ultimately abandoned, but in 1825, Chapman picked up an additional fourteen acres in Wayne County, just east of Ashland, for sixty dollars. (The land was sold for a ten-dollar loss seven years later.) He added another half acre in Ashland County—leased for forty years for a payment of twenty apple trees—the next year, in 1826. And then the central Ohio stakes clearly did begin to loosen. April of 1828 found him leasing a new half acre—"where the said John doth plant an Apple Nursery"—halfway across the state in Allen County. The same month and for the same terms—forty-year leases for forty apple trees—he secured another half acre not far to the north, in what would become Auglaize County. The end of that busy month of April 1828, he pledged himself to pay a thousand apple trees over ten years for "a certain enclosed lot or piece of ground" of indeterminate size, "lying below the Little Branch below Shanesville between the Little Lane and the River," also in Allen County, hard on the Ohio-Indiana border. After that, beginning in 1834 and with only one small exception, every piece of land he ever put money down on was over the line in Indiana: just shy of two hundred acres, bought over four purchases, in Allen County, Indiana, home to Fort Wayne; and another seventy-four acres in the northeast corner of Jay County, thirty-plus miles south of Fort Wayne, on or near the Wabash River.

Thus, by degrees—and sometimes not such gradual ones—this quintessential hill-and-valley man, a spawn of the Alleghenies and his own imagination and determination, became something else: a flatlander, mostly; a Hoosier, a colloquialism that first appeared in print in 1832, just as John Chapman was settling into the Fort

Wayne area, and a word whose supposed meaning—an "ignorant rustic, a hillbilly or rube"—might on the surface seem to apply to Chapman but certainly does not in any deeper sense.

❦

Looked at one way, all this amounted to nothing more than a lateral transfer. What the Muskingum River system had been in the first decade of the nineteenth century—the foot- and boat-path that civilization followed into the interior of Ohio—the Wabash and Erie Canal, which began construction in 1832, was meant to be for Indiana, and as he had been in Ohio, Chapman was there waiting with his apple tree nurseries when the lead edge of settlement was expected to push through. ("Expected" is the key word here since the canal was inevitably delayed, plagued by engineering shortfalls, and soon overtaken by the railroad.)

As earlier pioneers had recalled first seeing Chapman floating down the Ohio or up the Muskingum in that odd catamaran of his own design, so later ones would have their first memories of him shaped by water and boats, seeds and apple trees. Brockman Bower of Putnam County, some fifty miles due east of Fort Wayne, remembered watching Chapman floating down the Blanchard River in a canoe loaded with apple trees meant for settlers along the Blanchard, the Auglaize, and the Maumee Rivers. John W. Dawson didn't arrive in Fort Wayne until 1838, at age eighteen, but he knew Chapman well during his last years and was certain that the old nurseryman had been in and around the city since at least the start of the 1830s and had arrived with considerable flourish.

"In 1830," Dawson wrote, "he was seen one autumn day, seated in a section of a hollow tree which he improvised for a boat, laden with apple seed fresh from the cider presses of a more eastern part of the country paddling up the Maumee river, and landing at Wayne's fort, at the foot of Main Street, Fort Wayne."

(Dawson, in fact, appears to be an unusually reliable source. Abraham Lincoln would later appoint him territorial governor of Utah. After that, Dawson returned to Fort Wayne as owner and editor of the local *Sentinel* newspaper.)

Substitute the pitch and roll of Richland County for the swampy reaches of Putnam County, turn the confluence of rivers that created Fort Wayne into the confluence of rivers that led settlers to Marietta or Mount Vernon, and it's tempting to think that Chapman was just repeating his own history—déjà vu all over again. Even the early historians in both venues tended to treat him the same. Echoing the Ohioan A. Banning Norton, Jay County, Indiana, historian M. W. Montgomery refers to Chapman as "an oddity called Johnny Appleseed," who once had been a fine businessman, but an accident had caused "a partial derangement of his mind." As Montgomery's account suggests, though, more than Chapman's map coordinates were changing. The stories about him were changing, too, and the stories in the end are just about all we have to go on if we are to know this enigmatic figure beyond the sum total of his travels, transactions, and business models.

❦

John Chapman turned sixty in September 1834. He was no longer running double marathons—if he ever had—to warn of imminent Indian attacks, no longer felling trees like a man possessed or happily sliding down the Allegheny River on an ice floe. He still walked more in a year than many people walk in a lifetime, still lived more outdoors than in and in all kinds of weather, but the oral tradition that surrounds these later, western years is altered in degree and in kind from the tales of his youth and middle years.

The earliest recorded sighting of Chapman in western Ohio—
at Urbana, in 1826, just as he was turning fifty—has him doing
what might have seemed almost unthinkable a decade earlier:
contemplating legal action with regard to one of his nurseries.
Sometime earlier, Chapman had planted a nursery in surrounding
Champaign County, with the permission of the landowner. Now,
the farm had changed hands, and there was a question whether the
new owner would claim the trees as his own. Chapman took the
problem to the county's leading jurist, Colonel John H. James, for
advice.

"He did not seem very anxious about it," James later recalled,
"and continued walking to and fro as he talked, and at the same
time continued eating nuts."

Another subject, though, seems to have made Chapman considerably more restless. James had only recently married Abigail
Bailey, the youngest daughter of Francis Bailey of Philadelphia,
in many ways the fountainhead of the New Church in America.
Abbe and Chapman's connections were potentially multiple: John
Young had married one of the Barclay sisters, raised in Francis
Bailey's household. Another of the Barclay sisters, Hester, might
have hosted Chapman and his brother in Bedford, Pennsylvania,
on that initial trudge over the Alleghenies. Having established the
possibilities, James asked Chapman if he would like to visit with
Abbe, but Chapman, in James's words, "declined, referring to his
dress, that he was not fit, and he must yet go some miles on his
way."

Who could have imagined this carefree, rag-tag nomad being
so self-conscious in his youth? But the eccentricities of a young
man living at the raw edge of the wilderness are not always viewed
the same as the oddities of an aging man once the rawness has
started to wear off. Chapman continued to travel back and forth

across eastern Ohio until at least the late 1830s and quite possibly into the early part of the next decade. He was welcomed in many homes along the way, as he always had been, but on more than a few occasions, reservations crept in. According to one family tradition, the proprietor of a tavern on the Muskingum River at Lowell, Ohio, recorded in his diary that Chapman would arrive annually on his migrations back and forth to western Pennsylvania. The proprietor wrote that he would feed Chapman without charge, then point him to the barn for the night, so that his "wee beasties"—i.e., lice—would not contaminate the other guests. (The diary, unfortunately, has long been lost.)

"Maple Shade," the 1802 Putnam family mansion on the high bluffs of the Ohio near Belpre, was another common calling ground on his treks east and west. Chapman was loosely related to the Putnams, through his half siblings, but his welcome at Maple Shade seems to have been anything but warm. In an interview with West Virginia state historian Ray Swick, a Putnam descendant who wished to remain anonymous gave the following account, as it had passed down through a relative I'll identify only as "D."

"They had no use for him. D's father said that Johnny Appleseed was nothing but a bum—that all he did was come and sponge on people. He could come and stay and eat and eat and eat until you finally shoved him out and sent him on his merry way. . . . Whenever he was coming, D said his dad was really mad—didn't want him around."

According to this same Putnam descendant, Chapman was always put in what was known as the Peddler's Room—a second-floor bedroom with a restricted entrance and no access to the rest of the house, for guests or presumably the vermin that came in with them. (For symmetry, Maple Shade—minus the 1818 wing that contained the Peddler's Room—was moved in 1986 to

Blennerhassett Island, where John Chapman might or might not have planted an orchard while the estate owner and Aaron Burr plotted treason inside.)

Even his own family was wary of Chapman's hygiene. He seems to have dropped in on his half brother Nathaniel back in the Duck Creek area only infrequently at best, but even on those relatively rare occasions, Nathaniel's wife, Amorrillah, is said to have insisted he bathe thoroughly in the creek and wash his clothes before she would allow him in the house.

❦

In his youthful years, Chapman had amused young boys by sticking pins into those deeply callused feet and treated young girls with tiny gifts of this and that, including an amber water flask still on display at the History Center in Fort Wayne. Now, in his wintry season, Chapman seems to have been far more inclined to take children on his knee, especially the girls, and bounce them there while he told stories of olden days. Rosella Rice had a clear memory of Chapman babbling happily to a baby he was holding. Eliza Rudisill, the daughter of a celebrated Lutheran minister in Fort Wayne, recalled sitting in Chapman's lap, listening to his "tall tales" of Indians and the frontier.

With what seems to have been great regularity, this doting grandfather-like figure was asked why he had never taken a wife and had children of his own. The stories were always out there: He had been unlucky in love back in New England, or unsuccessful in Perrysville. He had taken an acute interest in two girls and sought to have them educated as his protégés and perhaps even a later wife, only, in one case, to have the parents reject his offer and, in the other, to become enraged when he found the girl, now grown to age fifteen, holding hands with a boy her own age.

David Ayers claimed to have known Chapman for a good fifteen years, from his own teens in the early 1820s into the late 1830s. After watching the much older man doting on his six-year-old sister, Ayers recalled, "I asked him why he had no wife. He said he would not marry in this world, but would have a pure wife in heaven." To a greater or lesser degree—one spouse sometimes in the afterlife, sometimes two—that always seems to have been Chapman's response: Either on his own or through Swedenborg's eyes, Chapman had visited the spirit world and knew what wonders awaited him there if he only continued to live properly and think right in his physical manifestation.

Indeed, in this closing act of his life, the New Church and Swedenborg's writings were clearly much with John Chapman. In 1972, Bill Cook of Glendale, Ohio, a suburb of Cincinnati, set down on paper memories that had been passed down from his grandfather, John Henry Cook. The older Cook had been a young man, traveling as an aide to his businessman-father, when he first encountered Chapman distributing New Church tracts that he had obtained through John Young. Chapman "carried these tracts in his hat," according to Cook's grandfather. "He wore a pyramid of three hats. The first was only a brim. Next came his cooking pot. Surmounting all was a hat with a crown. The sum total was, if extremely odd, rather ingenious. It enabled him to carry not only his kettle but his treasure of sacred literature, sandwiched between the pot and the crown of the uppermost hat. The books were kept dry and his hands were left free to deal with seed bags and tools."

"He wore a pyramid of three hats. The first was only a brim. Next came his cooking pot. Surmounting all was a hat with a crown."

Bill Cook writes that whenever his grandfather found himself headed in the same direction as Johnny Appleseed, he would invite the old man to travel along, providing him with food and lodging along the way. Many thought Johnny addled by then, if not demented, but John Henry Cook "believed him to be intelligent and full of pleasant story and good advice." In 1844, in what proved to be their last meeting, the two men, young and old, traveled north from Cincinnati together to what is now

Glendale, stopping at a little chapel known as the Pentecost in the Back Woods that had been raised on a camp-meeting ground and was soon to be abandoned. Inside, John Henry Cook took one end of a pew while Johnny settled comfortably at the other end, "as if he were quite used to sitting there." Bill Cook recalled his grandfather's telling him "how the humble old man's soul rose and stretched its wings as he felt secure and joyful. His gentle, clear voice singing Psalms."

The story continues exaggerated, even down to its final details. Not only is John Henry Cook so moved by Chapman's reverence that he converts to the doctrines of the New Church, but he also rescues and restores the pew he and Chapman last sat on, and today—now reverently known as the "Appleseed Pew"—it can be seen in the foyer of the Glendale New Church, on the site of that old meeting ground.

Such anecdotes, in fact, are plentiful over the broad sweep of John Chapman's frontier life and are almost predictable. Chapman both preached his news right fresh from heaven and lived it every day, and the personal example he set was a powerful draw for a theology that otherwise required an almost academic submersion to fully grasp. Here, too, though, something new is at work in these final years: a doctrinal rigidity, a certain peevishness. Chapman *knew* the path to heaven, he knew which wagon was going that way, and as he aged, he became less and less tolerant of those who wouldn't climb aboard.

Some of this surfaced as early as 1819, in Chapman's mid-forties, when he was spending the night in the cabin of a Quaker named Henry Roberts, near Mount Vernon. The two had had a cordial relationship for many years, but this time Chapman noticed that Roberts was reading Hosea Ballou's *Treatise on Atonement,* one of the foundation books of the Universalist Church movement, by a man often referred to as the father of American Universalism. Chapman soon took up the treatise and should have found much to admire in it. How could he help but respect an author who would write, "Preaching is to much avail, but practice is far more effective. A godly life is the strongest argument you can offer the skeptic." That's Chapman's life in neat summation. But finally, it seems, Chapman couldn't bear Ballou's and the Universalist movement's broader argument that in Christ's crucifixion and atonement all mankind is saved, and all, whatever the sins or virtues of their earthly lives, will find perfect joy in the life to come. According to A. Banning Norton, Chapman threw down the book in disgust at this point. He hadn't denied himself the pleasures of children or the joys of the flesh in this world for *that*!

David Ayers, who knew Chapman when he was in his fifties and beyond, would later write that despite Chapman's religious enthusiasm, people "paid little attention to the New Church . . . doctrine, it was not orthodox, neither popular, and old Johnny was ragged."

Ragged, and in some accounts almost sad. In 1839, in his mid-sixties, Chapman stopped at the Van Wert County, Ohio, home of Alexander McCoy to ask for a piece of ground where he could start one of his nurseries. McCoy refused him—he had just arrived in the county, near the Indiana line, and as yet had no cleared land to offer—but according to a history of the county, Chapman lingered on nonetheless. "He stood near the fire, where they were burning brush, and seemed to hate to leave the warmth. He was thinly clothed, his pantaloons were much too short and he wore on old pair of shoes without stockings." (Another settler in the area did give him a plot, the history goes on to record, and an orchard grown from the seedlings went on to produce many apples "equal to the best grafted fruit.")

Four years later, by now almost seventy, Chapman surfaces grumpily in an early history of Defiance County in the northwest corner of Ohio. "He was often in this neighborhood, intent on planting apple trees but always harmless and lonely," the anonymous historian recounts. "Johnny Appleseed attended a camp meeting at the farm now owned by Arrowsmith & Ridenour, in 1843. . . . He frequently rebuked the young men for their levity and appeared much displeased if they were not attentive hearers."

❧

Even Chapman's beloved New Church seems to have distanced itself from him during the last decades of his life. In that report to the First General Convention in 1817, Chapman had been "a very extraordinary missionary of the New Jerusalem . . . almost independent of corporeal wants and sufferings." Five years later, at the Fifth General Convention, the story continued: "Having no family, and inured to hardships of every kind, his operations are unceasing." And then . . . Chapman basically is dropped from Church annals until 1847, when an obituary, two years late in arriving, proclaims him "probably the most romantic figure in New Church History."

What happened in between can perhaps be gleaned from the voluminous correspondence of one of the Church's early Philadelphia stalwarts, William Schlatter. In May 1817, Schlatter writes an acquaintance that he has sent "some books to Mr. Chapman" and wonders if his correspondent knows of Chapman and whether the books have been received. Three years later, on March 20, 1820— with his own finances almost ruined by the Panic of 1819— Schlatter writes directly to Chapman, in response to Chapman's correspondence of a month earlier.

I refer you to my last letter, dated 20th Feb. in reply to your inquiry about the Book in which I informed you the society had it not in their power to [enter] into the arrangement you desired, say to barter books for land at fair price, and also that I wanted [you] to answer me. I referred you to our friends Wright and Marcus Smith of Cincinnati who have lately published some of Emanuel Swedenborg's works and might find it [possible] to exchange some for land. I informed you our Book society were indebted to the English society for the books imported, and that we could not on that account barter them but only sell for cash. I hope you will receive that letter. I directed it [to] Richland County, Ohio, it was the only direction I had.

The same exasperation—What happened to the response I sent earlier? How can I get in touch with you?—is present later in the letter as well, when Schlatter moves on to Chapman's request to have Silas Ensign, the Mansfield cleric, licensed as a New Church preacher. "We beg leave to point out the regular mode of application, which no doubt your society of readers will cheerfully comply with . . . ," Schlatter responds. "It is all important, to have some regular order in those matters. . . . This has been the uniform mode pursued with other societies and I make no doubt you will see the propriety of continuing the rule" (although it's hard, in fact, *not* to hear some doubt in Schlatter's own words). Two years later, in November 1822, Schlatter takes up Chapman again, complaining in a letter to Silas Ensign that "I have written him three if not four letters since I have had a line from him. I wish to know if he received my letters and the last books I sent." And with that Chapman disappears from Schlatter's correspondence as surely as he disappeared from the New Church annals generally until two years after his death.

Why? The reason might be as simple as compounded exas-peration. Communicating with an insistent frontier correspondent who only episodically had any sort of fixed address had to be chal-lenging. Or Chapman's general disappearance from New Church official records might have had to do with internal struggles within the Church itself. In an undated "Letter to the Receivers of the Heavenly Doctrines on the Want of Union" that appears to have been written sometime in the 1840s, Otis Clapp runs through a laundry list of issues dividing liberal and conservative forces within the New Church:

- New "Rules of Order" for church Conventions, adopted in 1838, that ran to "four chapters, fourteen articles, and sixty-two sections." According to Clapp, the new rules had led some to fear "that an attempt was making to convert the Convention into an ecclesiastical court."

- Questions about who could initiate new "Societies" and ad-minister the Holy Supper. Clapp had led an effort in the very early 1840s to allow missionaries to do this work in areas where officially appointed clergy were few and far between—most of North America, in fact, since as of 1841 the Church counted only twenty-seven ordained ministers in just four states. That effort, Clapp tells us, died the way many initiatives do in bu-reaucracies: in committee, slowly over two years.

- Questions, too, about whether "old church baptism" was valid now that Swedenborg and the church founded on his teachings had led the way into the New Dispensation of Christianity. (The finding of the Church's 1839 Convention: Old church baptisms have "no efficacy whatsoever, because the Lord has left that Church.")

Wherever one might ultimately come down on these issues, they wouldn't seem to leave much room for a wilderness prophet of known crackpot tendencies, which suggests another reason for Chapman's prolonged disappearance from the New Church record: embarrassment. After all, this was an organization that strove not just for orderly procedures but for respectability—a church with blue-blood Philadelphia roots, constructed on the writings of one of the acknowledged great minds of the eighteenth century—and its leading western proponent was a half (and sometimes more than half) naked man who appears to have talked incessantly about the spirit world and slept in hollow logs whenever he could.

Oddly enough, that very spirit world is what might have caused church elders their greatest consternation. Swedenborg freely acknowledged his own travels in the land of the dead and reported back on his findings at prodigious length, but his followers erected a firewall between their founder's spirit travel and the spiritualism—mediums, contacting the dead, rappings, etc.—that became so popular in the 1840s and beyond, and that frequently involved references back to the Swedish spirit-world traveler. In an 1847 bestseller, Andrew Jackson Davis, a Poughkeepsie, New York, shoemaker's apprentice, talked of his conversation with the spirit of Swedenborg himself. The next year, the Fox sisters, also from upstate New York and avid Swedenborgian readers, launched their international career as mediums. By then, though, the church founded on Swedenborg's revelations had already slammed that door closed. In September 1845, only six months after John Chapman's death, *New Jerusalem Magazine* issued what amounted almost to a New Church encyclical on what it called "open intercourse with the spirit world."

There was no risk in Swedenborg's entering the spirit world and communicating with angels because his own interior had been "opened by divine truths *even to the Lord*, for into those truths the

Lord flows in with man, and when the Lord, heaven also flows in," as Swedenborg himself wrote in *Heaven and Hell*. To those, though, who were in a less elevated state and less far advanced in what Swedenborg termed the "regenerate life," the danger was great, the article warns:

> No one can hold "rational intercourse with the angels, until the life of hell is destroyed and the life of heaven implanted; and this we are told cannot be done suddenly, by which we are to understand, from what is taught in many other passages, that it is a long, gradual, and progressive work; that it cannot be accomplished in a day, or a year, or a few years, but requires many years"—so many, indeed, that Swedenborg himself did not have his spiritual senses opened "until he was fifty-seven years of age."

Was that what John Chapman was doing out at his wilderness encampments and throughout much of his life of relentless self-denial? Opening his interior to divine truths? Trying to communicate with angels as his master and guru had? Is this what scared off his chroniclers? Maybe Chapman was the New Church's own Wild Child. Perhaps all that primitivism—the nuts, the berries, the all-but-loincloths, those hollow-log beds—was Chapman's attempt to recapture in his own life what Swedenborg referred to as "the men of the most Ancient Church," the ones who "had the knowledge of true faith by revelations for they spoke with the Lord and with angels, and were also instructed by visions and dreams, which were most delightful and paradisiacal to them."

Even the Church's own obituary for its most ardent evangelist captures some of this ambiguity. Chapman is described as "a picturesque, eccentric philanthropist, of whom a thousand tales, amusing, pathetic and inspiring, are still being told." Who can say what made a group once so eager to claim its frontier evangelist go antsy? All that can be shown with any certainty is that as John Chapman he essentially dropped off the New Church radar screen after a grand opening splash, while as Johnny Appleseed, he continues to flourish as a Church poster boy and icon more than a century and a half after his death. But with Chapman/Appleseed, that's an old story.

11.

FINAL RITES

T he John Chapman who died in William Worth's cabin
near the St. Joseph River in March 1845 is an absolute
bundle of queerness and competing claims. Maybe he
died on the eleventh of March, 1845, as some court papers indicate, or on the eighteenth, as the then weekly *Fort Wayne Sentinel*
suggested in its edition of March 22, 1845, and as the later Fort
Wayne newspaper owner and editor John Dawson also contends.
The court papers included notice that the Worth family, which
charged a small boarding fee, had levied the Chapman estate for
March 10, but not after that, a clear suggestion that he had left
this world the next day. For its part, the newspaper reported that
Chapman had died "Tuesday last"—March 18, a date that meshes
well with both the supposed circumstances that brought on Chapman's death and the detailed weather entries kept by an amateur
local meteorologist, Rapin Andrews. For the seventeenth, Andrews recorded in his diary: "Cloudy. Snow showers." The next day,
as Chapman perhaps lay dying or was already dead, the temperature plunged from twenty-nine at noon to nineteen in the evening.

Yet another document—a claim against Chapman's estate
submitted by Richard Worth, William's son, for care and funeral
expenses—seems to set the death date a day earlier, on the seventeenth.

Expence of sickness ten dollars
Expence for laying him out three dollars forty four cts
Expence of coffin to Samuel Flutter Six Dolar
March the 17, 1845

Richard Worth would later recall Chapman's going quickly—"passing to the spirit land"—soon after taking sick. Perhaps he did take ill on the tenth and died on the eleventh, and it took Richard another six days to submit his claim. Or maybe Richard got the date wrong, or predated the claim, for now-mysterious reasons. John Dawson had Chapman's illness lasting about two weeks—a prolonged period that fits with no other known theory and contradicts the *Fort Wayne Sentinel* obituary, which reported that "[Chapman's] death was quite sudden. We saw him in our streets only a day or two previous."

In a pair of articles that appeared in the *Fort Wayne Sentinel* on October 21 and 23, 1871, Dawson states as "indisputable facts" that Chapman was buried "in a beautiful natural mound at the family burying ground set apart by David Archer . . . which may be seen by the passer up the towing path of the Feeder [Canal, to the western bank of the St. Joseph River]. At the east side of this mound, near its foot, Johnny Appleseed was buried."

Seventy years later, Fort Wayne attorney H. A. S. Levering, representing opposing views, mounted a seemingly credible argument that Dawson had the burial spot all wrong. Chapman, Levering contended, had died and been laid in the ground on the east side of the St. Joseph, on land known as the Roebuck Farm. William Worth proved a hard person to pin down. He had never owned the cabin in which Chapman presumably died. Rather he seems to have appropriated an Indian cabin abandoned about 1821 when the Delawares were pushed still farther west, this time beyond the

Missouri River. The Worth clan generally was another matter, and an even more confusing one.

Various Worths, Levering showed, had then lived on both sides of the river. Levering even produced a key (if dead) witness, who had been shown the burial location by Christian Parker, who added "I should ought to know where he was buried because I buried him." Unfortunately for the Roebuck Farm proponents, the notarized testimony of another prize witness, Eben Miles Chapman, alleged grandson of John Chapman's brother Andrew, fell apart when it was learned that while Chapman had many half brothers, he had none by that name.

Levering, in any event, was effectively beating a dead horse. In 1916, almost a quarter century earlier, the Indiana Horticultural Society picked a spot near the top of the knoll that Dawson had fingered, surrounded it with a low iron fence, declared it to be Chapman/Appleseed's burial site, and installed a plaque that reads:

JOHN CHAPMAN

JOHNNY APPLESEED

DIED 1845

Nineteen years later, the local Optimist Club added to the enclosure an inscribed granite boulder brought from a tract along the Maumee River where Chapman had been growing fifteen thousand apple tree seedlings at the time of his death. That marker reverses the names ("Johnny Appleseed"/John Chapman) and adds "He lived for others," his dates (1774–1845), and depictions of an apple and an open "Holy Bible." Still later, in September 1965, the Men's Garden Clubs of America in conjunction with the Johnny Appleseed National Memorial Foundation added further gravesite improvements and yet another plaque, which reads, "In fond memory of John Chapman, endearingly known as Johnny Appleseed." Being thrice memorialized, though, does not necessarily make the site right. Like the man and the details of his death, Chapman's grave is at best an approximation.

❦

His *Fort Wayne Sentinel* obituary paints a predictably singular and saintly portrait of John Chapman, while also noting that he was "better known by the name of Johnny Appleseed." (The "Johnny," in fact, seems to have come into common usage only in the very last years of his life. As late as 1840, when he bought a pocketknife at a Fort Wayne trading firm, the purchase was entered under "John Appleseed.") Chapman, the obituary informs, was easily recognizable by

> the eccentricity and the strange garb he usually wore. . . . He is supposed to have owned considerable property, yet he denied himself almost the common necessities of life—not so much perhaps from avarice as from his peculiar notions on religious subjects. He was a follower of Swedenbourgh [*sic*], and devoutly believed that the more he endured in this world the less he would have to suffer and the greater would be his happiness hereafter—he submitted to every privation with cheerfulness and content, believing that by so doing he was securing snug quarters hereafter. In the most inclement weather he might be seen barefooted and almost naked, except when by chance he picked up articles of old clothing. . . .

As noted earlier, the details of Chapman's own history are scant and frequently wrong when they are mentioned—he was not a native of Pennsylvania; he had not lived for some years past in the Cleveland area; he was halfway through his seventieth year, not over eighty—but the space given to the obituary, almost three hundred words, seems generous, and the writing lively. Taken in isolation, in fact, this feels like star treatment—as if the editors had rolled out an extra arsenal of prose highlights to celebrate the life of this odd man who dwelt among them. The fact is, though, that the newspaper's obituary writer (or writers) employed a lively style whoever the subject and appeared to find saintliness in one and all.

The next week, for example, in an obituary almost a third longer than Chapman's, the *Sentinel* noted the passing of John Edsall, age thirty-seven, whose death also was very sudden—"a severe and violent constipation of the bowels, which in a few hours terminated his existence, in spite of all the efforts of his physician, who attended him . . . with more than a brother's care"—and whose life held similar intimations of godliness. Despite being nearly crippled by rheumatism in his youth, Edsall had prospered as a Fort Wayne tailor, selflessly helped to raise and educate five siblings after the death of his mother, and been held in the highest esteem by his fellow citizens. "We never witnessed a larger attendance at a funeral; the Presbyterian church was crowded with citizens of all ranks and classes. . . ."

In that same March 29, 1845, edition—in a short front-page feature on the New York State Lunatic Asylum, at Utica—the *Sentinel*'s editors also seem to be suggesting that an excess of religious fervor such as Chapman often exhibited is not always to be divinely hoped for. Since its opening in 1843, 550 patients have been admitted to the New York asylum, the article recounts, and 291 since released as cured (185), improved (61), unimproved (22), or dead (23). Of the 259 remaining patients, most are said to have become insane from "fanatical excitement," and of those, the greatest number (77) seem to be suffering from perhaps incurable "religious anxiety."

John Chapman might have been insane, or demented, or fanatical, and he was certainly religious in the extreme, but he never appears to have suffered from religious anxiety, curable or otherwise. Still, the unavoidable truth is that, even by his own standards, Chapman was in a sorry state at the end of his life. More than twenty-five years after the fact, the same Samuel Flutter (also spelled "Fletter") who had dressed Chapman for burial and built his coffin would describe his final wardrobe as "the waists of four pairs of pants. These were cut off at the forks, ripped up at the sides and the fronts thrown away, saving the waistband attached to the hinder part. These hinder parts were buttoned around him, lapping like shingles so as to cover the whole lower part of his body." Overtop it all, next to Chapman's skin, was a coarse coffee sack, Flutter went on, with holes cut out for the arms and head, and "what was once pantaloons."

No wonder A. C. Comparet, who was still a boy in 1845, remembered how, whenever Chapman returned anew to Fort Wayne, "our parents would say that he would have us out of town as a scare." "A scare" at the very least—Chapman must have been a terrifying site on first encounter, and Fort Wayne was no longer a raw frontier outpost. The Wabash and Erie Canal finally had business booming. By 1845, the city was closing in on three thousand residents, and growing by a hundred new houses annually. Nor did Chapman's peculiar attire leave him particularly well prepared for the fickle late-winter weather of eastern Indiana or for the wave of illness that seems to have surrounded his own death.

"There has been much sickness in this neighborhood for a few weeks past, causing the death of some of our best citizens," the *Fort Wayne Sentinel* noted a week after Chapman's obit appeared. Some victims had been carried away by something known as "Bilious Typhoid Pneumonia." Others, like Chapman, had succumbed to the winter, or cold, plague: "It commences with a chill, runs its course in a short time, assumes a typhus form and terminates in death. It requires energetic treatment; copious blood-letting, strong hot brandy toddy, plasters to the stomach and feet and hands, have been successfully tried. Salts as a cathartic, and followed by quinine, have been useful"—none of which seem to have been used on John Chapman, but why employ extraordinary measures of any sort in this instance? By every account, this was a death Chapman neither feared nor saw any reason to run from. Indeed, in Swedenborgian terms, it wasn't even a death as we generally conceive that word but a transition from the physical to the spiritual world that Chapman had been longing and preparing for virtually all of his adult years.

❦

What we do know for certain about the end of John Chapman's life is what he died in possession of, as recorded at probate court: a gray mare appraised at $17.50; two thousand apple trees at a nursery in Jay County on the Wabash River, valued at two cents per tree; the fifteen thousand apple trees at an Allen County nursery, along the Maumee, appraised at three cents per; two quarter sections of land in Allen County; other Allen County tracts of 5 acres, 18.7 acres, 35 acres, 42.11 acres, and 74.04 acres; land in Jay County valued at $222. On paper, it rounds out to a nice estate. In practice, the largest and smallest parcels—the two quarter sections, and the five-acre holding—as well as the thirty-five-acre piece all were eventually sold for back taxes on the property: $13.17 in all, less than the combined cost of Chapman's coffin, his burial preparations, and the doctor who looked in on the dying man in his final hours. By December 1855, when the estate administrator submitted his final report, everything else that comprised John Chapman's worldly wealth had been sold off for $409, a little more than $9,300 in contemporary dollars, nothing to be sneezed at, but by then, too, claims on the estate had gobbled up every bit of it because—for all his many virtues—Chapman seems to have met very few of his personal financial obligations during at least the last half decade of his life.

Joseph Hill of Adams County, Indiana—which Chapman often passed through in his regular commute between Allen and Jay Counties—claimed to have provided board for the aging nursery-man for a total of fifty-three weeks between 1837 and his death, at an average cost of a little less than $2 per week: $104 in all, all past due. William Worth, who was sheltering Chapman at the time of his death, submitted his own bill for "Bording five weeks since the year 1840," for a total of $8.75. Perhaps Chapman thought these were all charity boardings, or friendship ones, and the bills never appeared until once he was gone, but it should be noted that the only class of people David Ayers could ever remember Chapman railing against were landlords.

The largest of Chapman's creditors, by far, was nearly his own flesh and blood: William Broom, Persis's husband and either Chapman's right-hand man for much of his time in Indiana or—witness the probate-court claims—his under- or unpaid serf. Chapman was in his grave (wherever it might have been) less than three weeks before Broom came forward to claim that he was owed $140 for clearing and fencing 11¾ acres "on the lands of John Chapman Deceased" and another $15 for his work to date on "building one log house," where Chapman might have intended to live out his final years. In the end, Broom's claims consumed nearly 40 percent of the total Chapman estate and helped reduce the balance on the probate books to zero.

❦

Much the same could be said, at least metaphorically, of the effect time has worked on the account books of John Chapman's physical presence on this earth. Wisps can be found here and there, tantalizing hints—a name in a ledger book, an amber flask connected by family lore, the GPS coordinates of places that might once have woven themselves somehow into Chapman's life story. But as Shelley wrote of Ozymandias and those famous "vast and trunkless legs of stone" in the desert, almost nothing of John Chapman beside remains.

The white frame house at the northwest corner of Second and Main Streets in Greensburg, Pennsylvania, where John Young quite possibly introduced Chapman to New Church doctrines, was most recently a four-story bank clad in cheap metal and now sits vacant. The site of Young's "summer house," all of a mile away and another strong candidate for where Chapman first met Swedenborg, is today a part of Seton Hill University.

Near Dexter City, Ohio, a seven-foot monument built of stones sent from every state in the union is dedicated "In Memory of John Chapman, Famous 'Johnny Appleseed' . . . Without a Hope of Recompense, Without a Thought of Pride, John Chapman Planted Apples Trees, and Preached, and Lived, and Died." The Duck Creek settlement where his father and stepmother moved in 1805 was nearby. Somewhere up the hill behind the monument is a cemetery where members of Chapman's family might be buried. To reach the monument, you can drive Route 821 some eighteen winding miles north of Marietta, crisscrossing back and forth across Duck Creek much as the Chapman-Cooleys might have done on foot more than two centuries earlier. Or you can follow Interstate 77, which connects Marietta and Cleveland. Take the Dexter City exit and head north at the bottom of the exit ramp, across from Adultmart, a sprawling megastore for pornographic books and videos.

In Mount Vernon, the two prime lots that Chapman bought back when the city was mostly someone's vision are the home of Knerr Tire, Inc. His small orchard to the west and the millrace that helped define it were first partially obliterated when the Army Corps of Engineers slightly changed the course of the Kokosing River; then what survived became part of a railroad bed and later the urban street grid. The larger orchard to the east is covered by apartment buildings and a Salvation Army Center for Worship and Service. Twenty-six miles due north in Mansfield, the blockhouse where settlers took refuge while Chapman ran for help and in warning has been moved from the center of the original city to a tranquil treed spot known as South Park and is now used as a Boy Scout meeting hall.

Southeast down Route 39 on the road to Perrysville, an Ohio Historical Marker denotes the site of the Delaware Indian village known as Greentown. "John Chapman (Johnny Appleseed) had an amicable relationship with the Delaware," the sign informs us, "owned land throughout the Black Fork Valley, and was known to have visited Greentown on his travels throughout Ohio." No mention of the Greentown torching that launched the cascade of events that led to Chapman's race to Mount Vernon. Four miles farther down the road is Perrysville itself, where Chapman seems to have fallen in love and been spurned. Signs at either end of the pleasant, one-stoplight town note that it is the "Home of Craig Weber Welterweight Champ."

Of the trek from this land west to Indiana, there is really nothing but guesswork. Robert Price speculates that Chapman followed a "land bridge," a geological hump that runs from Lake Erie southwest toward Fort Wayne. Chapman's land and nursery dealings and the occasional sightings of him in western Ohio might suggest a more direct route west from Mansfield, roughly along the line of current U.S. 30. Either route converges eventually on Chapman's last act in the Fort Wayne area and his final resting place, that still slightly disputed knoll in Johnny Appleseed Park.

When I visited the site on a mid-April afternoon, the apple

trees that surround the enclosure had just come into bloom, a beautiful and fitting tribute from nature itself, and just about the same time they had come into bloom in 1845, according to the diaries of Rapin Andrews. A nearby sign installed by an organization called American Forests—"People Caring for Forests and Trees Since 1875"—makes the claim that one of the trees is "the Direct Descendant of the Johnny Appleseed Apple Tree." Not far to one side, utility lines cut through the park on low, erector-set towers. On the other side, two hundred feet down the hill from the knoll, begins the vast macadam expanse of Fort Wayne's Memorial Coliseum parking lot. Meanwhile, 430 miles back east in Bedford, Pennsylvania, where the Chapman brothers might have begun their western lives, Hester Barclay—John Young's cousin-in-law and a bedrock of the early New Church—lies in lovely Historic Memorial Park under a tombstone whose inscription perfectly captures the essence of death as Swedenborg conceived it: "Here lies the body of Hester Barclay, who changed her mode of existence February 8th, 1796 . . ."

If we get to do in death what we so devoutly hope for and believe in during life, then surely this is what happened to John Chapman on that chilly March morning in 1845, just on the edge of old Fort Wayne: He changed his mode of existence. He transformed into spirit—and into the myth of Johnny Appleseed.

12

APPLESEED UNBOUND

~

No generation fully appreciates the change it has undergone. Events are too close at hand. Perspective is inevitably collapsed. Stirring epithets such as "the Greatest
Generation" or romantic ones like "the Jazz Age" are awarded
posthumously, the same as medals for firefighters dead in the line
of duty. To those who live through such times and moments, the
struggles and joys of daily existence often leave little room for
grander historical thoughts.

So it must have been with John Chapman. He had lived hard,
even by frontier standards, and remarkably long for a man who
paid so little heed to his own physical well-being. At late as 1845,
the year of his death, average life expectancy was still a little over
forty years, up only slightly from the time of the Revolution. Perhaps that was uniqueness enough for him. He had survived against
the odds and self-imposed circumstances, even prospered in his
very singular way, and, through Swedenborg, he was living in the
very first century of the New Dispensation, the opening moments
of a postmillennial world. What more could anyone ask or need to
know?

Yet whether John Chapman noticed it or not, the Western
world turned all but upside down during his lifetime. Chapman
had been born in a royal colony, came of age in what amounted to

a Third World country, and would die in a regional power soon to become a global economic force. Capitalist democracy—the dream of the New World—had become the defining aspiration of the Old World too, but not its only one. On February 22, 1845—less than a month before Chapman's death—Friedrich Engels wrote Karl Marx from Elberfeld, Germany, to report on the progress of agitation in the German confederation. "Every day brings us new supporters. . . . The most stupid, indolent, philistine people, hitherto without any interest in anything in the world, are beginning almost to rave about communism." Marx himself had recently been expelled from Paris and was resettling in Brussels. The first volume of *Das Kapital*, Marx's magnum opus, wouldn't be published until 1867, but already battle lines were being drawn that would help define the political future of much of the twentieth century.

Nowhere, though, did this tide of change crest higher than in America. Indeed, John Chapman's adult life wandering the trails and waterways of Ohio and Indiana parallels almost exactly the great age of expansion that Daniel Walker Howe writes of in *What Hath God Wrought: The Transformation of America, 1815–1848*. Canals (the Erie, the Wabash, and others), the steamboat, railroads, Samuel F. B. Morse's electric telegraph (the biblical "What hath God wrought" was the first message Morse sent) had all served to liberate Americans "from the tyranny of distance," as Howe puts it: "Neither Alexander the Great nor Benjamin Franklin [America's first postmaster-general] knew anything faster than a galloping horse."

As isolation disappeared and communication improved, manners and morals changed as well. Church attendance roughly doubled between the birth of the nation and the middle of the nineteenth century, while average alcohol consumption sank by as much as 70 percent. Cities grew. People were living closer together. Richard Hoe's 1843 invention of the steam-driven rotary printing press helped create common understandings and expectations. Nearly naked hermits—John Chapman's signature style for most of his life—were throwbacks to an earlier epoch of the national life.

As late as 1829, Frances Milton Trollope, that arch observer of New World customs and the mother of the celebrated English novelist Anthony Trollope, was still portraying Cincinnati as little more than an overbuilt hog abattoir:

> If I determined upon a walk up Main-street, the chances were
> five hundred to one against my reaching the shady side without
> brushing by a snout fresh dripping from the kennel; when we
> had screwed our courage to the enterprise of mounting a certain
> noble-looking sugar-loaf hill, that promised pure air and a fine
> view, we found the brook we had to cross, at its foot, red with
> the stream from a pig slaughter-house; while our noses, instead
> of meeting "the thyme that loves the green hill's breast," were
> greeted by odours that I will not describe, and which I heartily
> hope my readers cannot imagine; our feet, that on leaving the
> city had expected to press the flowery sod, literally got entangled
> in pigs' tails and jaw-bones: and thus the prettiest walk in the
> neighbourhood was interdicted forever.

Seven years later, William Holmes McGuffey began publishing his famous *Eclectic Reader*s in Cincinnati. The next year, two local artisans—candle maker William Procter and soap maker James Gamble—teamed up to form what would eventually become one of the world's leading industrial enterprises. By 1852, eight thousand steamboats were tying up annually at Cincinnati's docks, better than twenty-two a day, almost one every hour. The following year, the city could boast the nation's first all-paid fire department and the world's first steam-powered fire engines. By then, too, Cincinnati was one of the leading centers of the Abolitionist movement—home to Harriet Beecher Stowe until shortly before she began writing *Uncle Tom's Cabin*.

As with Cincinnati, so it was with much of the rest of the nation. In all sorts of ways, the place was bursting out of its seams. New president James K. Polk took up America's remarkable growth in a lengthy inaugural address delivered March 4, 1845, just two weeks (or maybe only one) before John Chapman's death. "But eighty years ago our population was confined on the west by the ridge of the Alleghanies," Polk told the assembled members of both houses of Congress. "Within that period—within the lifetime, I might say, of some of my hearers—our people, increasing to many millions, have filled the eastern valley of the Mississippi, adventurously ascended the Missouri to its headsprings, and are already engaged in establishing the blessings of self-government in valleys of which the rivers flow to the Pacific. The world beholds the peaceful triumphs of the industry of our emigrants." And then Polk got to perhaps the central point he wanted to make that day: "To us belongs the duty of protecting them adequately wherever they may be upon our soil. The jurisdiction of our laws and the benefits of our republican institutions should be extended over them in the distant regions which they have selected for their homes."

The Mexican War wouldn't erupt until two years later, but a fight was already in the offing. The outgoing Congress had approved annexation of Texas, a cause dear to the heart and political fortunes of Polk and his fellow Democrats, and sure to incite passions in America's southern neighbor. But while war was expected—some might even say sought—the new president was already thinking past Texas and its attendant political questions, such as slavery. "The title of numerous Indian tribes to vast tracts of country has been extinguished. . . . It is confidently believed that our system may be safely extended to the utmost bounds of our territorial limits," including the territory long in question that "lies beyond the Rocky Mountains." "Our title to the country of the Oregon is 'clear and unquestionable,'" Polk said, "and already are our people preparing to perfect that title by occupying it with their wives and children."

This, of course, was America's Manifest Destiny, and an 1845 map shows just how far the nation had come toward achieving it in a scant six decades. Florida, which entered the Union the day before Polk's address, was the twenty-seventh state so admitted. Once the edge of the frontier, Ohio (the seventeenth state) and then Indiana (nineteenth) sat comfortably midstream in this parade of growth. Iowa, Missouri, Arkansas, and Louisiana formed America's official westward border, but beyond that were territories and Indian districts straight to the Pacific set up like dominos and as sure to fall as rain in a hurricane. Texas was a large push, to be sure, but only one of many. To use Polk's haunting legal verb, any other claim—Mexican, British, Indian, Spanish, etc.—was certain to be *extinguished* as well.

As early as 1831, the German philosopher Georg Wilhelm Friedrich Hegel had written that America was "the land of the future . . . in the time to come, the center of world-historical importance will be revealed there." Already his prophecy was coming true. Fulfillment was everywhere. Transformation was the air the nation breathed, the water it drank, the food by which it sustained itself, and yet John Chapman seems not to have changed at all. He *was* the wilderness at the start of the nineteenth century; he was its after-echo by the time of his death, at almost mid-century. Perhaps that explains the hold Johnny Appleseed has so long exercised on the American imagination: The Garden of Eden had been tamed, the Holy Experiment of Union and democracy was careening toward the Civil War, almost nothing was as it once had been, but this one great innocent lived on. Still, without what amounted to a journalistic miracle of sorts, the Myth of Johnny Appleseed, maybe the most enduring and endearing of all American folk tales, might never have gotten off the ground.

❦

For a quarter century after his death, John Chapman's chroniclers were a distinctly regional lot. T. S. Humrickhouse, of Coshocton, was responsible for the first posthumous profile of Chapman—an April 1846 article for *Hovey's Magazine of Horticulture.* Chapman, according to Humrickhouse, pursued his nursery work with such zeal that he came "to be regarded by the few settlers, just then beginning to make their appearance in the country, with a degree of almost superstitious admiration." But Humrickhouse, a frequent *Hovey's* contributor, was more interested in Chapman's theories of apple propagation, which he found to be advanced "obscure and illiterate though [Chapman] was," and the author was clearly hedging his bet as to whether the pioneer pomologist was posthumous or not. "Recently, his visits have been altogether intermitted," Humrickhouse wrote. "Our hope is, that he may yet live in the enjoyment of a green old age, happy in the multitude of its pleasing reminiscences." Happy Chapman might well have been in his New Jerusalem heaven, but he had been in his grave more than a year when the *Hovey's* article made its appearance.

The next year, 1847, Henry Howe, an entrepreneurial reporter who had already published successful "historical collections" of five other states—Massachusetts, Connecticut, New York, Pennsylvania, and Virginia—added Ohio to his roster and included a brief profile of Chapman that revealed the shocking news of his near marriage in Perrysville and the more mundane fact of his snuff habit. But Howe, too, assumed that Chapman was alive, by now two years after his death, and wasn't able to correct that on the record for more than four decades, until his revised history of the state appeared in 1889.

An 1858 work of historical fiction—*Philip Seymour*, by Mansfield, Ohio, minister James F. M'Gaw—went a long way toward establishing the broad details of Chapman's death. M'Gaw's brother, T.N., also a minister, had the account straight with Richard Worth, son of the man in whose cabin Chapman had died, and Richard's memory of that event—as delivered through the M'Gaws—was soon to form the standard version of John Chapman's last days. Still, the 1847 death date survived even Richard Worth's supposed firsthand recollection, and so it has continued to soldier on through history, even today peppering the Internet.

Four years after M'Gaw, in 1862, Chapman and Appleseed even got an elegant regional chronicler, in A. Banning Norton, and a memorable superlative: "the oddest character in all our history." Somewhere in these first decades after his death, Johnny might also have been the recipient of a brief eulogy for the ages: Sam Houston's stirring "Farewell, dear old eccentric heart . . . ," supposedly delivered on the floor of Congress. But the evidence is thin at best.

The eulogy appears to have made the leap from purely fictional accounts to a 1926 article for the Chicago Historical Society ("Johnny Appleseed: The True Story," by James Lattimore Himrod), and from there to a 1967 address before the Brooke County, West Virginia, Historical Association by Frank Chapman, great-great-grandson of John Chapman's half brother Nathaniel, to a 1986 compilation of American folklore by Kemp P. Battle, which also has Johnny arriving in Pittsburgh on a Conestoga wagon and tarrying there a dozen years as per Walt Disney, and on to a 1998 book, *Forgotten Heroes*, that bears the imprimatur of the Society of American Historians. But I could find no record of any such speech, and, in fact, Sam Houston didn't take his Texas Senate seat until almost a year after Chapman was in the ground.

As with so much other Appleseed lore, though, there are dots to connect that make the eulogy faintly possible, or at least the search fun. Sam Houston didn't take his Senate seat until 1846, but as a former member of the House (1823–26, from Tennessee, before moving on to Texas), he had the privilege of its floor and might indeed have claimed it for the purpose of celebrating an American original, much as he was.

Houston, it turns out, was also intimately familiar with William Stanbery, one of Chapman's earliest champions in Newark, although not in the best of ways. Back in the spring of 1832, representing Licking County in Congress, Stanbery managed to grievously insult Houston when he appeared in the House with a delegation from the Cherokee Nation. Threats ensued, and two weeks later, when the two met on Pennsylvania Avenue, Houston gave Stanbery a hard rap on the head with his hickory cane, then wrestled him to the ground. Undeterred, Stanbery drew a pistol, held it to Houston's chest, and fired point blank. But the pistol failed to discharge, and rather than die in Stanbery's arms, Houston resumed the attack with his cane. In subsequent legal proceedings, the Texan was represented by Francis Scott Key, who must have done a good job, because his client basically escaped with nothing more than a five-hundred-dollar fine, which he never paid.

Two decades later, in 1852, Stanbery was long retired from Congress and living back in Licking County when Houston, then nearing the end of his first Senate term, appeared in Newark to lob verbal grenades at the Whig Party and its presidential standard bearer, General Winfield Scott, but the newspaper account of Houston's speech makes no mention of (a) a Stanbery-Houston reunion or (b) more critically, whether Houston used the occasion to praise the late nurseryman whose apple trees probably still graced the county's hillsides.

Perhaps the most compelling argument against the legitimacy of the Sam Houston eulogy, though, is the simple fact that when W. D. Haley took the Appleseed myth national in the November 1871 issue of *Harper's New Monthly Magazine*, he made no mention of it. In an account that included virtually everything then known or suspected about the life of John Chapman, this is an absence that speaks volumes.

❦

Context is everything in understanding how Johnny Appleseed was sprung almost full-born on the broad American public, and in this case, the context is threefold. First is *Harper's New Monthly Magazine* itself. Launched in 1850 by the publisher Harper & Brothers, in large part to showcase its own books and authors, the magazine achieved a circulation of fifty thousand copies within six months and kept growing from there. A decade later, *Harper's* was selling on average two hundred thousand copies a month— one magazine for every 150 Americans. No periodical of its day boasted comparable circulation, and none could claim a more distinguished list of contributors: Charles Dickens, William Makepeace Thackeray, George Eliot, Herman Melville, Mark Twain (whose name was misspelled in one memorable byline as Mark Swain), Theodore Dreiser, Horace Greeley, Horatio Alger, Henry James, etc., as well as art by Frederic Remington, Winslow Homer, and others.

It is undoubtedly an exaggeration to say that when *Harper's* spoke, people listened, but *Harper's* was the mass communication of its day. Its circulation was transcontinental. And the magazine had a reputation for taking on serious subjects in a serious way. The "Editor's Scientific Record" for the same issue that brought

America news of Johnny Appleseed noted that water levels were declining in the Great Salt Lake, Dr. Livingston was still missing in Africa, a new species of giant salamander had been discovered in China, and the plant cundurango was exciting interest as "a supposed specific for cancer and other diseases." The "Editor's Historical Record" that followed reported on political corruption in New York City, noted that twenty-five thousand working men in the same city had recently demonstrated in support of the "eight-hour movement," and tallied the results of legal proceedings in France, where nearly two dozen communists had been put on trial for torching public buildings: seven sentenced to death, two more to life in prison with hard labor, and the rest to lesser sentences, fines, and/or deportation. In short, for lending legitimacy to an almost lost and never more than regional folk hero and for embedding him in the national conscience, there could hardly have been a better medium than *Harper's*.

Time counts as well. Just as the moment had been right seventy years earlier when John Chapman first appeared on the edge of the Ohio Country, so the moment was now right for "Johnny Appleseed—A Pioneer Hero," as *Harper's* titled its seven-page article. The Civil War had been over for half a decade, but it was hardly forgotten. One in every fifty Americans alive at the start of the war was dead at the end of it. A president had been assassinated. His smoldering successor—hailed at the start of the war as the "greatest man of his age" in the pages of the *New York Times*—had proven one of the most divisive politicians in American history. The economy of the South remained in ruins, its social order in collapse, yet already Jim Crow laws were beginning to rise from the ashes. Reconstruction had torn apart both houses of Congress. In another five years it would basically be abandoned altogether in the shameful political compromise that gave the nation the presidency of Rutherford B. Hayes. To borrow from the title of George

Fort Milton's 1930 history of Andrew Johnson and Reconstruction, this was "the Age of Hate," and here was a genuine American hero who was all about love—of his fellow citizens, of all God's creatures, of all creation.

Finally, there is W. D. Haley himself. He disappears in most accounts of the *Harper's* article—is the messenger and nothing more—and indeed it's a stretch to construct a hard-and-fast account of the man. But here, too, exists a trail, and an intriguing one. On March 6, 1890, the *Salinas* (California) *Weekly* reported the death of a Captain W. D. Haley as follows: "A well-known journalist and Grand Army man, died in San Jose last Sunday, after a lingering illness, aged 62 years. Captain Haley's latest venture was the Santa Margarita 'Times,' which failing health compelled him to abandon several months ago. His death was hastened by a wound received in the war of the rebellion, which never completely healed."

More than thirty years earlier, Haley had also appeared in a history of All Souls Unitarian Church in Washington, DC. Born in England and a Harvard student before being called to the ministry early in the 1850s, Haley had taken over the Unitarian church in the nation's capital in 1858 and served there until 1861, when he entered the Union army as chaplain of the 17th Massachusetts Volunteers, rising eventually to the rank of Captain. "After the Civil War," the brief profile concludes, "he would seem not to have resumed the ministry, but to have chosen the life of a wandering printer and newspaper correspondent, which led him finally to California, where he died in San Jose in 1890."

Bingo! But can we say for certain that the W. D. Haley who preached from the Unitarian pulpit and later died in California is the same W. D. Haley who orchestrated Johnny Appleseed's national debut? Not really, though we do know that Haley's profile of the "Pioneer Hero" was his second article for *Harper's* and that the first, written in 1859, was a lengthy description of the public buildings and emerging glories of Washington, DC. And with that further piece of evidence, we can begin to make some fairly solid assumptions about Johnny's first great muse.

Like Chapman, Haley was a man of religious bent, brought to the ministry in a branch of Christianity perhaps more sympathetic to the Swedenborgian message than any other. On the great issue of his younger years, slavery, he had been a foursquare abolitionist. As a minister in Alton, Illinois, before coming to Washington, Haley led the fight against slavery, even after his church had been broken into and its windows demolished. The author of the Washington church history notes, with irony, that Haley was called to a church in the capital that had been bitterly split over the very same issue. Haley also appears to have had a natural affinity with and curiosity about Native Americans. In 1855, according to the church historian, he traveled among the Chippewas and obtained "much valuable scientific and literary information." As with Chapman, Haley seems to have been an inveterate wanderer, another of those American nomads working their way from coast to coast. What's more, he had seen the horrors of war, and apparently carried with him on his travels and unto his death a battlefield wound. It's hard, in fact, to imagine John Chapman's finding a more empathetic chronicler, and all that sparkles like diamonds in Haley's treatment of Johnny Appleseed.

In his very first sentences Haley sets a nostalgic tone that pervades the whole article: "The 'far West' is rapidly becoming only a traditional designation; railroads have destroyed the romance of frontier life, or have surrounded it with so many appliances of civilization that the pioneer character is rapidly becoming mythical." From there, he moves on to make Johnny Appleseed the emblem of this paradise lost and a measure of just how far into the darkness of modernity America had traveled in its first hundred years.

The march of Titans sometimes tramples out the memory of smaller but more useful lives, and sensational glare often eclipses more modest but purer lights. This has been the case in the popular demand for the dime novel dilations of Fenimore Cooper's romances of border life, which have preserved the records of Indian rapine and atrocity as the only memorials of pioneer history. But the early days of Western settlement witnessed sublimer heroisms than those of Indian torture, and nobler victories than those of the tomahawk and scalping knife.

Among the heroes of endurance that was voluntary, and of action that was creative and not sanguinary, there was one man, whose name, seldom mentioned now save by some of the few surviving pioneers, deserves to be perpetuated.

And in fact, that's exactly what the article did: rescued a name almost lost to memory, adorned it with folklore, and perpetuated Johnny Appleseed for generations to come.

Earlier accounts by Henry Howe, A. Banning Norton, Rosella Rice, and others all echo through the pages of Haley's article: the lashed-together canoes and their "long and toilsome voyage" up the Muskingum waterways and into the Black Fork, shoes forgone to a family with even less than he had, Johnny's odd headgear (both the tin mush pan and the long-visored pasteboard kind), the respect accorded him by even "the rudest frontiers-man," that red-hot iron with which he treated cuts and bites alike, Swedenborg and the "news right fresh from heaven," Johnny's miracle run through the night in the War of 1812, his abhorrence of grafting, the skeeters not burned ("No Brahmin could be more concerned for the preservation of insect life"), the rattlers abided, the deeds not recorded, Johnny's star turn in the "primitive Christian" drama, his beautiful death, and on and on. Haley, after all, was doing what journalists often do—synthesizing a life and pulling together all that was then known about it. Haley's closing tribute, though, clearly flowed from the pen of a reporter accustomed in an earlier career to extolling the dead from the front of a church.

> Thus died one of the memorable men of pioneer times, who never inflicted pain or knew an enemy—a man of strange habits, in whom there dwelt a comprehensive love that reached with one hand downward to the lowest forms of life, and with the other upward to the very throne of God. . . . Now, "no man knoweth of his sepulchre;" but his deeds will live in the fragrance of the apple blossoms he loved so well, and the story of his life, however crudely narrated, will be a perpetual proof that true heroism, pure benevolence, noble virtues, and deeds that deserve immortality may be found under meanest apparel, and far from gilded halls and towering spires.

W. D. Haley's account does contain errors. He has Chapman as Jonathan, not John (a common problem for more than a century after his death). He writes that there is "good reason for believing that Chapman was born in Boston, in 1775"—a year off and the wrong city, although those facts would not be authenticated until the 1930s. Haley also uses the 1847 death date, one large reason why even a silver bullet in the heart won't kill it.

The article was no sooner in print than John W. Dawson took to the pages of his own *Fort Wayne Sentinel* to point out these shortcomings and more. Chapman's landholdings had been more extensive than Haley credited. His headgear also included a "crownless hat, limbered with rough usage, which he often ran his hand through and carried on his arm." Penurious in the extreme, Chapman complained of tavern charges whenever he was forced to take a meal at one. He would sometimes do day labor at harvest time. "Captain James Barnett, deceased, used to say that Johnny

Appleseed was the best hand he hired to husk corn." Most egregious to the Indiana editor and publisher, Haley has the "primitive Christian" story set in Mansfield when—according to Dawson—it was a demonstrable fact that the preacher in question, Adam Payne, was a Hoosier and the famous incident had occurred not in central Ohio but on the streets of Fort Wayne in 1830, not long before Payne was killed by Indians and his head mounted on a pole as a trophy of war.

But quibbles and real errors aside, W. D. Haley's *Harper's* article not only rescued John Chapman from what almost certainly would have been an ever-diminishing spot in regional American history, but also served for three-quarters of a century as the foundation on which virtually all other treatments of the Appleseed myth were raised. Haley provided the timbers and the building blocks. Everything else was tweaking. And for the next seventy-five years, a host of writers and poets, biographers, memoirists, hagiographers, and public reformers great and small tweaked both man and myth with abandon.

❦

Johnny was the son of a Revolutionary War hero and schooled at Harvard, in some of these early, post-Haley accounts. (Reverend Hillis's novel is probably more responsible for the Harvard degree than any other source.) In other accounts, Johnny seemed to have just walked out of the woods into life. He planted his trees south into Virginia and as far west as Oregon and the Pacific. In yet another account, he rises suddenly among the combatants on Lookout Mountain, in that cloud-wrapped battle of November 1863, more than eighteen years after his death. Robert Price has chronicled alleged Johnny meetings with George Washington, Daniel Boone, John James Audubon, Abraham Lincoln (and Lincoln's father), and more. In his 1945 book *Pleasant Valley,* the Pulitzer

Prize–winning author, celebrated conservationist, and Mansfield, Ohio, native Louis Bromfield invokes his great-aunt Mattie to add to the list of Appleseed's encounters Lazare, the Lost Dauphin of France, "that curious and mysterious character who, as a young man, spent much time in our Ohio country"—a description that might be equally applied to Chapman himself.

As late as the early 1950s, when Price was finishing his biography, a tradition persisted in Missouri that Johnny had married an Indian girl there and lived with her on Turkey Creek in Ralls County until one day "he walked into the tepee, gazed longingly at his baby, then walked away, never to be heard of again." In March 1955, the highly popular Classics Illustrated Junior comic-book series—a prized research tool of indolent junior-highers of the era (I was one)—produced a Johnny Appleseed issue that had him planting orchards "as far West as Illinois, Iowa, Michigan, and Missouri." Closer to his own time and territory, a story endured that on one of his last ramblings through Ohio Johnny was eastward bound from Iowa. Johnny's apple seeds might have gotten to all those places—he had a habit of giving things away to strangers in need who were passing through—but again, no evidence exists that he ever crossed the Mississippi River or got anywhere near it.

In the nonfiction foreword to his 1904 novel, Newell Dwight Hillis dates the peculiarities of Appleseed's character to 1815, when Chapman became lost in the forest and fell victim to a near-fatal attack of typhoid or malaria. "Months later," Hillis informs, "when he reappeared on the edge of the settlement, he wore one of his apple sacks for garments and had an old rusty tin pan on his head; he was dazed and out of his mind." Chapman had evidently been a scholar earlier in life; now, he "entered in to a new phase of his career"—the "strange and crazy old man" years, which ended according to Hillis in 1835, a full decade ahead of the fact. Nonetheless, Hillis writes, "Save Colonel Clark, he is the most striking man of all the generation that crossed the Alleghanies." Which "Colonel Clark" is not specified, but the reference most likely is to George Rogers Clark, the Indian fighter and Revolutionary War hero and older brother to William Clark, of Lewis and Clark fame. Appropriately enough, in yet another stretching of the Appleseed myth, Chapman serves as a scout under George Rogers Clark's command, although Clark's greatest moments came well before Chapman was any taller than a wagon wheel.

Eleanor Atkinson evokes a similar mixture of heroism, mystery, and something approaching tragedy in the foreword to her popular 1915 novel *Johnny Appleseed: Romance of the Sower.* "Jonathan Chapman, the nurseryman of Puritan breed," was "half mystic, half poet, a lover of nature and of his fellow-man . . . always in the van of migration, consecrated to the blossoming of the wilderness." And yet this "beautiful life of self-sacrifice . . . came in old age, to some end obscure and lonely." *Quel dommage,* one wants to add, if only because French seems proper for such a sentiment so expressed.

Circumstances changed, too, and the myth adjusted to embrace them. Atkinson's novel went a long way toward introducing the "Pittsburgh years" into the Chapman/Appleseed story, and the story slid over to make room for them. America's Edenic past became even more past. Johnny was increasingly emblematic of an era most Americans could no longer recall or even barely imagine. By the time Henry A. Pershing wrote *Johnny Appleseed and His Time: An Historical Romance* in 1930, the author could lament that "modern appliances of telegraph, telephone, television, radio, and many other like inventions have left nothing for romance to build upon." As Michael Pollan recounts in *The Botany of Desire,* the Volstead Act of 1919 and the nearly fifteen years of Prohibition that followed left apple growers scrambling for a new identity. Almost simultaneously, the hard winter of 1917–18, when late December temperatures in New England fell to minus forty degrees and below, savaged apple orchards throughout the Northeast and into Virginia and Ohio. Hard cider was yesterday's news and the distillation of a yesteryear economy. An apple a day was where the fruit was heading, and as he always had been, Johnny was a few steps in front of the game when the future arrived, with a healthy, lush, plump, flavorful apple waiting in hand, and never mind that he never seems to have sold an apple per se in his life.

❦

"If you don't know where you are," the writer Wallace Stegner once said, "you don't know who you are." A corollary might be, if you don't know who you are, you can be from anywhere and do anything. So it was with John Chapman. For at least the last half of his life and almost ever since his death, he has been pretty much whatever one wanted to make of him. Not surprisingly for a literary character so hard to pin down, poets have probably done best with Johnny Appleseed. The myth comes with just enough fact to anchor it to the page, and more than enough ephemera for the poetic imagination to have free range.

In their poem "Johnny Appleseed," from the 1933 collection *A Book of Americans,* Rosemary and Stephen Vincent Benét capture the essence of the myth in nine quatrains of almost doggerel verse that nonetheless manage to raise their subject to heroic stature and cut to the heart of his appeal:

The stalking Indian,
The beast in its lair,
Did no hurt
While he was there.
For they could tell
As wild things can,

Johnny Appleseed

That Jonathan Chapman
Was God's own man.

A decade earlier, in "In Praise of Johnny Appleseed," another celebrated literary figure of the time, Vachel Lindsay, tackled the same basic myth in an almost exactly opposite fashion—a poem nearly as complicated as the poet himself. Lindsay acknowledged his debt to W. D. Haley right at the beginning and inherited Haley's mistakes as well—the birth and death dates, Jonathan instead of John—but otherwise his work is strikingly original.

Born to wealth in Springfield, Illinois, Lindsay declined to follow his father into the medical profession, becoming instead an American troubadour. For several summers, he wandered on foot from state to state, trading recitations of his poetry for food and shelter—doing with verse much as John Chapman had done with apple seedlings and snippets of his Swedenborgian texts. Whether writing (in his most famous poem) about Salvation Army founder William Booth marching into heaven—"Booth led boldly with his big bass drum"—or how Johnny Appleseed "ran with the rabbit and slept with the stream," Lindsay knew the feel and sound of footfalls on the open road and untilled land, and like a true troubadour, he was also determined to bring music and poetry together. Lindsay's stage recitations of his poems were famous, and his Appleseed ode is filled with a combination of stage directions and concertmaster notes: "To be read like old leaves on the elm tree of Time. Sifting soft winds with sentence and rhyme." "While you read, hear the hoofbeats of deer in the snow. . . ." "To be read like . . . heartbeats of fawns that are coming again when the forest, once more, is the master of man." Like that last stage direction, this is also a poem absolutely steeped in nostalgia for a purer and lost America, and for the simple nurseryman that Manifest Destiny had outraced and left behind:

"Johnny stood near the fire, where they were burning brush, and seemed to hate to leave the warmth. He was thinly clothed, his pantaloons were much too short and he wore an old pair of shoes without stockings."

At last the Indian overtook him, at last the Indian hurried past
  him;
At last the white man overtook him, at last the white man hurried
  past him;
At last his own trees overtook him, at last his own trees hurried
  past him. . . .
And the real frontier was his sunburnt breast.

Edgar Lee Masters—Lindsay's biographer and friend, and arguably his superior as a poet—takes matters a step further in his book-length poem *Toward the Gulf.* Just as John Chapman disappeared into Johnny Appleseed, so Masters has Appleseed disappearing into his life's work and becoming the orchards he planted:

Johnny Appleseed said, so my father told me:
I go to a place forgotten, the orchards will thrive and be here
For children to come, who will gather and eat hereafter.
And few will know who planted, and none will understand.

Maybe, in fact, that's every apple man's ultimate dream.

❧

Playwrights and commentators got in the act as well. How could they resist a life so dramatic? Arnold Sundgaard and Marc Connelly's musical *Everywhere I Roam* opened on Broadway—at the National Theater on West Forty-First Street—on December 29, 1938, with twenty-five-year-old Norman Lloyd starring as Johnny and winning accolades for one of the top-ten Broadway performances of the year, even though the show lasted exactly thirteen performances. "It begins 100 years ago in a sort of prairie Garden of Eden," a *Time* magazine reviewer wrote in the January 9, 1939, issue, days before the curtain rang down for the last time. "The toiling farmer drips with honest sweat, his steadfast wife brings him cool water from the spring, and Johnny Appleseed moseys by, planting apple trees." That cool spring water out on the prairie might have been what doomed the production: The Dust Bowl was then in its eighth year of crippling drought, not to be relieved until the rain finally returned that September. Nostalgia was tempting, but John Steinbeck's *The Grapes of Wrath*, published only four months later, was more to the point.

More intriguing in many ways is the Appleseed musical that was never made. The papers of Kurt Weill and his wife, the actor-singer Lotte Lenya, suggest that Weill was contemplating his own version of the Appleseed life and legend. Imagine what Weill and his Marxist collaborator on *The Threepenny Opera*, Bertolt Brecht, might have done with such a deeply textured character and fundamentally conflicted American story. At one level, John Chapman was a proto-capitalist, land speculator, and frontier entrepreneur par excellence. What's more, religion wasn't merely his opiate; it formed the core of his being. But what was Chapman's life about if it wasn't the famous Marxist dictum: "From each according to his ability, to each according to his needs"?

Indeed, politics might have been what attracted Howard Fast to the Chapman story. Fast's 1942 juvenile novel *The Tall Hunter* is fairly standard Appleseed fare, even if far better written than most of it: Embittered tall hunter slays Indians left and right while hunting for his abducted wife, until he happens to meet Johnny, who teaches him understanding and forgiveness, then reunites hunter and wife. But Fast himself was hardly a neutral observer. A prolific writer, he joined the Communist Party USA in 1944, two years after finishing *The Tall Hunter*, and was briefly imprisoned in 1950 for contempt of Congress after refusing to name names before the House Un-American Activities Committee. Blacklisted in Hollywood and New York, he self-published his most famous novel, *Spartacus*, in 1951, two years before he won the Stalin Peace Prize.

Whether he was writing about Roman slaves or American patriots such as Thomas Paine, Fast liked heroes willing to rise up against the establishment and the cruelty of the times. And, in his own way, John Chapman fits that formula just fine. The Appleseed myth might have worked the kinks out of his resume, just as Disney would flatten the rough spots, but John Chapman was never, ever a simple man. And yet, of course, simplicity is just what the world wanted from him, and what the times increasingly demanded.

❦

Johnny Appleseed embodies "the America that has never been interested in money or public opinion, that has been friendly, sensible, and brave instead of aggressive and bloody, that has nurtured life instead of destroying it, and that has been sensitive to the beauty of this continent, and done something to create here a civilization. Johnny Appleseed stands for ourselves at our best." Thus, Charles Allen Smart declared in the August 1939 issue of *Harper's Magazine* as storm clouds darkened over Europe, and civilization, however defined, once more seemed at risk. Smart was an Ohioan—born in Cleveland and living on an inherited farm near Chillicothe, along the same Allegheny escarpment where Chapman had roamed for so many years—and, of course, he wrote those words in the successor to the magazine in which W. D. Haley had expressed strikingly similar sentiments about the same mythic figure, in the aftermath of another war. That might be nothing more than coincidence, but it does emphasize how little history changes at its core from generation to generation. This time, though, something new was in the mix: Hollywood.

13

Blessings Three

~

The story of Johnny Appleseed's debut on the silver screen can be told, in part, through letters discovered in the archives of the Johnny Appleseed Educational Center and Museum at Urbana University in west-central Ohio—a school and a city rich with Chapman associations. Urbana, recall, was where the Greentown Indians were being removed to during the War of 1812 when came the horror that launched John Chapman on his famous run. Urbana was also where Chapman met with attorney John James to discuss possible legal proceedings regarding one of his orchards—and also declined James's invitation to visit his wife, a part of the Barclay-Young clan who introduced the nurseryman to Swedenborg. James, for his part, donated the land on which Urbana College rose in 1850 as the second coeducational college in America (seventeen years after Oberlin) and the only Swedenborg-affiliated college west of the Alleghenies—the fulfillment of a wish long held by Chapman, although half a decade after his death.

The first president of the college, botanist Milo Williams, was well acquainted with Chapman, shared many common interests with him, and reportedly committed to paper what probably would have been the most lengthy and illuminating portrait of Chapman by any of his contemporaries, but that manuscript, too, has gone missing. Urbana University's Johnny Appleseed complex is located in the combined Bailey and Barclay Halls, named for Francis Bailey, the Philadelphia printer generally considered the Father of the New Church in America, and for Bailey's ward Hester Barclay, sister-in-law to John Young etc. The place crawls with connections, direct and indirect. And central to this discussion, the museum is also the repository of the papers of Florence Murdoch, the longtime secretary of the Swedenborgian Church in Cincinnati and the hub around which the epistolary history of Johnny's film career turns.

On December 19, 1944, Caroline Dunn, librarian at the William Henry Smith Memorial Library of the Indiana Historical Society, wrote to Murdoch, who apparently had heard rumors that an Appleseed movie was in the works and wanted to be certain that the New Church's most famous apostle was going to be well treated.

The Indiana Division of the State Library, it turned out, had indeed been contacted by someone from Metro-Goldwyn-Mayer, seeking articles and other resources about the life of Chapman/Appleseed. The MGM official, however, was either in the dark or unconcerned that Walt Disney was also in the chase, and on that subject Caroline Dunn had definite opinions. An animated Walt Disney version of the Appleseed story, she felt, would be far superior to the normal Hollywood fare. She only hoped that the Disney studio wouldn't end up producing something "peculiar and horrible—movies so often do."

Three and a half years later, with the MGM movie scrapped and Disney's animated version of Johnny's life headed to theaters nationwide, Murdoch was convinced that "something peculiar and horrible" was exactly what the Disney Studio had done. On May 26, 1948—the day before the cartoon classic *Melody Time* was released—Murdoch wrote Walt Disney to correct the error of his ways.

Her letter begins on a high note. Murdoch had learned that the cartoon celebrates Johnny's "Blessings Three," and in her official capacity as secretary of the New Church Library, she wanted to express her approval. The "Blessings Three"—"love and faith and an apple tree"—caught the spirit of the New Church just right. After that, though, the tone grows more heated. Publicity for the movie showed Johnny goaded on to greatness by a sourpuss apparition in a coonskin hat—Johnny's "Guardian Angel"—and for Murdoch that was playing far too fast and loose with the spirit world that was central to Swedenborg's vision and sacred in New Church belief. Murdoch demanded of Disney "what process of reasoning" had led his studio to such a "strange conception," which she feared would poison the minds of the legions of children who were sure to see the film.

What to do? Murdoch had several suggestions: perhaps a traditional angel, or a child could lead Johnny on if an angel wouldn't do. At the least, couldn't Disney change the name "guardian angel" to "spirit of the frontier"?

Walt Disney never replied, and the last-second corrections Murdoch requested never were made. And that's probably just as well, because, without his guardian angel (think of a diminutive Jed Clampett with acid reflux), Disney's Johnny Appleseed never would have gathered the gumption to leave his nonexistent farm near Pittsburgh, much less cross the Ohio into the Terra Incognita of the Northwest Territory. In Disney's "The Old Settler: Johnny Appleseed and Johnny's Angel," one of seven cartoon shorts making up *Melody Time,* poor Johnny is "such a sawed-off, scrawny fellow" (despite being by all accounts absolutely the average height of the time, about five feet nine) and "weren't no pioneer, and he know'd it" (notwithstanding that he had walked across the mountains of Pennsylvania, survived brutal winters and a hostile environment) and "ain't got the muscle or the breadth of chest" (ludicrous on the face of it) to join the pioneer parade heading west.

Worse, there's not even a hint of the intellectual intensity that John Chapman would have needed to wrestle his way into Swedenborg's truths, as he obviously did. (In Lancashire, England, according to New Church historian Ophia D. Smith, early Swedenborgian enthusiasts were known appropriately as "Top o' the Brow folks.") Almost worst of all, Johnny is burdened the entire cartoon through by Dennis Day's Irish tenor voice, perfect maybe for "Danny Boy" but not really the thing for, say, shouting out "The Spirit of the Lord is upon me, and he hath anointed me to blow the trumpet in the wilderness . . ." on a dead run, in the middle of the night, in the deep of the forest.

But that's Hollywood. And the myth had long before become decoupled from the man—a fact driven home at the very beginning of "The Old Settler" when the narrator places him in the long tradition of Paul Bunyan, John Henry of the thirty-pound hammer, and Davy Crockett, only one of whom can, like Johnny Appleseed, claim a solid historical antecedent. (John Henry is a wild card—perhaps pure fiction, perhaps an ex-slave or a former prisoner. No convincing documentation has ever been found.) In American folklore, all roads seem to lead through the Disney studios, and no tale emerges unchanged by the experience. Indeed, in the preface to *Boone: A Biography*, Robert Morgan laments how hard it is "to rescue figures like Daniel Boone and Johnny Appleseed from the distortions of television and Walt Disney."

Still, my almost five-year-old grandson adored the cartoon, as five-year-olds have been doing now for better than six decades. And if the Disney studio took the Appleseed myth and pushed it over the top, the storyline was already heading that way, and studio executives were more than prepared to defend their work. In a lengthy response to Florence Murdoch, dated June 23, 1948, Hal

Adelquist, manager of Disney's Story Department, explained how the animated film and particularly Johnny's Guardian Angel came to be.

To begin with, Adelquist wrote, the Appleseed story had been painstakingly researched, and the "guardian angel" was in keeping with the known facts about Johnny's life. He was, after all, a simple frontiersman who believed both that his tree planting was divinely inspired and that heavenly spirits walked among us. Why, then, shouldn't he have a bouncy imp in a coonskin hat urging him on?

Adelquist closed his letter with a flourish, broadening his defense to encompass not only Johnny's Angel but the cartoon as a whole and the film industry in general. Disney's Johnny Appleseed interpretation, he wrote Murdoch, was the closest cinema had ever come "to a sermon on . . . brotherly love and unselfishness." And that, in a way, sums up the evolution of the myth itself.

W. D. Haley took a mixture of biography, legend, and folklore concerning an often saintly man and packaged it into a mythic figure for the American public. Three-quarters of a century later, Walt Disney Studios took the myth Haley had done so much to formalize; wrapped it around a simple, almost simpleton saint; added a musical score with a refrain that neatly encapsulates this trimmed-down life—"Oh, the Lord's been good to me!"—and rendered the whole into a sermon on brotherly love and unselfishness that has now been retold in countless and always uplifting children's books, juvenile yarns, videos, classroom units, Sunday school syllabi, and much, much more. "A sweet juvenile entertainment," *New York Times* reviewer Bosley Crowther called the animated film, "in the familiar Disney inspirational style." Exactly. This truly is the cartoon that launched a thousand homilies.

One should add, too, that it was a film treatment that finally satisfied even the redoubtable Florence Murdoch. On September 23, 1955, more than seven years after she had Hal Adelquist's explanation in hand, Murdoch wrote him back, expressing admiration for the film treatment and enclosing, for the Disney organization's consideration, a "suggested outline for Johnny Appleseed Junior Clubs." Why not?

🍎

Disney hegemony aside, the Cult of Saint Johnny over the last half century–plus is a many-splendored and gloriously diverse thing. The Henry Cooper Log Cabin Museum in the City Park of Parkersburg, West Virginia, has on display a roughly 2.5-foot forked branch from an apple tree supposedly planted by " 'Johnny Appleseed' or Jonathan Chapman" in Belpre, Ohio—just across the Ohio River—about 1803 and sawed down to the ground some 132 years later. Maintained by the Centennial Chapter of the Daughters of American Pioneers, the museum displays the branch in a weakly lit second-floor showcase, along with a mastodon tooth discovered in Africa and a stuffed golden eagle and peacock. As I studied the branch, I kept thinking of those dank reliquaries in European cathedrals, where for a euro's worth of illumination you can peek at the shinbone of some long-ago saint.

That same spirit—artifacts of the blessed—prevailed for many years at the Dawes Arboretum, five miles south of Newark, Ohio. Opened in 1929, the Arboretum is the brainchild of Bertie Dawes and her husband, Beman, founding president of the forerunner to the Pure Oil Company and younger brother of Charles Dawes, Calvin Coolidge's vice president and winner of the 1925 Nobel Peace Prize. Bertie and Beman Dawes laid the groundwork for their long-held dream in 1917 by purchasing the 140-acre "Old Brumback farm," where John Chapman might have planted one or more orchards as early as 1801. (As we've seen, Licking County sources differ on the matter.) By 1929, the Daweses had expanded their holding to 293 acres and overseen the planting of more than fifty thousand trees from all around the world. Today, the grounds have grown almost sevenfold again, to nearly two thousand acres and some five thousand different types of woody plants. It's a truly lovely spot, a green oasis only a few minutes off Interstate 70. By the late 1970s, though, the main obsession of the Arboretum seems to have been legitimatizing its Appleseed connections.

In a monograph published by the Arboretum in 1979 to coincide with its celebration of John Chapman's 205th birthday and the founding of the Johnny Appleseed Foundation, C. Burr Dawes, son of Beman and Bertie, writes not only about his own blood relationship with Chapman, via John's half brother Davis, but also about the formative influence his ancestors had on the future Johnny Appleseed's early years. Daweses, Chapmans, and Simondses (Elizabeth Chapman's family) had been intermarrying since early Colonial Ipswich, the author contends. Indeed, according to C. Burr Dawes if no one else, it was his family that took in young John and Elizabeth Chapman after their mother's death, and his great-etc.-grandmother Anna (Lawrence) Simonds who taught Johnny both his "fair copperplate script" and the reading skills that ultimately would lead him to Swedenborg and his texts. (All of which, of course, makes Johnny the something-somethingth cousin not only of the George Bushes but of a Nobel Prize winner and U.S. vice president!)

The provenance of the Arboretum's apple orchards, though, is the real subject of Dawes's attention, and on this he mounts a defense worthy almost of the Shroud of Turin, even producing affidavits signed and notarized by descendants of some of the area's earliest settlers. In one, Lura Eliza Beard Davis recalls how her grandfather, Andrew Beard, would drive her in his horse and buggy by land later bought for the Arboretum, pointing to old trees and proclaiming, "Johnny Appleseed planted that apple tree." The affidavit is signed and dated March 29, 1979. By the time it was published later that year by the Arboretum, Lura Davis was dead.

The other document, notarized November 18, 1979, and jointly signed by Claude C. Crist and Viola Weekley Crist, husband and wife, is far richer in detail. Viola Crist had moved into the Brumback farm in 1912, at age six, to live with Rebecca Brumback, stayed there until Beman Dawes bought the place in 1917, and remained close to Rebecca until her death in 1937. More than forty years later, Viola was still serving as the keeper of Rebecca's memories.

Rebecca, Viola recalled, had frequently recounted her father's tales about Johnny Appleseed: how he would stay a week at a time, putting in new apple trees and tending to ones he had previously planted all around the area. Johnny slept with the hired men, Viola remembered Rebecca's saying. In the evenings, he would entertain children with tales of his travels and "the Indians and wild animals he'd made friends with." As always, there were scripture readings, too, for the family and help. Like Lura Davis, Viola Crist ends her affidavit by swearing for the record that the Arboretum apple trees are, at least in part, genuine Appleseeds.

The Dawes Arboretum today makes no claims as to the Appleseed provenance of any of its trees or orchards. Indeed, its information desk seems slightly embarrassed by the suggestion. But the bill of particulars that once supported those claims—the case that C. Burr Dawes worked so hard to make and Viola Crist did much to support—ends up sounding very much like the standard reservoir of memories and experiences that got Johnny sainted in the first place. He planted. He was humble. He carried the Wonderful Word to owners and hired hands alike. And when the sun grew low and the children gathered around, he told tales of his life on the American edge, among the fading artifacts of the New Eden: friendly Indians, loving wolves, beneficent bears. The truth is, Disney didn't have to do any work at all. The story was always there, waiting for the Master's hand.

❦

Oddly for a man whose own financial life was largely a mess, Johnny Appleseed also has become a minor saint of commerce. Florence Murdoch never could find a sponsor for her Johnny Appleseed Junior Clubs, but today, children up to age thirteen can join their local Johnny Appleseed Junior Ecology Club, a creation of the banking industry meant to teach kids to save the old-fashioned way, a few dimes at a time. (The "ecology" part would seem to be a lesson about how small seeds grow into big savings.)

Mighty apple trees from little pips was also the theme of the "Johnny Appleseed: Planned Giving Pioneer" promotion launched in the summer of 1999 by Union Hospital of Dover, Ohio, and it ran all through a full-page ad for the John Hancock Mutual Insurance Company that appeared in major magazines in the mid-1950s. Under a magnificent illustration by F. M. Davis that shows a robust Johnny striding boldly through an orchard bursting with apple blossoms, the ad begins, "He planted seeds for us to reap," and goes on to conclude: "Americans understand Johnny Appleseed. We are a nation of planters for the future. We have always tried to live so that our sons and daughters would enjoy the blossoming of the work we do."

So far, so good, but in between its simple opening and elegant closing, the John Hancock ad manages to carry the elasticity of the Chapman/Appleseed biography to dizzying heights. His real name was Jonathan, the ad copy tells us. He walked into Pittsburgh two hundred years ago—circa the mid-eighteenth century, decades before Chapman was born and back when Pittsburgh itself was nothing more than a very imperiled fort—and there built a log cabin, planted apple trees, and "sat down to watch them grow." And thus it goes until, just as happens in the Disney cartoon, "one night [Johnny] went to sleep under an apple tree and did not wake up again." Bye-bye, William Worth family. So long, Fort Wayne.

As the John Hancock ad suggests, Johnny Appleseed might also be considered the patron saint of misinformation—or perhaps of information so multilayered that the original facts are all but lost and what remains is wherever the narrator wants to take the story. That was certainly the case in November 1999 when Representative Mark Souder of Indiana claimed the House floor to extol his district's wonders, including Johnny Appleseed. In lengthy remarks, Souder noted that John Chapman had been born in Ohio, that his father was a preacher, that the first written order for his apple trees dates to 1818, and on and on—a catalog of butchered facts that grows even more breathtaking when one considers that Souder (a) had access through the Congressional Research Service to some of the nation's most experienced archival investigators and (b) used to boast on his House website (before resigning his seat in May 2010, in the face of a sex scandal) that he was "one of Congress's strongest supporters of our nation's national parks, monuments and historical sites." What history, one wants to ask? And whose? But weirdness is part of Johnny Appleseed's legacy, too—one more place where his sainthood seems assured.

❧

When and where the truly strange began to creep into the Appleseed myth is anyone's call. This was, after all, a man considered superlatively odd in his own lifetime, in a frontier wilderness teeming with singularity. But something happened to the myth—a wheel began to come loose—just about the same time that American society itself started to come unglued, in the mid-1960s.

Pacifism had always been an honorable strain in the national story—deeply rooted in the dense tangle of religious strains that had helped shape the country—and John Chapman, who traveled defenseless through the frontier, could easily have served as its poster boy. Now, with the Vietnam War and its protestors building to a crescendo, pacifism took on a sharper edge, and that part of the Appleseed myth hardened with it. "America, Love It or Leave It!"—what would Chapman have made of that line in the sand from half a century back? Probably nothing. He loved what America was, the physical place, this "fresh, green breast of the new world," as F. Scott Fitzgerald once wrote. The ideological battles over what America should be and do had already been solved, to his mind. America was the New Jerusalem, the epicenter of a New Dispensation. The Second Coming had come and gone. God was in charge.

So, too, with Emerson's self-reliant man. Who was more so than Chapman? And what American essay has done more than Emerson's famous "Essay on Self-Reliance" to limn the quintessential national character? Yet as the 1960s segued into the decades beyond, self-reliance began to morph (in some instances) into mountain men, and mountain men (in even rarer instances) into the Ted Kaczynskis of the evening news. And inevitably Chapman and Appleseed and the entire idea of self-reliance American-style morphed with them. Oddballs became kooks; and kooks, cranks and cult leaders and very, very occasionally lone avengers.

Johnny Appleseed was still saintly—how could he be otherwise?—but as the second half of the twentieth century moved forward, his sanctity began to gain an occasional up-with-the-organization edge, like the culture at large. Back in August 1952, the *Hallmark Hall of Fame* followed up the all-star cavalcade of historical figures celebrated in its opening season—the poetic Brownings, Roger Williams, Florence Nightingale, Girl Scouts founder Juliette Low, smallpox conqueror Edward Jenner, Abigail Adams, etc.—by launching season two with a Johnny Appleseed biography whose title was self-explanatory: "Crabapple Saint."

Thirty-five years later, Johnny was back in prime time—the subject of an episode on *Shelley Duvall's Tall Tales & Legends*—but now with a twist. Elf-like comedian Martin Short played Johnny. His obsessions included not only seeds and trees, but also the beautiful Betty Nature (nineteen-year-old Molly Ringwald, fresh from *Pretty in Pink*), and their mutual enemy was the puffed-up mayor of fictional Smithville, none other than the Hollywood dynast Rob Reiner. That's a show one doesn't have to watch to see. Indeed, it's a show one *shouldn't* watch—as dull an hour of "entertainment" as possible.

Even in still images, Johnny seemed to come strangely unglued from himself and his own mythic past as the twentieth century wore on. Disney aside, there had always been basic agreement on what John Chapman looked like, going back to even before the four illustrations that accompanied W. D. Haley's 1871 *Harper's* article: normal height, piercing eyes, hair and beard mostly long and unkempt, rawboned and sinewy as one might expect of a man who lived on the fruits of the forest and walked in his lifetime the equivalent of at least several times around the globe, dressed mostly in rags. Yet in September 1966, when Johnny Appleseed made his debut on a U.S. postage stamp—the launch of a new "American Folklore" series of first-class (then five-cent) stamps— the person walking out of a giant-apple background is something else almost entirely: trim beard; belted short-sleeve tunic; pants neatly tucked into unscuffed buckskin boots; in one hand a shovel held over his shoulder; in the other, a sack presumably filled with seeds; what might be a metal pan on his head but also resembles a miner's helmet without the headlight; hooded eyes looking straight ahead.

Perhaps the stamp design—by Robert Bode, a New York ad agency art director—is simply meant to be the anti-Disney Appleseed. No one could ever say that *this* version lacked the gumption to migrate west, just as no one would confuse Bode's somewhat moody Davy Crockett stamp, issued the next year in the same folklore series, with the Fess Parker version of Crockett that a generation of schoolchildren grew up with in the 1950s. But the overall impression of the Appleseed stamp, its muscular purposefulness, recalls nothing so much as Bolshevik poster art of the 1930s: Workers of the world, unite! Even loner nurserymen and itinerant prophets.

Maybe, in fact, Chapman/Appleseed was a genuine radical—a religious Marx, a Jesus of Nazareth for moderns—or maybe he was just another fallen idol, another American hero who didn't quite pan out. In a December 17, 1974, article that appeared in that great chronicler of bad behavior, the *National Enquirer*, U.S. Department of Agriculture historian Dr. Wayne Rasmussen takes the Appleseed myth apart limb by limb. Johnny was "a miserly speculator," he tells reporter James M. Quinlan. The apple seed business was all about financing his land deals, the orchards all about securing his land claims, and the proof is in the ratios, according to Rasmussen. "While he planted only a few acres of apple trees, he claimed and bought thousands of acres and turned around to sell the land at a profit to farmers who were following the frontier west."

This was historical revisionism, tabloid-style, but by the mid-1970s, an important new Appleseed constituency could not have cared less if the apple business was Johnny's front for flipping properties, if Swedenborg was just a cover story, or even if Lucy in the Sky (with Diamonds) was carrying Johnny's love child. By then, the American backwoods were filling with self-styled Johnny Appleseeds sowing cannabis seeds far and wide as they dreamed of a new Utopia of the Stoned. (The phrase "Johnny Appleseed of Pot" recently produced nearly ten thousand hits on Google.) If Walt Disney's cartoon launched a thousand homilies, Johnny himself gave impetus to hundreds of lifestyles, not all of them productive.

One could spend months picking out the most inventive, the weirdest, the most historically inaccurate, and the just plain wackiest Appleseed reference from all the choices available. For sheer fun, the Midwest League's Fort Wayne TinCaps—named for that never-proven mush pan Johnny might have worn on his head—is definitely a frontrunner. How many other American folk heroes can claim a Class-A baseball team as a namesake? For discordance, there's Project Appleseed, which has appropriated the name of this consummate pacifist and unarmed traveler of the wilderness for a program that mixes rifle marksmanship and lessons about the Revolutionary War and lost liberties. But Patti Smith's explanation of how she came to open her 2005 poetry collection *Auguries of Innocence* with a meditation on Johnny is hard to top. The poem, she told an online interviewer, was built out of a brew of Johnny Appleseed, one of her "favorite people in American history"; Ralph Nader, who "has a great affection for Johnny Appleseed"; H. P. Lovecraft, an early-twentieth-century master of the "cosmic horror" school of fiction; and (appropriately) an on-board encounter with the spirit world:

> I was actually on a plane going to a political rally for Ralph Nader, and as I was sitting on the plane, I looked over and saw a vision of Johnny Appleseed, just floating about, in the plane.

I don't know what he was doing on Northwest Airlines, but I thought "Well, I saw Johnny Appleseed on the plane; it's best to write about it." So I wrote this poem on the plane. But in the center of it, I wound up also reflecting a bit on H. P. Lovecraft, because there is something of him in Johnny Appleseed, as well. Something of his generous obscurity. [And indeed the poem is titled "The Lovecrafter."] So Ralph Nader, Johnny Appleseed, and H. P. Lovecraft all find their way into this little poem. I'd be happy to go to the prom with any of them.

Surely, this has to be among the strangest trio of possible prom dates imaginable, but Smith's story reminds us that the Myth of Johnny Appleseed is a very big tent indeed—large enough for messianic critics of the corporate state and thrift-bank savings programs alike; for a real frontiersman, a legendary nurseryman, and the spectral emanation of both; for elfin Appleseeds and macho ones; for lifers and day-trippers and the heavily tripped out; for sermonettes and cautionary tales and cosmic horror stories.

❦

Johnny Appleseed is where we go to rediscover American innocence and to be reminded that this world really is about more than getting and spending, and that life has—or should have—higher goals and greater challenges than riches and clout. As the *New York Times* editorialized on April 1, 1951, channeling W. D. Haley and Charles Allen Smart:

> The men of his day who sought and gained wealth, power and prestige are long forgotten. Still remembered, as fresh as Ohio apple blossoms, is the simple man who took no care for the things of the morrow as he walked through early American history and brushed close to people's hearts. Perhaps it was because,

after all, wealth and power and prestige may not be so hard to achieve; many a man gets them. Johnny Appleseed aimed at something much tougher: to leave the world a more neighborly place than he found it.

Two centuries before there was a Simplicity Movement, John Chapman had created a lifestyle that was simplicity itself—a level of consumption that would drive the national economy back to a barter system if it were widely practiced. Like the Greek Cynics, he shunned ease and comfort that he might spend his days in the presence of true virtue. Snuff, the occasional tool, a rare tavern meal or night under a rented roof, the Swedenborg books—that was all of the earth's resources he seems to have needed, and the books he recycled to a fare-thee-well. Johnny didn't merely live lightly on the land; he barely touched it, even though he walked it constantly.

"'Tis the gift to be simple, / 'Tis the gift to be free, / 'Tis the gift to come down where you ought to be," the old Shaker hymn goes. "And when we find ourselves in the place just right, / It will be in the valley of love and delight." Could there be a better forty-three-word summary of John Chapman's life?

Long before all but a handful of people realized what a fragile creation this earth is, Chapman and Appleseed were there, too, coddling Nature as if she were a newborn baby. And that finally might be the greatest gift of both. John Chapman had scripture urging him on—not only the Bible, but Swedenborg as well: "All things in the world exist from a Divine Origin . . . clothed with such forms in nature as enable them to exist there and perfect their use and correspond to higher things." But however it came to be, by God's hand or as nothing more than a cosmic accident, and by whatever label one comes to the challenge—creation care, evangelical environmentalism, secular green, planetary survivalist—this whirling globe of ours does need someone to show us how to love it better. As he always was in life, Johnny Appleseed is waiting out there even now, at that razor-thin line between present and future, man and myth, the real and the imagined, ready to lead the way.

My Johnny

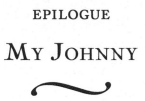

A close friend—a lawyer with a Sufi's heart—has a vision of John Chapman building his bramble enclosures, planting his seeds, then twirling Sufi-like the whole night long in rapturous concord with whatever he conceived of as the Universal Divine. I can see that. Chapman, Appleseed, whatever you call him, might have out-Swedenborged Swedenborg. God talked to him through every tree, every leaf, every rock, every beast great and small, every atom of creation. How could he not twirl in joy? Johnny's famous loneliness might not have been so lonely after all. As William Dean Howells once wrote, "If his belief was true and we are in this world surrounded by spirits, evil or good, which our evil or good behavior invites to be of our company, then this harmless, loving, uncouth, half-crazy man walked daily with the angels of God."

I can see also Henry David Thoreau in Chapman—two children of New England living deliberately in nature. Indeed, at the very moment John Chapman lay dying in William Worth's cabin in Fort Wayne, Thoreau was digging the foundation for his celebrated cabin at Walden. But for all his intellectual independence, Thoreau never cut the lifeline. Walden was within easy walking distance of the world he had always known. Even as he was rhapsodizing on life in the woods, Thoreau was still carrying laundry home to his mother. Not so Chapman. From his early twenties on, maybe before, he had no tether left.

In an article for the December 1979 *American Heritage* magazine, Edward Hoagland suggests that if Chapman had left a diary behind, he might today be compared to John James Audubon or George Catlin, the great Indian portraitist. I like that. Certainly, his diary would not have been what Thoreau's writings were: a relentless critique of the Industrial Revolution. Chapman lived his critique. The nature he loved and gave himself over to vibrated through his entire being. Like Walt Whitman, Chapman sang "the body electric."

Years ago, I spent a long night with the Washington, DC, Emergency Psychiatric Response Team, heroic men and women tending to the certifiably insane who had been deinstitutionalized from area hospitals. Most of those they treated that night were living in the city's parks, often short walks from the Capitol or the White House. These were women convinced they were men who had been castrated by demons; men essentially baying at the moon. One man told me that when he walked down the street and saw the stars overhead, he was convinced each star was part of an intergalactic space fleet that was looking to him for direction. "If I turn right, they turn right," he told me. "If I turn left, they go left. What if I turn the wrong way?" We found him paralyzed, in the middle of an intersection. The sky was full of stars.

I can't help but recall those people when I think of Johnny Appleseed. They were dressed roughly the same, in odd bits of cast-off clothing, sometimes with talismanic meaning. They smelled horribly, as John Chapman must have. Voices exploded in their heads; their brains were on fire. Occasionally, their eyes almost glowed as they talked, as his were said to. By our modern definitions, John Chapman almost certainly was insane. As the old adage goes, if you talk to God, it's prayer. If God talks to you, it's schizophrenia.

I think, too, of the woods that surround the office where I have written much of this book—of how light shines through the trees, of what a simple joy it is to turn away from these words and walk among the black walnuts and locusts and hawthorns that wait beyond my windows, beckoning me to join them. "There is a pleasure in the pathless woods," Lord Byron wrote in *Childe Harold.* "There is society, where none intrudes." And so it surely was for John Chapman. To go easy in this busy world. To walk those pathless woods and feel the dappled sunlight on your skin. To shine and be simple. That's Johnny Appleseed to me.

ACKNOWLEDGMENTS

This book began with a suggestion made more than two decades ago by my friend and colleague Dick Victory. A thousand thanks to him.

Joe Besecker, Director of the Johnny Appleseed Society at Urbana University, opened wide the Society's collections and archives for my inspections. Many thanks to him, as well, and to a host of historical society workers and volunteers, and librarians in Massachusetts, Pennsylvania, West Virginia, Ohio, and Indiana, for helping guide my research. Any listing is bound to be incomplete, but here's a start, working roughly westward: Farida Pomerantz of the Storrs (Public) Library in Longmeadow, MA; Michelle Gray and Marianne Battista of the Warren County (PA) and Venango County (PA) historical societies, respectively; West Virginia State Parks & Forests historian Ray Swick; Ken Finkel of the Washington County (OH) Historical Society; Linda Showalter, Special Collections Librarian at Marietta College; Dan Fleming of the Newark (OH) Public Library; Jim Gibson, head of the Knox County (OH) Historical Society; and Randy Elliot of the History Center in Fort Wayne, Indiana, part of the Allen County–Fort Wayne Historical Society. Their work is invaluable in preserving local and regional records and memory.

Any author who tackles Johnny Appleseed stands, of necessity, on the shoulders of Robert Price and his superb 1954 biography, *Johnny Appleseed: Man and Myth*, and I'm no exception. Price, in turn, benefited greatly from the counsel and research of what I have come to think of as the Two Late Florences: Florence Murdoch, secretary of the Swedenborgian Church in Cincinnati, and

Florence Wheeler, longtime librarian in Leominster, MA. I, too, am in their debt.

Carroll Odhner, Director of the Swedenborg Library at Bryn Athyn College outside Philadelphia, and Rev. Kurt Horigan Asplundh of the General Church of the New Jerusalem gave generously of their time so that I might better understand the New Church and John Chapman's place in its history. Arthur Humphrey and Jean Woods were equally generous in illuminating Chapman's ties to John Young, who almost certainly introduced the future Johnny Appleseed to the compelling visions of Emanuel Swedenborg.

My literary agent, Rafe Sagalyn, believed in this book from first mention. Alice Mayhew, my editor, has been wonderfully encouraging and helpful when I have needed it most, as has Karen Thompson. Heartfelt thanks all around.

Of friends and family, I'm multiply blessed. Ben Lamberton, Brewster Willcox, Dan Rapoport, Scott Shane, Robinson Duncan, Wendy and Vaughn Clatterbuck, Winslow McCagg, Nancy Talley, Doug Bartley, and the late Roger Chavez among many, many others asked key questions, provided obscure answers, suggested further reading, and patiently lent ears to sometimes rambling musings. Charlie and Cornelia Saltzman put me in touch with Penn State University pomologist Jim Schupp, who with great care walked me through the mysteries of the apple seed. My son, Nathan, helped shape and guide this book; my daughter, Ihrie, has illustrated it beautifully. Grandson Caper, age 5, reintroduced me to a child's delight in the Walt Disney version of Johnny Appleseed's life. As always, Candy, my wife, has been first reader and chief sounding board.

The faults of this book are mine; any credit is broadly shared.

I'm also grateful to the following sources and organizations for permission to quote from the works cited.

Ohio Historical Society: Mss. 951 (Buttles Family Paper, Letter from Lura Ann Bristol to Levi Buttles, 30 September, 1869) and VFM 1620 (Julia Buttles Case Papers, Letter from Ruhamah Mays to Elizabeth, wife of Captain Job Case, 23 August, 1805).

Johnny Appleseed Foundation: Robert Price, *Johnny Appleseed: Man and Myth* (copyright © 1954 by Robert Price).

Harper's Magazine: Charles Allen Smart, "The Return of Johnny Appleseed" (copyright © 1939 by Harper's Magazine. All rights reserved. Reproduced from the August issue by special permission).

Brandt & Hochman Literary Agents, Inc.: Rosemary and Stephen Vincent Benét, "Johnny Appleseed" (from *A Book of Americans* by Rosemary and Stephen Vincent Benét, copyright © 1933 by Rosemary and Stephen Vincent Benét; copyright renewed © 1961 by Rosemary Carr Benét).

American Philosophical Society: John Meurig Thomas, "Rumford's Remarkable Creation," *Proceedings*, 142, 4, 1998.

University of Rochester Library Bulletin: Peter Stadnitski, "Advance Information on an American Land Speculation" (trans. R.W.G. Vail), XXIV, 2 & 3, Winter-Spring 1969.

NOTES

1: Right Fresh from Heaven

1 *"the morning-glory leaves about his gray beard":* Memories of Rosella Rice, cited in H. S. Knapp, *A History of the Pioneer and Modern Times of Ashland County from the Earliest to the Present Day* (Philadelphia: J. B. Lippincott & Co., 1863), 33.

3 *skins had been selling for as much as ten dollars each back then:* Fortescue Cuming, *Cuming's Tour to the Western Country: 1807–1809* (Cleveland: A. H. Clark Co., 1904), 137.

3 *"and by far more vicious & wicked":* James H. O'Donnell III, *Ohio's First Peoples* (Athens, OH: Ohio University Press, 2004), 43.

4 *"the oddest character in all our history":* A. Banning Norton, *A History of Knox County, Ohio, from 1779 to 1862 Inclusive* (Columbus, OH: Richard Nevins, 1862), 50.

4 *"Generations yet to come shall rise up and call you blessed":* Cited in William E. Leuchtenberg, "John Chapman (Johnny Appleseed)," *Forgotten Heroes: Inspiring American Portraits from Our Leading Historians,* ed. Susan Ware (New York: The Free Press, 1998), 15.

4 *"as we, who knew him, have learned to love him":* Framed quote hanging on the wall of the Johnny Appleseed Educational Center and Museum, Urbana University, Urbana, OH.

10 *"spiritual character of the visible, audible, tangible world":* Emerson's oration "The American Scholar" was delivered before the Phi Beta Kappa Society in Cambridge, MA, on August 31, 1837.

13 *"he manifested that singular character attributed to him":* W. M. Glines, *Johnny Appleseed by One Who Knew Him* (Columbus, OH: K. J. Heer Printing Co., 1922), www.archive.org/stream/johnnyappleseedb00glin/johnnyappleseed b00glin_djvu.txt.

14 *1954 biography* Johnny Appleseed: Man & Myth: Robert Price, *Johnny Appleseed: Man & Myth* (Bloomington: Indiana University Press, 1954). This is an essential work on John Chapman, gracefully written and painstakingly researched.

2: Roots

17 *"I have as much as I need for the present":* Lost for more than a century and a half, Elizabeth Chapman's letter first appeared in print in 1936, in a

booklet published by the Fort Wayne, Indiana, Johnny Appleseed Memorial Commission.

18 *"Crossed the Appalachians, / And was 'young John Chapman'":* Vachel Lindsay, *Collected Poems* (New York: Macmillan, 1923).

22 *"a handsomer man never walked our main street":* Grace P. Amsden's history of Concord, written in the 1950s, is unpublished. An electronic version of the book is available at ci.concord.nh.us/Library/concordhistory/concordv2.asp?siteindx=L20,08,05.

25 *"an ingenious inventor, and an exceptionally innovative scientist":* John Meurig Thomas, "Rumford's Remarkable Creation," *Proceedings,* American Philosophical Society, vol. 142, no. 4, 1998, 597.

25 *the young cousin who would eventually gain a reputation that dwarfs his own:* Online sources for the genealogy of the Symonds-Simonds-Simons family are too numerous to list here. For a good, brief history of Count Rumford, see Reverend Samuel Sewall's 1868 account, "Life Story of Benjamin Thompson, Jr.," part of his *History of Woburn, Middlesex County, Mass.,* available at www.homeofourfathers.com/lisbeth/benjaminthompsonjrlifestory.htm.

26 *spelled out Johnny Appleseed's paternal heritage in detail for the first time:* Florence Wheeler, "John Chapman's Line of Descent from Edward Chapman of Ipswich," *The Ohio State Archeological and Historical Quarterly* 48 (January 1939). Wheeler's work is masterful.

27 *before his own death of smallpox, on December 7, 1760:* Mid-eighteenth-century dates can be particularly confusing. Great Britain and its possession officially adopted the Gregorian calendar in 1752, but many town and church record keepers in New England continued to use the Julian calendar. Thus, for example, one set of records has John Chapman dying in Tewksbury on December 7, 1760, at age forty-six years and five days, and another dying in the same place on January 23, 1761, at age forty-six years and eighteen days. They are, however, almost certainly the same John Chapman.

29 *overlooking Boston harbor, in mid-June 1775:* Company records give Nathaniel's height as five feet nine inches, exactly the average height of the day, and the same height his son, John, would eventually attain. At six feet two—taller in his boots—George Washington towered over the men he commanded.

30 *but it does suggest considerable mitigation:* Robert Price's supposed slighting of Nathaniel Chapman's military service can be found in Price, *Johnny Appleseed,* 16. George Huff's extensive rebuttal, the source of the quotes that follow, is in the collection of Storrs (public) Library, Longmeadow, MA.

32 *the son he had rarely seen since John was well shy of a year old:* For more on the Cooley family in Longmeadow, see *Proceedings of the Centennial*

Celebration of the Incorporation of the Town of Longmeadow, October 17th 1883, published by the Secretary of the Centennial Committee, under Authority of the Town, 1884; and *Reflections of Longmeadow: 1783/1983*, ed. Linda M. Rodger and Mary S. Rogeness, published by the Longmeadow Historical Society.

32 *frame home that dates back to at least 1695:* Tradition holds that the house in which the Chapman-Cooley family was raised once stood in the meadow after which Longmeadow was named. Later, it was disassembled and moved to 135 Bliss Street. Still later, it was moved again, one lot south to 14 Fairfield Terrace, where, with additions and modifications, it still stands.

3: Breaking Away

37 *"the mighty army that for two hundred and fifty years has been marching westward"*: *Proceedings of the Centennial Celebration of the Incorporation of the Town of Longmeadow*, 105. Then living in Chicago, Reverend Charles R. Bliss was serving as general secretary of the Congregational Church's New West Education Commission, whose object was "the promotion of Christian civilization in Utah and adjacent States and Territories." And he clearly did not like what his travels had revealed to him of life on the frontier. Far better these westerners should heed the example of Longmeadow's founders, who "commissioned in [God's] providence to build a town . . . put into their work not only toil and daring and endurance, but fidelity to moral ideas, and obedience to divine instructions. Would that the founders of the countless towns now springing up in the far West were actuated by similar principles, but as the spent ripples on a lee-shore so are the conservative influences of justice, intelligence and religion upon many of those towns. A revival of the rigid and uncompromising virtues that brought our fathers here, and sustained them till their work was grandly done, is needed from the Atlantic to the Pacific ocean; and upon its coming, we cannot doubt, rests the safety of the republic."

38 *the Swedenborgian Church of North America:* The J. Appleseed history of Johnny Appleseed can be found at www.swedenborg.org/jappleseed/history.html. In 1890, doctrinal issues and an internal dispute over the authority of Swedenborg's texts caused the New Church to split into two groups: the General Convention of the New Church, based in Bryn Athyn, just outside Philadelphia, and the Swedenborgian Church of North America, headquartered in Newtonville, MA.

40 *northern end of what is now Allegheny National Forest:* Sherman Day, *Historical Collections of the State of Pennsylvania: Containing a Copious Selection of the Most Interesting Facts, Traditions, Biographical Sketches, Anecdotes,*

etc., Relating to Its History and Antiquities, both General and Local, with Topographical Descriptions of Every County and the Larger Towns in the State (Philadelphia: G. W. Gorton, 1843).

41   *"So I figured I would take the most expeditious way out"*: Interview with the author.

43   *"one false step might hurl horse and rider into the abyss below"*: Archer Butler Hulbert, *Historic Highways of America*, vol. 11, bk. 1, *Pioneer Roads and Experiences of Travelers* (Cleveland: The Arthur H. Clark Company, 1904), 28.

44   *slept not under blankets but between feather-filled mattresses:* For more on Francis Baily's travels, see Hulbert, *Historic Highways of America*, vol. 11, bk. 1, 106–38.

46   *in the Laurel Highlands, the snow lay four feet deep:* Data here is drawn mostly from Ben Gelber, *The Pennsylvania Weather Book* (Piscataway, NJ: Rutgers University Press, 2002), 34*ff.*

47   *where the winter weather is almost always more extreme:* Joseph Price's 1796 weather diary can be viewed online at www.lowermerionhistory.org/texts /price/price1796.html.

47   *"soon after which fell two feet of snow"*: S. P. Hildreth, *Pioneer History: Being an Account of the First Examination of the Ohio Valley, and the Early Settlement of the Northwest Territory* (Cincinnati: H. W. Derry & Co., 1848), 487.

50   *overwhelming the state and New England as a whole:* Winifred Barr Rothenberg, "The Invention of American Capitalism: The Economy of New England in the Federal Period," *Engines of Enterprise: An Economic History of New England,* ed. Peter Temin (Cambridge, MA: Harvard University Press, 2000), 69*ff.*

51   *down to 2.8 children by the middle of the next century:* For more, see Daniel Scott Smith, *Population, Family and Society in Hingham, Massachusetts, 1635–1880* (Ann Arbor, MI: Xerox University Microfilms, 1975).

54   *"hair-breadth escapes by flood and field"*: Cited in Carolee K. Michener, *Franklin: A Place in History* (Franklin, PA, Bicentennial Committee: 1995), 20*ff.*

4: Land, Ho!

55   *"These advantages are all of the greatest benefit to trade and agriculture"*: For Peter Stadnitski's complete report, see *University of Rochester Library Bulletin,* vol. 24, nos. 2 & 3, Winter–Spring 1969, lib.rochester.edu/index .cfm?PAGE=1013. The translation is by R. W. G. Vail.

58   *"Nothing was done to improve the land"*: Not all of Robert Morris's speculation proved so successful. He spent the years 1798–1801 in a Philadelphia prison, unable to meet his debts.

59   *"many who had planned to buy were turned away empty-handed":* Paul Demund Evans, *The Holland Land Company* (Clifton, NJ: A. M. Kelly, 1975), 28–29.

60   *in a valley ringed by old apple orchards:* For more, see *Travels in the Years 1791 and 1792 in Pennsylvania, New York and Vermont. Journals of John Lincklaen, Agent of the Holland Land Company* (New York: G.P. Putnam's Sons, 1897).

62   *sold, at prices ranging from $2.50 to $6:* Roughly $31 to $75 in current dollars.

63   *"fond of fun, fight and whiskey":* Warren County history is drawn largely from two sources: *History of Warren County, Pennsylvania,* ed. J. S. Schenck (Syracuse, NY: D. Mason & Co., 1887), and Sherman Day's 1843 history earlier cited. The Warren County Historical Society and its newsletter, *Stepping Stones,* are also valuable resources.

67   *the town that by then bore his name:* The anecdote that casts aspersions on Matthew Young's survivability can be found in Schenck, 403*ff.* Young is exonerated in Frances Ramsay, "A Profile of Matthew Young, Founder of Youngsville," *Stepping Stones* 8 (September 1963).

67   *trading post back where creek and river met:* The John Daniels ledger is in the care of the Warren County Historical Society. In its *Stepping Stones* newsletter of March 1955, the society provides a brief history of the ledger. "It came to the Court House with the papers of Mr. Ezra Trimm who died in 1893 leaving his estate for the benefit of the poor of Eldred Township. The book had been used as a scrap book and was filed away with the pertinent papers—and forgotten. One day, Mr. George Seavy, one of the County Commissioners, had occasion to consult the file. He was attracted by the beautiful old leather volume and picked it up to examine it. He was surprised to see the early dates appearing between the pasted clippings and took the book to Mr. Merle Deardorff who promptly sent it to Harrisburg. There the clippings were removed, the pages laminated, the contents microfilmed and the book returned to Warren County."

71   *four square miles of forest, meadow, scrub, and wilderness:* The county is still lightly settled, but as of the 2000 Census, population density was about fifty people per square mile, roughly two hundred times what it was two hundred years earlier.

73   *published in the* Warren Ledger *in 1854:* Lansing Wetmore's 1853 oration on John Chapman can be found in *Stepping Stones,* 885–87.

76   *pick surnames from the same narrow pool:* See H. Kenneth Dirlam's pamphlet "A Gatherer and Planter of Appleseeds," published by the Richland County (Ohio) Historical Society, circa 1956.

5: Down to Business

78 *"to alter, in whatever matter, the laws of property"*: Alexis de Tocqueville, *Democracy in America*, trans. Henry Reeve (Cambridge, MA: Sever and Francis, 1863), 314.

78 *trading-post ledger that has long since disappeared:* The ledger entry is noted in the 1879 *History of Venango County, Pennsylvania*, by J. H. Newton, reprinted in 1976 by (and available from) the Venango County Historical Society.

80 *"with the red men of the forest, as with his own race"*: Newton, *History of Venango County*, 595.

81 *"he drifted further westward"*: *History of Venango County, Pennsylvania*, vol. 1 (Chicago: Brown, Runk & Co., 1890), 562–63.

83 *the bite that introduced sin and death into the world:* The fruit and bite survive in the name and logo of Steve Jobs's computer company, although one suspects that Jobs is more interested in suggesting knowledge than in that common admonition of early American readers: "In Adam's fall sinned we all."

85 *Insula Pomorom, the "Isle of Apples"*: Sources here are primarily Berton Roueché, "One Hundred Thousand Varieties," *The New Yorker*, August 11, 1975; Marcel de Cleene and Marie Claire Lejeune, *Compendium of Symbolic and Ritual Plants in Europe: Trees and Shrubs*, vol. 1 (Ghent, Belgium: Man & Culture Publishers, 1999); and Mrs. M. Grieve, *A Modern Herbal: The Medicinal, Culinary, Cosmetic, and Economic Properties, Cultivation, and Folk-Lore of Herbs, Grasses, Fungi, Shrubs & Trees with All Their Modern Scientific Uses* (New York: Harcourt, Brace, & Company, 1931).

88 *are credited to Zane's nursery:* For more on nurseries on the Ohio frontier, see *Bulletin 326* of the Ohio Agricultural Experiment Station, July 1918; and James Morton Callahan, *Semi-Centennial History of West Virginia* (Semi-Centennial Commission of West Virginia: 1913), 343.

89 *to markets as far away as New Orleans:* R. Douglas Hurt, *The Ohio Frontier* (Bloomington: Indiana University Press, 1996), 243*ff.*

90 *there were always places to stop along the way:* Correspondence with the author. Arthur F. Humphrey is also the author of a fine article— "Greensburg: Johnny Appleseed's Spiritual Nursery"—which appeared in the Summer 2006 issue of *Westmoreland* (County, PA) *History*.

90 *"'the Pittsburgh, Fort Wayne and Chicago Railway Dept.'"*: Price, *Johnny Appleseed*, Appendix B: "John Chapman's Nurseries."

90 *"they must have been tenfold more so"*: W. D. Haley, "Johnny Appleseed: A Pioneer Hero," *Harper's New Monthly Magazine*, November 1871, 830*ff.*

93 *apple propagation by seed utterly unreliable:* I've been helped immeasurably in these pages by the counsel of Dr. Jim Schupp, Associate Professor of Pomology at Penn State University.

96   *corroborating evidence abounds:* For more, see Michael Pollan, *The Botany of Desire: A Plant's-Eye View of the World* (New York: Random House, 2001), chapter 1, "Desire: Sweetness, Plant: The Apple."

97   *thirty gallons of hard cider, and a quart of wine:* Virginia E. and Robert W. McCormick, *New Englanders on the Ohio Frontier: Migration and Settlement of Worthington, Ohio* (Kent, OH: The Kent State University Press, 1998), 243.

6: A Calling

100   *"the delight of the greater part of the students":* Sydney E. Ahlstrom, *A Religious History of the American People* (New Haven: Yale University Press, 1972), 415*ff.* The winner of the 1973 National Book Award, Ahlstrom's book is a magnificent piece of scholarship and easily accessible.

100   *"couthness" clearly counted not for a thing:* Charles A. Johnson, *The Frontier Camp Meeting: Religion's Harvest Time* (Dallas: Southern Methodist University Press, 1955). See especially chapter 2, "Seed Time."

106   *"and devoted my work to spiritual matters":* Quoted in "Emanuel Swedenborg" by Lars Bergquist (1986), part of the *Swedish Portraits* series published by the government-financed Swedish Institute.

108   *we cannot serve our neighbors as God intended:* Emanuel Swedenborg, *Heaven and Hell,* 3rd ed., trans. George F. Dole (New York: Swedenborg Foundation, Inc., 1984). For Swedenborg on the divisions of heaven, see 40; on thought-speech, 28; on dwellings in heaven, 141–42; on the malice that displays itself in hell, 482.

109   *were clearly influenced by Swedenborg:* www.swedenborg.org.uk/writers-influenced-by-swedenborg.

111   *"the New Church in America, if not in the world":* Reverend H. Clinton Hay's 1917 history is reprinted in *Our Daily Bread,* vol. 54, no. 9, September 2003—a monthly publication of the Swedenborgian Church.

112   *"with the* spiritual sense *of [God's] holy word":* John Hargrove, *A Sermon, on the Second Coming of Christ, and on the Last Judgment: Delivered the 25th December, 1804, Before Both Houses of Congress, at the Capitol in Washington* (Baltimore: Warner & Hanna, 1805).

113   *some time not long after the start of the new century:* For more, see Humphrey, "Greensburg: Johnny Appleseed's Spiritual Nursery."

116   *where he "baptized near 40 souls, old and young":* Robert Hindemarsh and Edward Madeley, *Rise and Progress of the New Jerusalem Church in England, America, and Other Parts* (London: Hodson & Son, 1861), 187.

116   *makeshift catamaran, bags packed with seed:* In a February 15, 1957, "American Notebook" piece on Johnny Appleseed for *The Christian Science*

Monitor, author Montagu Frank Modder suggests that the canoes might have been packed with rotting apples. Surely the seeds alone would have been easier and more pleasant to transport!

119   *destroyed by flooding a year later:* Charles R. Rector, "The Genesis of Blennerhassett Island," *The West Virginia Review* 11 (September 1932).

122   *"Here is news right fresh from heaven for you":* See *Our Daily Bread,* September 2003.

123   *"loses his wisdom, stammers, and falls prey to despair":* Swedenborg, *Heaven and Hell.* For the Three Heavens, see 46; for the spirit world after death, 358; for the balance between heaven and hell, 447.

7: In Country

125   *"the first swarming of the New England hive":* Newell Dwight Hillis, *The Quest of John Chapman: The Story of a Forgotten Hero* (New York: The Macmillan Company, 1904), 10, 19–23.

129   *magnified as they would never be again:* In *The Ohio Frontier,* R. Douglas Hurt notes that Ohio's Native Americans were also decimated by crop failure, famine, and smallpox that swept down the Ohio River Valley in 1762. "Sick and Dying everyday" was the way one observer described Ohio's Shawnee country that year. See 45*ff.*

131   *"convenient port holes for firing out of":* Hurt, *The Ohio Frontier,* 121.

131   *The New Eden finally was up for grabs:* Hurt, *The Ohio Frontier.* Chapter 4, "The Road to Hell," and chapter 5, "Fallen Timbers," provide an excellent overview of these Indian wars.

132   *the delightfully ironic name of William Playfair:* For more on the Scioto Company and William Playfair, see George W. Knepper, *Ohio and Its People* (Kent, Ohio: The Kent State University Press, 1989), beginning at 66. William Dean Howells's reflections on the land scam are found in *Stories of Ohio* (New York: Harper & Brothers, 1897), 174–78.

133   *Cutler seems to have been almost without peer:* Louis W. Potts, "Visions of America, 1787–1788: The Ohio of Reverend Manasseh Cutler," *Ohio History* 111 (Summer–Autumn 2002): 101–20.

134   *a bargain but not as great as one might suppose:* Hurt, *The Ohio Frontier,* 254–55.

135   *"the eye which he held triumphantly in the other":* Cuming, *Cuming's Tour to the Western Country,* 137–38.

137   *"God only can improve the apples":* Price, *Johnny Appleseed,* 46–60.

138   *"for a sleeping companion I can't see":* For more on Andy Craig, see Norton, *A History of Knox County,* 50*ff.*

139 *Indian land stretched for miles upon miles:* For more on John Stilley, see Norton, *A History of Knox County,* 103*ff.*

141 *"frighten any honest dutchman almost out of his wits":* Norton, *A History of Knox County,* 109.

141 *How* could *Chapman have been easily forgotten:* Norton's chapter devoted to Chapman begins at 128.

142 *farming and cheese making than in the healing arts:* Lori Scharf, " 'I Would Go Wherever Fortune Would Direct': Hannah Huntington and the Frontier of the Western Reserve," *Ohio History* 97 (Winter–Spring 1988): 5–28.

143 *any part of what they had helped to create:* Robert W. and Virginia E. McCormick, "New England Culture on the Ohio Frontier," 33*ff.*

144 *silver lining in the clouds overhead:* The description of Arora's sorrow over his father's death comes from a letter written by Lura Ann Bristol, of Worthington, Ohio, to Levi Buttles, Gambier, Ohio, on September 30, 1869 (MSS 951, Buttles Family Papers, Ohio Historical Society). Ruhamah Mays's descriptions of frontier times are contained in a letter sent by Mays, of Worthington, Ohio, to Elizabeth, the wife of Captain Job Case, in Granby, Connecticut, on August 23, 1805 (VFM 1620, Julia Buttles Case Collection, Ohio Historical Society).

145 *all part of his portable apothecary:* The noxious dog fennel (alternative names include "stinking mayweed") that Chapman wrongly advocated for malaria was long known as "Johnny weed," although that term today is more linked to cannabis.

146 *"they never would do him wrong":* Norton, *A History of Knox County,* 134.

8: The Plan

147 *grew in great, shrub-like clumps:* N. N. Hill, Jr., *History of Coshocton County, Ohio: Its Past and Present* (Newark, Ohio: A. A. Graham & Co., 1881). Hill's description of the early flora and fauna of the area begins on 257. Coshocton County, it should be noted, was originally part of Knox County.

148 *"especially as it was done in the course of a few weeks":* Letter from Reverend Daniel Story to Thaddeu Mason Harris, dated June 3, 1803. Cited in *Williams History of Washington County, Ohio: 1788–1881* (Cleveland: H. Z. Williams & Bro., 1881), 98.

150 *danger on all sides but mostly from the French and their Indian allies:* The *Journal of Christopher Gist, 1750–51,* is available online at donchesnut.com/genealogy/pages/gistjournal.pdf. The entries cited here begin on 5.

152 *"while he stared at his trophy in bewilderment":* Howells, *Stories of Ohio,* 177*ff.*

153 *"make a true Report thereof to the Company":* Gist, *Journal*, 2.

155 *Chapman was very much a part of it all:* Ben Butler, Dr. Henderson, and the tornado of 1808 can all be found in Norton, *A History of Knox County*, 57*ff.*

158 *"any private conveyance nearer than Newark or Zanesville":* Price, *Johnny Appleseed*, 73*ff.*

159 *"In short, all of them are reflections of their own hells":* Swedenborg, *Heaven and Hell*, 460.

160 *"one of the best customers the court had":* Norton's description of James Craig begins on 61.

160 *"gracious, respectable hospitality and business decorum":* Price, *Johnny Appleseed*, 68.

162 *the easily confused name of Johnny Goldthwaite:* Isaac Smucker, *Centennial History of Licking County, Ohio* (Newark, OH: Clark & Underwood, 1876). Comments on Chapman are on 48. The description of Catharine Stadden can be found on 72.

163 *supporters of the Swedenborg-based Church of the New Jerusalem:* Proof of global connectivity: I discovered the tenuous J. M. Smucker–Asplundh Tree Expert connection on, of all places, *Pravda*'s English-language website, engforum.pravda.ru/showthread.php?p=2848565.

163 *near Fallsburg, and St. Albans Township:* Notes of Ben Jones, cited in Price, *Johnny Appleseed*, 284n29.

166 *but it could be leased for ninety-nine years:* See Price, *Johnny Appleseed*, Appendix C: "John Chapman's Land Holdings."

167 *"zealously lived out—the Swedenborgian doctrine":* Knapp, *A History of the Pioneer and Modern Times of Ashland County*, 32.

168 *"protection against all danger, here and hereafter":* Knapp's chapter on John Chapman begins on 27. It should be noted that these early Ohio histories tend to recycle many of the same Chapman/Appleseed stories, often in the same or very nearly the same words.

169 *"his credentials as to the latter of these":* N. N. Hill's chapter on Chapman begins on 264.

169 *"from all entangling alliances in this":* Hill, *History of Coshocton County*, 264.

170 *the family finances must have been perilous:* Lucy Cooley did have at least one well-off relative follow her to Ohio. Cousin James Cooley, almost thirty years her junior, graduated from Yale and moved to Ohio in 1815 to practice law. In 1826, John Quincy Adams named him chargé d'affaires to Lima, Peru, where James Cooley died the following year.

171 *when John Chapman was turning six years old:* Hill, *History of Coshocton County*, 264.

172 *Chapman started frequenting the eastern edge of Indiana:* " 'Johnny Appleseed'—John Chapman," *Ohio History* 9 (April 1901), 307–8.

172   *himself descended from one of the stepsiblings:* See Frank O. Chapman's "John Chapman (Johnny Appleseed)," presented to the Brooke County (WV) Historical Association, April 20, 1967. (Chapman's talk is available online at brookcountywvgenealogy.org/JohnChapman.html.) Other accounts have Chapman appearing for a last time in Green Township, near Ashland, in 1843.

173   *"immemorial to the oldest inhabitants":* Williams *History of Washington County,* 587.

173   *"Her frequent, 'says she's' and 'says I's'":* Knapp, *A History of the Pioneer and Modern Times of Ashland County,* 33. The acidic characterization of Persis Broom comes from the pen of Rosella Rice, an ardent keeper of the Appleseed flame.

173   *John had befriended almost a decade earlier:* The bear story can be found in "The First Apples in Washington County," handwritten notes of Austin A. Middleswart, born 1837, available at the Washington County (OH) Public Library, History & Genealogical Room. The Silverheels account comes from C. Burr Dawes's "Johnny Appleseed in Marietta and the Muskingum Valley," *Tallow Light* 4 (February 1967). *Tallow Light* is a publication of the Washington County Historical Society.

9: Man to Myth

176   *"labors, angel-crowned, in heaven":* Rosella Rice, *Mabel: Or, Heart Histories* (New York: Follett, Foster, and Co., 1863).

177   *"a good old man, a friend, and a benefactor":* Knapp, *A History,* devotes considerable space to Rice's memories, beginning on 31.

177   *"tens of thousands at his death":* Ohio *History* 9, beginning at 305.

178   *"partake the proffered hospitality":* Knapp, *A History,* 74*ff.*

178   *"she was already engaged":* Henry Howe, *Historical Collections of Ohio: An Encyclopedia of the State,* vol. 1 (Norwalk, OH: The Laning Printing Co., 1896), 260.

179   *entangling foreign alliances:* www.shmoop.com/war-1812/timeline.html. For an in-depth look at the War of 1812, see A. J. Langguth, *Union 1812: The Americans Who Fought the Second War of Independence* (New York: Simon & Schuster, 2007).

183   *under the terms of Hull's surrender:* Price, *Johnny Appleseed,* 87*ff.*

184   *"the smoke of their ruined wigwams":* The most complete account of these events can be found at Knapp, *A History,* 525–32.

185   *That's when the horror began:* Norton's lengthy (and slightly different) description of these events in *A History of Knox County* begins at 136.

186   *"protect the settlers from their savage foes":* Ohio *History* 9, 309*ff.* "Jezreel" was the biblical seat of King Ahab.

186   *"midnight silence reigned without"*: Hill, *History of Coshocton County*, 266.

187   *"moonlight midnight with his piercing voice"*: Cited in Price, *Johnny Apple-seed*, 94.

190   *"payment in Books of the New Church"*: The New Church documents that follow are all available for inspection at the library of Bryn Athyn College, on the north side of Philadelphia. The library is an excellent and highly accessible source for all such matters.

10: The Last Frontier

195   *luck and skill and, yes, undaunted courage:* The essential book on the Lewis and Clark expedition is Stephen Ambrose, *Undaunted Courage: Meriwether Lewis, Thomas Jefferson, and the Opening of the American West* (New York, Simon & Schuster, 2007). The title reverses a phrase Thomas Jefferson used in a memorial to Lewis, written after his death—a memorial that could apply equally to John Chapman: "Of courage undaunted, possessing a firmness and perseverance of purpose which nothing but impossibilities could divert from its direction. . . ."

199   *"he has made all things for good"*: See Price, *Johnny Appleseed*, 115*ff*. E. Vandorn's reminiscences were in the form of a letter that appeared in two installments in the weekly (Mansfield) *Ohio Liberal* newspaper of August 13 and August 20, 1873.

200   *inside a huge hollowed-out sycamore tree:* Price, *Johnny Appleseed*, 51.

203   *on or near the Wabash River:* Price, *Johnny Appleseed*, Appendix C.

204   *but certainly does not in any deeper sense:* See www.indiana.edu/~molpage /What%20is%20a%20Hoosier.pdf for a fuller treatment of "Hoosier." The Indiana poet James Whitcomb Riley once suggested that "Hoosier" was a corruption of "Whose ear?" and traced back to the debris of vicious barroom brawls once common in the state and all across the frontier.

205   *"at the foot of Main Street, Fort Wayne"*: Dawson's recollections are largely contained in two letters to the *Fort Wayne Sentinel*, published October 21 and 23, 1871.

205   *"a partial derangement of his mind"*: M. W. Montgomery, *History of Jay County, Indiana* (Chicago: Church, Goodman, and Cushing, 1864), 209.

206   *"he must yet go some miles on his way"*: Knapp, *A History*, 28–29.

208   *before she would allow him in the house:* C. Burr Dawes, *Tallow Light* 15 (1), 27–28. Amorrillah Chapman's name is sometimes spelled "Amirella."

208   *"tall tales" of Indians and the frontier:* Eliza Rudisill's memories can be found in a 1971 brochure published by Trinity (Lutheran) Church, Fort Wayne, in celebration of its 125th anniversary. The church was founded by Eliza's father, Henry Rudisill.

209 *"have a pure wife in heaven"*: Price, *Johnny Appleseed*, 164.

211 *site of that old meeting ground:* The complete story of the "Appleseed Pew" is available from the Glendale (Ohio) New Church, www.newchurch.org /societies/cincinnati/johnnyAppleseed.

212 *"and old Johnny was ragged"*: Price, *Johnny Appleseed*, 134–35, sums up both the Henry Roberts and the David Ayers accounts.

212 *apples "equal to the best grafted fruit"*: *History of Van Wert County, Ohio, and Representative Citizens* (Chicago: Richmond & Arnold, 1906), 143.

213 *"displeased if they were not attentive hearers"*: *History of Defiance County* (Chicago: Warren, Beers, & Co., 1883), 270.

213 *"most romantic figure in New Church History"*: See *Annals of the New Church*, 1847, 533–34, for the full obituary.

215 *"the Lord has left that Church"*: Otis Clapp's undated "Letter to the Receivers of the Heavenly Doctrines on the Want of Union" is in the collection of the H. Furlong Baldwin Library of the Maryland Historical Society, in Baltimore.

216 *their international career as mediums:* Timothy Miller, ed., *America's Alternative Religions* (Albany: SUNY Press, 1995), 77*ff*.

217 *"most delightful and paradisiacal to them"*: Swedenborg quote cited in *The New Jerusalem Magazine* for 1845–46, vol. 19 (Boston: Otis Clapp, School Street, 1845), 19.

11: Final Rites

219 *plunged from twenty-nine at noon to nineteen in the evening:* Rapin Andrews's weather calculations can be found in Price, *Johnny Appleseed*, 239.

220 *"March the 17, 1845"*: Fort Wayne is rich in historical resources for anyone pursuing John Chapman. The 1845 newspapers cited in these pages are available, on microfilm, at the main building of the Allen County Public Library. Photocopies of the original Chapman estate papers can be found nearby at the Records Management Division of the Allen County Probate Court. The History Center, operated and maintained by the Allen County–Fort Wayne Historical Society, has extensive archives, including the 1871 John Dawson articles cited here and the H. A. S. Levering communications concerning Chapman's burial site. "Johnny Appleseed: The Man Behind the Myth," by Steven Fortriede—vol. 66, no. 1 (2003) of the historical society's semiannual publication, *The Old Fort News*, available from the History Center—is an excellent condensation of the Chapman story. Fortriede's account of the flap over Chapman's death and burial sites is especially thorough.

224 *"what was once pantaloons"*: As Robert Price notes (*Johnny Appleseed*, 235), Samuel Flutter's memory of Chapman's final attire had had many years to

ripen. Still, the level and exactness of detail—and the fact that the description is so unromantic—lends it considerable credence.

224 *"would have us out of town as a scare":* "Reminiscences of A. C. Comparet," Occasional Publication of the Allen County–Fort Wayne Historical Society, 1962.

229 *diaries of Rapin Andrews:* Fortriede, "Johnny Appleseed," 13, 15n59.

12: Appleseed Unbound

232 *"beginning almost to rave about communism":* The Marx-Engels letters can be read at marxists.catbull.com/archive/marx/works/1845/letters/45_03_07 .htm.

232 *"anything faster than a galloping horse":* See interview with Daniel Walker Howe, *National Review Online,* November 30, 2007. Jill Lepore's "Vast Designs: How America Came of Age," *The New Yorker,* October 29, 2007, is also an excellent source of commentary on Howe's book. See www .newyorker.com/arts/critics/books/2007/10/29/071029crbo_books _lepore.

233 *"thus the prettiest walk in the neighbourhood was interdicted forever":* Frances Milton Trollope, *Domestic Manners of the Americans* (London: Whittaker, Treacher, & Co., 1832), 85.

235 *"occupying it with their wives and children":* James K. Polk's inaugural address is available in its entirety at www.presidency.ucsb.edu/ws/index.php ?pid=25814.

235 *"world-historical importance will be revealed there":* Quoted in Daniel Walker Howe, *What Hath God Wrought: The Transformation of America, 1815–1848* (New York: Oxford University Press, 2007), 305. The quote is taken from Hegel's *Introduction to the Philosophy of History,* first published posthumously in 1840. Hegel died in 1831.

236 *"multitude of its pleasing reminiscences":* The *Hovey's* article is available online through the Hathi Trust Digital Library—see vol. 12 (1846), beginning at 132. Edited by C. M. Hovey, the publication was officially known by the ambitious title of *The Magazine of Horticulture, Botany, and All Useful Discoveries and Improvements in Rural Affairs.*

238 *almost a year after Chapman was in the ground:* James Himrod's article, perhaps the seed of the story, has Chapman dying March 11, 1847, which makes the sequencing work far better. Kemp Battle tells us also that the first thing Johnny's baby eyes ever saw was a branch filled with apple blossoms, which would leave him functionally blind until he was roughly seven months old.

239   *still graced the county's hillsides:* For more, see Dan Fleming's "Sam Houston's Ties with Licking County" at www.wclt.com/news/special/articledetail.cfm?articleid=25146.

240   *better medium than* Harper's: All quotes that follow from W. D. Haley's article are taken from "Johnny Appleseed—A Pioneer Hero," *Harper's New Monthly Magazine,* November 1871, 830–37.

241   *"where he died in San Jose in 1890":* The *Salinas Weekly* obituary notice is at www.newspaperabstracts.com/link.php?id=3097. For more on W. D. Haley's tenure as a minister in Washington, DC, see Jennie W. Scudder, *A Century of Unitarianism in the National Capital* (Boston: The Beacon Press, 1922), 61*ff.*

242   *emerging glories of Washington, DC:* W. D. Haley, "Washington in 1859," *Harper's New Monthly Magazine,* December 1859.

245   *mounted on a pole as a trophy of war:* As noted earlier, Dawson's amendments and clarifications appeared in the October 21 and 23, 1871, editions of his *Fort Wayne Sentinel.*

246   *"spent much time in our Ohio country":* Louis Bromfield, *Pleasant Valley* (New York: Harper & Brothers, 1945), 26–35.

247   *"generation that crossed the Alleghanies":* Hillis, *The Quest of John Chapman,* ix–x.

247   *French seems proper for such a sentiment so expressed:* Eleanor Atkinson, foreword to *Johnny Appleseed: The Romance of the Sower* (New York: Harper & Bros., 1915).

248   *"you don't know who you are":* Wallace Stegner was paraphrasing another iconoclastic writer and thinker, Wendell Berry. The quote is cited in an online column posted February 18, 2009, by Timothy Egan of the *New York Times.*

249   *"Was God's own man":* Rosemary and Stephen Vincent Benét, *A Book of Americans* (New York: Rinehart & Co., 1933).

250   *"the real frontier was his sunburnt breast":* Lindsay, *Collected Poems,* 82–90. The poem cited in the previous paragraph is Lindsay's "General William Booth Enters into Heaven."

251   *"and none will understand":* Edgar Lee Masters, *Toward the Gulf* (New York: The Macmillan Co., 1918).

251   *"Johnny Appleseed moseys by, planting apple trees":* The unsigned review appeared in the January 9, 1939, issue of *Time* magazine. The entire review is available at www.time.com/time/magazine/article/0,9171,771292,00.html.

252   *version of the Appleseed life and legend:* The Weill and Lenya papers include a clipping from the September 16, 1940, issue of *Scholastic Journal* that refers to a radio script about Johnny Appleseed, written by Bernard C.

Schoenfeld, plus nine pages of notes about Chapman/Appleseed taken from multiple other sources. See Joy H. Calico, *Brecht at the Opera* (Berkeley: University of California Press, 2008), 218n105.

253 *"Johnny Appleseed stands for ourselves at our best":* Charles Allen Smart, "The Return of Johnny Appleseed," *Harper's Magazine,* August 1939, 225–34.

13: Blessings Three

256 *Murdoch wrote Walt Disney to correct the error of his ways:* Caroline Dunn's December 19, 1944, letter to Florence Murdoch; Murdoch's May 26, 1948, letter to Walt Disney; and Hal Adelquist's lengthy, June 23, 1948, reply to Murdoch can all be found in the archives of the Johnny Appleseed Educational Center and Museum at Urbana University, in Urbana, Ohio.

258 *to join the pioneer parade heading west:* "The Old Settler" is one of seven cartoon shorts incorporated into *Melody Time.* The others are: "Once Upon a Wintertime," with Frances Langford singing; "Bumble Boogie," built around a swing version of Rimsky-Korsakov's famous "Flight of the Bumblebee"; "Little Toot," this time with the Andrews Sisters handling the vocals; "Trees," yes, the Joyce Kilmer classic with help from Fred Waring and the Pennsylvanians; "Blame It on the Samba," in which Donald Duck treads the boards; and "Pecos Bill," ably assisted by Roy Rogers, the Sons of the Pioneers, and others.

258 *"Top o' the Brow folks":* Ophia D. Smith, "The Beginnings of the New Jerusalem Church in Ohio," *Ohio State Archeological and Historical Quarterly* 61 (July 1952), 239.

258 *"from the distortions of television and Walt Disney":* Robert Morgan, *Boone: A Biography* (Chapel Hill, NC: Algonquin Books, 2008). When Morgan visited the Johnny Appleseed Museum at Urbana University, he told director Joe Besecker that he had initially been torn between writing about Boone or John Chapman. Understandably so.

259 *"familiar Disney inspirational style":* Bosley Crowther, "The Screen," *The New York Times,* May 28, 1948.

261 *the future Johnny Appleseed's early years:* C. Burr Dawes's "Johnny Appleseed: Early Ohio Horticulturist" was published by the Dawes Arboretum of Newark, Ohio, in 1979. A copy, including the affidavits mentioned in the pages to follow, is available from the Newark (OH) Public Library.

264 *where his sainthood seems assured:* Representative Mark Souder spoke to the House about Johnny Appleseed on November 2, 1999. His full remarks are available at thomas.loc.gov/cgi-bin/query/F?r106:1:./temp/~r106Zw2YnQ:e25278:.

269 *"go to the prom with any of them":* The interview is available on Patti Smith's

website and at www.kaapeli.fi/aiu/ps/auguries2.html. Smith's *Auguries of Innocence* is available, in paperback, from Ecco Press.

270 *"correspond to higher things":* Swedenborg's quote is cited in Edward Hoagland's "Johnny Appleseed: The Quietly Compelling Legend of America's Gentlest Pioneer," *American Heritage,* December 1979, 61–70—an eloquent condensation of John Chapman's life and legend.

Epilogue: My Johnny

273 *"walked daily with the angels of God":* From "A Foolish Man, A Philosopher, and a Fanatic," by William Dean Howells. "A Foolish Man . . . ," from *Stories of Ohio,* is available online at www.readbookonline.net/read OnLine/15547/.

274 *the great Indian portraitist:* Hoagland, "Johnny Appleseed," 62.

SELECTED BIBLIOGRAPHY

Biographies and Biographical Sketches

Glines, W. M. *Johnny Appleseed by One Who Knew Him*. Columbus, OH: K. J. Heer Printing Co., 1922.

Haley, W. D. "Johnny Appleseed: A Pioneer Hero." In *Harper's New Monthly Magazine*, November 1871.

Hoagland, Edward. "Johnny Appleseed: The Quietly Compelling Legend of America's Gentlest Pioneer." In *American Heritage*, December 1979.

Leuchtenberg, William E. "John Chapman (Johnny Appleseed)." In *Forgotten Heroes: Inspiring Portraits from our Leading Historians*, ed. Susan Ware. New York: The Free Press, 1998.

Price, Robert. *Johnny Appleseed: Man and Myth*. Bloomington, IN: Indiana University Press. 1954.

Johnny Appleseed in Fiction and Poetry

Atkinson, Eleanor. *Johnny Appleseed: The Romance of the Sower*. New York: Harper & Bros., 1915.

Benét, Rosemary, and Stephen Vincent Benét. "Johnny Appleseed." In *A Book of Americans*. New York: Rinehart & Co., 1933.

Fast, Howard. *The Tall Hunter*. New York: Harper & Row, 1942.

Hillis, Newell Dwight. *The Quest of John Chapman: The Story of a Forgotten Hero*. New York: The Macmillan Company, 1904.

Lindsay, Vachel. "In Praise of Johnny Appleseed." In *Collected Poems*. New York: Macmillan, 1923.

Pershing, Henry A. *Johnny Appleseed and His Time: An Historical Romance*. Strasburg, VA: Shenandoah Publishing House, 1930.

Pioneer Life & Times

Cuming, Fortescue. *Cuming's Tour to the Western Country: 1807–1809*. Cleveland: A. H. Clark Co., 1904.

Evans, Paul Demund. *The Holland Land Company*. Clifton, NJ: A. M. Kelly, 1975.

Gelber, Ben. *The Pennsylvania Weather Book*. Piscataway, NJ: Rutgers University Press, 2002.

O'Donnell, James H., III. *Ohio's First People*. Athens, OH: Ohio University Press, 2004.

Hildreth, S. P. *Pioneer History: Being an Account of the First Examination of the Ohio Valley, and the Early Settlement of the Northwest Territory*. Cincinnati: H. W. Derry & Co., 1848.

Howells, William Dean. *Stories of Ohio*. New York: Harper & Bros., 1897.

Hulbert, Archer Butler. *Pioneer Roads and Experiences of Travelers*, vol. 11 of *Historic Highways of America*. Cleveland: The Arthur H. Clark Company, 1904.

———. *Waterways of Westward Expansion, the Ohio River and Its Tributaries*, vol. 9 of *Historic Highways of America*. Cleveland: The Arthur H. Clark Company, 1903.

Hurt, R. Douglas. *The Ohio Frontier*. Bloomington, IN: Indiana University Press, 1996.

Knepper, George W. *Ohio and Its People*. Kent, OH: The Kent State University Press, 1989.

Lincklaen, John. *Travels in the Years 1791 and 1792 in Pennsylvania, New York and Vermont: Journals of John Lincklaen, Agent of the Holland Land Company*. New York: G. P. Putnam's Sons, 1897.

McCormick, Virginia E., and Robert W. McCormick. *New Englanders on the Ohio Frontier: Migration and Settlement of Worthington, Ohio*. Kent, OH: The Kent State University Press, 1998.

Local & Regional Histories

Callahan, James Morton. *Semi-Centennial History of West Virginia*. Semi-Centennial Commission of West Virginia, 1913.

Day, Sherman. *Historical Collections of the State of Pennsylvania: Containing a Copious Selection of the Most Interesting Facts, Traditions, Biographical Sketches, Anecdotes, etc., Relating to Its History and Antiquities, both General and Local, with Topographical Descriptions of Every County and the Larger Towns in the State*. Philadelphia: G. W. Gorton, 1843.

Hill, N. N., Jr., *History of Coshocton County, Ohio: Its Past and Present*. Newark, Ohio: A. A. Graham & Co., 1881.

History of Defiance County. Chicago: Warren, Beers, & Co., 1883.

History of Van Wert County, Ohio, and Representative Citizens. Chicago: Richmond & Arnold, 1906.

History of Venango County, Pennsylvania, vol. 1. Chicago: Brown, Runk & Co., 1890.

Howe, Henry. *Historical Collections of Ohio: An Encyclopedia of the State*, vol. 1. Norwalk, OH: The Laning Printing Co., 1896.

Knapp, H. S. *A History of the Pioneer and Modern Times of Ashland County from the Earliest to the Present Day*. Philadelphia: J. B. Lippincott & Co., 1863.

Montgomery, M. W. *History of Jay County, Indiana*. Chicago: Church, Goodman, and Cushing, 1864.

Newton, J. H. *History of Venango County, Pennsylvania.* Franklin, PA: Venango County Historical Society, 1976 (reprint).

Norton, A. Banning. *A History of Knox County, Ohio, from 1779 to 1862 Inclusive.* Columbus, OH: Richard Nevins, 1862.

Proceedings of the Centennial Celebration of the Incorporation of the Town of Longmeadow, October 17th 1883. Longmeadow, MA: Secretary of the Centennial Committee, 1884.

Rodger, Linda M., and Mary S. Rogeness, eds. *Reflections of Longmeadow: 1783/1983.* Longmeadow, MA: Longmeadow Historical Society, 1983.

Schenck, J. S., ed. *History of Warren County, Pennsylvania.* Syracuse, NY: D. Mason & Co., 1887.

Smucker, Isaac. *Centennial History of Licking County, Ohio.* Newark, OH: Clark & Underwood, 1876.

Williams History of Washington County, Ohio: 1788–1881. Cleveland: H. Z. Williams & Bro., 1881.

Apples

de Cleene, Marcel, and Marie Claire Lejeune. *Trees and Shrubs,* vol. 1 of *Compendium of Symbolic and Ritual Plants in Europe.* Ghent, Belgium: Man & Culture Publishers, 1999.

Grieve, Mrs. M. *A Modern Herbal: The Medicinal, Culinary, Cosmetic, and Economic Properties, Cultivation, and Folk-Lore of Herbs, Grasses, Fungi, Shrubs & Trees with All Their Modern Scientific Uses.* New York: Harcourt, Brace, & Co., 1931.

Pollan, Michael. *The Botany of Desire: A Plant's-Eye View of the World.* New York: Random House, 2001.

Religion & Emanuel Swedenborg

Ahlstrom, Sydney E. *A Religious History of the American People.* New Haven: Yale University Press, 1972.

Bergquist, Lars. "Emanuel Swedenborg," pamphlet in *Swedish Portraits* series. Translated by Paul Britten Austin. Stockholm: The Swedish Institute, 1986.

Hargrove, John. *A Sermon, on the Second Coming of Christ, and on the Last Judgment: Delivered the 25th December, 1804, Before Both Houses of Congress, at the Capitol in Washington.* Baltimore: Warner & Hanna, 1805.

Hindemarsh, Robert, and Edward Madeley. *Rise and Progress of the New Jerusalem Church in England, America, and Other Parts.* London: Hodson & Son, London, 1861.

Johnson, Charles A. *The Frontier Camp Meeting: Religion's Harvest Time.* Dallas: Southern Methodist University Press, 1955.

Selected Bibliography

Miller, Timothy, ed. *America's Alternative Religions*. Albany: SUNY Press, 1995.
Swedenborg, Emanuel. *Heaven & Hell*. Translated by George F. Dole. New York: Swedenborg Foundation, Inc., 1984.

Early American History, Customs, and Notable Figures

Ambrose, Stephen. *Undaunted Courage: Meriwether Lewis, Thomas Jefferson, and the Opening of the American West*. New York: Simon & Schuster, 2007.
de Tocqueville, Alexis. *Democracy in America*. Translated by Henry Reeve. Cambridge: Sever and Francis, 1863.
Howe, Daniel Walker. *What Hath God Wrought: The Transformation of America, 1815–1848*. New York: Oxford University Press, 2007.
Langguth, A. J. *Union 1812: The Americans Who Fought the Second War of Independence*. New York: Simon & Schuster, 2007.
Morgan, Robert. *Boone: A Biography*. Chapel Hill, NC: Algonquin Books, 2008.
Rothenberg, Winifred Barr. "The Invention of American Capitalism: The Economy of New England in the Federal Period." In *Engines of Enterprise: An Economic History of New England*, edited by Peter Temin. Cambridge: Harvard University Press, 2000.
Trollope, Frances Milton. *Domestic Manners of the Americans*. London: Whittaker, Treacher, & Co., 1832.

INDEX

Index

ABOUT THE AUTHOR

Howard Means is the author of many books, including *The Avenger Takes His Place: Andrew Johnson and the 45 Days That Changed the Nation*, *Colin Powell: A Biography*, the novel *CSA*, and *The Banana Sculptor, the Purple Lady, and the All-Night Swimmer*, studies in eccentricity coauthored with Susan Sheehan. A former senior editor and senior writer at *Washingtonian Magazine*, he lives in the village of Millwood, Virginia, with his wife, Candy.